Microsoft® SharePoint® 2010 FOR DUMMIES®

by Vanessa L. Williams

WILEY

Wiley Publishing, Inc.

Microsoft® SharePoint® 2010 For Dummies®

Published by
Wiley Publishing, Inc.
111 River Street
Hoboken, NJ 07030-5774

www.wiley.com

About the Author

Vanessa L. Williams is a professional Web consultant based out of Indianapolis. She has developed Web-based solutions for a long time, specializing in ASP.NET and SharePoint for the past five years.

Dedication

For Mom who's not here anymore, and Simone who is.

Author's Acknowledgments

Writing these books is always a whirlwind tour of SharePoint's functionality. There's just never enough time to explore it all. Toward that end, I relied on many people to help pull together this book.

I would especially like to thank Pam Fozo and Lisa Woods, my co-authors and technical reviewers. The book never would have made it to a finished product without the patience and prodding of my editors, Jean Nelson and Jen Riggs. And Katie Feltman deserves special thanks for bearing the brunt of so many missed deadlines.

I've worked on many great projects over the past several years. Thanks to my colleagues and clients at Allegient in Indianapolis for all the great opportunities. Also, thanks to the many readers who have reached out over the years with comments, questions, suggestions, and opportunities. I'm grateful to the SharePoint and .NET communities online, in Indy, and elsewhere who continue to be a great source of inspiration.

Of course, this book wouldn't be here without the great work of the product teams in Redmond. I'm still excited about this product!

As usual, you can reach me online at www.sharepointgrrl.com.

Publisher's Acknowledgments

We're proud of this book; please send us your comments at http://dummies.custhelp.com. For other comments, please contact our Customer Care Department within the U.S. at 877-762-2974, outside the U.S. at 317-572-3993, or fax 317-572-4002.

Some of the people who helped bring this book to market include the following:

Acquisitions, Editorial, and Media Development

Project Editor: Jean Nelson

Senior Acquisitions Editor: Katie Feltman

Copy Editor: Jen Riggs

Technical Editor: Pam Fozo

Editorial Manager: Kevin Kirschner

Media Development Project Manager: Laura Moss-Hollister

Media Development Assistant Project Manager: Jenny Swisher

Media Development Associate Producers: Josh Frank, Marilyn Hummel, Douglas Kuhn, and Shawn Patrick

Editorial Assistant: Amanda Graham

Sr. Editorial Assistant: Cherie Case

Cartoons: Rich Tennant (www.the5thwave.com)

Composition Services

Project Coordinator: Lynsey Stanford

Layout and Graphics: Nikki Gately, Joyce Haughey

Proofreaders: Rebecca Denoncour, Christine Sabooni

Indexer: Sharon Shock

Publishing and Editorial for Technology Dummies

Richard Swadley, Vice President and Executive Group Publisher

Andy Cummings, Vice President and Publisher

Mary Bednarek, Executive Acquisitions Director

Mary C. Corder, Editorial Director

Publishing for Consumer Dummies

Diane Graves Steele, Vice President and Publisher

Composition Services

Debbie Stailey, Director of Composition Services

Contents at a Glance

Introduction 1

Part I: Collaborating with Team Sites 9
Chapter 1: Getting to Know Your Team Site 11
Chapter 2: Sharing Your Documents 23
Chapter 3: Working with Lists 41
Chapter 4: Creating Custom Lists 53
Chapter 5: Getting a New View 69
Chapter 6: Subscribing to Feeds and Alerts 87
Chapter 7: Yours, Mine, and Ours: Social Networking 97

Part II: Taking Your Team Site to the Next Level 115
Chapter 8: Configuring Libraries and Lists... 117
Chapter 9: Working with Web Pages 137
Chapter 10: Working with Web Parts 145
Chapter 11: Finding Your Way around a Team Site............................. 155
Chapter 12: Securing Your Team Site... 169
Chapter 13: Creating New Sites.. 185

Part III: Putting On Your Webmaster Hat 199
Chapter 14: Getting Started with Portals and Web Sites 201
Chapter 15: Approving Content for Publication 215
Chapter 16: Creating Page Layouts with SharePoint Designer 231
Chapter 17: Rolling Up Content to the Home Page............................. 253
Chapter 18: Configuring Site Navigation 265

Part IV: Putting a Bow on It.................................... 277
Chapter 19: Changing the Look and Feel of Your Site........................ 279
Chapter 20: Branding Your SharePoint Site 291
Chapter 21: Managing Site Assets.. 307

Part V: Enterprise Services 317

Chapter 22: Content Types and Metadata...319
Chapter 23: Exploring Enterprise Search...337
Chapter 24: Business Intelligence in SharePoint 349

Part VI: The Part of Tens..................................... 361

Chapter 25: Ten Governance Items 363
Chapter 26: Ten Ways to Master SharePoint 369

Index 375

Table of Contents

Introduction *1*

No, Really, What Is SharePoint?...2
Who Should Read This Book...4
How to Use This Book...4
Foolish Assumptions...4
How This Book Is Organized 5
    Part I: Collaborating with Team Sites............................5
    Part II: Taking Your Team Site to the Next Level 6
    Part III: Putting On Your Webmaster Hat........................6
    Part IV: Putting a Bow on It..6
    Part V: Enterprise Services 6
    Part VI: The Part of Tens 7
Icons Used in This Book 7
Where to Go from Here..7

Part 1: Collaborating with Team Sites *9*

Chapter 1: Getting to Know Your Team Site 11

Requesting Your Team Site 11
Viewing Your Team Site in the Browser 13
Contributing to a Team Site 14
    Uploading documents 15
    Adding calendar items 16
    Social networking...17
Customizing Your Team Site..19
    Introducing the Ribbon 19
    Modifying the home page 20

Chapter 2: Sharing Your Documents.........................23

Defining Document Libraries 24
Getting Your Documents into a Library 24
    Uploading a single document 25
    Uploading multiple documents.....................................25
    Uploading documents with Windows Explorer 28
    Uploading documents into a folder...............................30

Working with Documents 32
    Using the Edit menu 32
    Editing a document's properties 33
    Checking documents in and out 34
    Sending a link to your document 37
  Recovering Deleted Documents 38

Chapter 3: Working with Lists **41**
  Getting to Know SharePoint's Lists 42
    Creating a new list 44
    Using the Ribbon to manage lists 46
  Entering Data in SharePoint Lists..47
  Customizing List Forms 49
  Taking Lists Offline..50

Chapter 4: Creating Custom Lists. **53**
  Planning Your Custom List..54
  Creating Custom Lists...54
  Adding Columns to Your List..56
    Getting to know column types 57
    Validating data entry...60
  Working with the Title Column..62
  Importing a Spreadsheet as a List 63
  Taking Your List to the Next Level: Calculated and Lookup Columns ...65
    Creating a calculated column...65
    Using a lookup column 66

Chapter 5: Getting a New View. **69**
  Viewing the View 69
  Getting to Know Your View Formats...70
  Creating a Standard View 71
    Choosing columns for your view 73
    Filtering lists with views 74
    Grouping results 76
    Allowing editing options 76
    Choosing a display style 78
  Managing List Data in a Datasheet View....................................79
  Using Ad Hoc Views 81
  Creating a Calendar View 81
  Displaying Tasks in a Gantt View 82
  Managing Existing Views 83
    Modifying your views 83
    Setting the default view..83
    Other SharePoint built-in views 84
  Displaying Views via Web Parts...84

Chapter 6: Subscribing to Feeds and Alerts .... .87

Viewing RSS Feeds 87
Reading Feeds with Outlook 89
Displaying RSS Feeds of Other Sites.....................................90
Alert Me 92

Chapter 7: Yours, Mine, and Ours: Social Networking .... .97

Sharing and Tracking Using the Ribbon 98
Tagging for Yourself and Others 98
"My" Site and Other "My" Stuff...101
Using Your Tags and Notes Page..103
Information Sharing with Blogs and Wikis 104
   Lone voice in the corporate wilderness? Creating a blog site.....105
   Posting to a blog 106
   The whole is greater than the sum of its parts: Using wikis
      to collaborate and coauthor 107
Communicating with Discussion Boards..............................110
   Creating a discussion board...110
   Posting and replying to a subject 111
   Viewing discussions 112

Part II: Taking Your Team Site to the Next Level *115*

Chapter 8: Configuring Libraries and Lists .... .117

Accessing List Settings 118
Configuring the General Settings 120
   Changing the title, description, and navigation.............121
   Versioning settings 122
   Advanced settings 124
   Validation settings 128
   Rating settings..129
   Audience Targeting settings 129
   Metadata Navigation settings 129
   Per-Location Views settings 130
   Form settings 131
Permissions and Management Options 131
   Permissions for This Document Library (or List) setting 132
   Workflow settings 133

Chapter 9: Working with Web Pages .... .137

Understanding SharePoint Web Pages 137
   Why wiki pages?..138
   What about Web Part pages? 138
   Choosing a Wiki Content page over a Web Part page
      or vice versa 139

Creating a New Wiki Content Page 140
 Finding and linking other Wiki Content pages 141
 Categorizing your wiki pages 142
Creating a New Web Part Page 143

Chapter 10: Working with Web Parts 145

Adding a Web Part to Your Page 145
Choosing the Right Web Part 147
Changing Web Part Properties 150
Connecting Web Parts 152

Chapter 11: Finding Your Way around a Team Site 155

Navigating Your Team Site 155
 Getting acquainted with the Ribbon 157
 Going global with the Top Link bar 157
 Using the Welcome menu 158
 Tracking back with breadcrumbs 159
 Getting specific with the search box 161
 Getting help 162
Staying Local with the Quick Launch bar 162
Exploring Administrative Options 165
 Site Actions 165
 Site Settings 166

Chapter 12: Securing Your Team Site 169

Using SharePoint Groups 170
Securing Lists, Libraries, and Documents 175
 Breaking inheritance 175
 Viewing a group's permissions 178
 Checking a user's permissions 179
Granting Administrative Access 180
 Viewing permission assignments 180
 Managing SharePoint Designer access 183

Chapter 13: Creating New Sites 185

Getting Acquainted with Templates 185
Understanding Site Hierarchy 188
Creating a New Site 191
Creating Your Own Site Templates 194
 Creating a template from an existing team site 194
 Creating a template from a publishing site 196

Part III: Putting On Your Webmaster Hat *199*

Chapter 14: Getting Started with Portals and Web Sites 201
Exploring SharePoint's Publishing Site...202
Creating and Editing Pages..204
Adding Content to Your Page 205
Adding content to your page..206
Changing the page's layout...207
Setting Page Layout Defaults..210
Changing the Master Page of a Site 213

Chapter 15: Approving Content for Publication 215
Deciding Whether to Use Content Approval or Approval Workflows.....215
Choosing the Content Approval Option (Everything in Moderation).....216
Is it drafty in here? Turning on Content Approval 217
Identifying Approvers..218
Casting an approving eye...219
Disapproval: Not just for stern parents 220
Getting alerts on approval/rejection status 220
Configuring Approval Workflows 221
Approval workflow options 221
Setting up an Approval workflow...223
Initiating a workflow 225
Approving an item 227
Checking the status of an Approval workflow 229

Chapter 16: Creating Page Layouts with SharePoint Designer 231
Getting Inside a SharePoint Page Layout...232
Working with content placeholders 235
Page layouts and styles...237
The relationship between the page layout and a master page....237
Making Decisions before You Start 238
Creating New Page Content Fields 239
Creating a site column for page content.......................................240
Adding your publishing content site column to a
content type used by page layouts..241
Adding your site column to the page layout 243
Creating a New Page Layout..245
Putting Containers and Controls in Your Layout 248
Using the Edit Mode Panel 250

Chapter 17: Rolling Up Content to the Home Page **253**

Publishing Web Parts 253
    Rolling up content 254
    Displaying a site's hierarchy 257
    Creating custom displays with the Summary Link Web Part 258
Starting from Scratch 261

Chapter 18: Configuring Site Navigation **265**

Configuring Dynamic Navigation 265
    Configuring global navigation 266
    Configuring current navigation 268
Configuring Static Navigation 269
Looking at Alternative Ways to Generate a Navigation Menu 272

Part IV: Putting a Bow on It 277

Chapter 19: Changing the Look and Feel of Your Site **279**

The Look and Feel Section of Site Settings 280
Changing Your Site Icon 281
Changing the Theme of Your Site 283
    A note on fonts 286
    A word on usability 286
    The benefits of themes 287
Creating a Custom Theme for SharePoint 2010 Using PowerPoint 288

Chapter 20: Branding Your SharePoint Site **291**

Comparing Publishing and Collaboration Branding Options 292
Branding Parts and Pieces 293
CSS Primer 296
    Anatomy of a CSS rule 297
    CSS resources 298
The Style Library and the Master Page Gallery 299
    Contents of the Style library 299
    Viewing images used for predefined master pages 300
    Master Pages and Page Layouts gallery 301
Uploading an Alternate Style Sheet 302
Custom Branding 304

Chapter 21: Managing Site Assets **307**

Figuring Out What to Put Where 307
    Using libraries to store content 309
    Putting Web page content in default locations 310
    Deploying content in folders or libraries 311

Packaging Your Assets..311
    Creating a solution in Visual Studio 312
    Uploading and activating a solution................................314
Collecting Statistics..315

Part V: Enterprise Services 317

Chapter 22: Content Types and Metadata 319

Understanding Intrinsic and Extrinsic Metadata.......................319
I Never Metadata I Didn't Like..320
    Creating a term store..321
    Importing a term set file...322
    Adding a managed metadata column to a list or library 324
Getting Personal with Folksonomies..326
Understanding Content Types..328
    Creating a new site content type 329
    Associating a content type with a list or library...........................331
    Publishing site content types...332
Using Columns 333
    Creating a new site column 334
    Reusing site columns..335

Chapter 23: Exploring Enterprise Search.......................337

Tweaking Search..337
    Enabling search..338
    Using the search center 339
    Scoping out 342
    Adding your own search results.......................................344
    Removing search results..345
    Reviewing search analytics 347
    Customizing the Search Box Web Part..............................347

Chapter 24: Business Intelligence in SharePoint.................349

Calling All Data Wranglers...350
Business Intelligence Tools in the SharePoint Toolkit 351
The New Business Intelligence Center Site Template.....................354
    Creating the site...354
    Reviewing the site's pre-created content 355
    Monitoring key performance with status lists and
        scorecards..356
    Dashboards — PerformancePoint Services and
        Excel Services 357

Part VI: The Part of Tens............................ 361

Chapter 25: Ten Governance Items 363
Failure Is Not an Option (Neither Is Looking Away and Whistling) 363
Get Executive Buy-In and Support....................................364
Build an Effective Governance Group 364
Find the Right Level...364
Yours, Mine, Ours: Decide Who Owns What.........................365
(Re)visit Social Networking Policies 365
Design and Branding 366
The Content Managementy Bits 366
Reuse Web Parts...367
Keep Things Current: Web Operations Management 367

Chapter 26: Ten Ways to Master SharePoint 369
Reading Developer Blogs...369
Finding Local User Groups 370
Building a Virtual Lab...370
Getting Information from the Horse's Mouth 371
Starting with a Good Foundation.....................................372
Borrowing from Others..373
Getting Certified..373
Taking a Peek under the Covers 373
Digging Deeper under the Covers.....................................374
Deconstructing a SharePoint Site.....................................374

Index.. 375

Introduction

*W*ith everyone connected via internal networks and externally with the Internet, more organizations are using Web sites — both inside and outside their organizations. Think about where you work. Your company probably has at least one Web site on the Internet, and probably several more, such as a brochureware site, an e-commerce site, and product microsites.

Internally, Human Resources may have its own self-service portal. Your department may have a Web site for posting documents to share with others. Another group may post reports to a site. Nowadays, Web sites are ubiquitous.

Web sites have some really great things to offer. They're *standards-based,* which means it's easy for them to talk to each other. They're easy to search. They can be visually stunning or plain Jane. They require nothing more than a browser to interact with — even on a mobile phone!

Microsoft SharePoint Server 2010 is a product that takes advantage of the best of the Web to help you be more productive at work. Not just you, but also your coworkers, department, division, and even your Information Technology (IT) department.

Take everything you know about Web sites and then add to that the ability to manage and search documents, publish reports and business information, track contacts, display information from other databases, and collaborate using blogs, wikis, and discussion boards. You can use SharePoint's Web sites to store, track, secure, and share all the stuff you do at work.

Do you know how to create Web pages? Do you know how to create links from one page to the other? Do you know how to configure a Web site for search and document storage? With SharePoint, you can do all these things without any technical skills.

And that's what this book shows you how to do. SharePoint 2010 is intended to be a self-service environment, and this book helps you get the most out of the platform.

No, Really, What Is SharePoint?

Maybe you're a whiz at Word or a spreadsheet jockey with Excel. Going forward, you're going to have to be just as good at Microsoft SharePoint Server 2010 to get the most out of your desktop Office client applications. Microsoft is continuing to integrate functionality once locked up in client applications, or not available at all, with SharePoint. For example, using SharePoint 2010 with Office 2010, you can create an online gallery of your PowerPoint slides, display interactive spreadsheets in Web pages, or reuse information from your company's databases in Word documents. You can even use Visio 2010 to automate your business processes using SharePoint.

Officially, Microsoft represents SharePoint 2010 as a "business collaboration platform for the Enterprise and Web." *SharePoint* is a set of different products from Microsoft that allows businesses to meet their diverse needs in the following domains:

- **Collaboration:** Use SharePoint's collaboration sites for activities, such as managing projects or coordinating a request for proposal.

- **Social networking:** If you work in a large company, you can use SharePoint as a Facebook for the Enterprise experience that helps you track your favorite coworkers and locate people in expertise networks.

- **Information portals and public Web sites:** With SharePoint's Web content management features, you can create useful self-service internal portals and intranets, or you can create visually appealing Web sites that are actually easy for your business users to maintain.

- **Enterprise content management:** SharePoint offers excellent document- and record-management capabilities, including extensive support for metadata and customized search experiences.

- **Business intelligence:** SharePoint is an ideal platform for providing entrée into your organization's business analysis assets. You can use insightful dashboards that allow users to get the big picture at a glance and then drill down to get more detail.

- **Business applications:** Use SharePoint to host sophisticated business applications, integrate business processes' backend databases and your SharePoint content, or simply use SharePoint as the means to present access to your applications.

The functionality I discuss in the preceding list is delivered by two core products:

✔ **SharePoint Foundation 2010** is the underlying software platform that delivers all the building block functionality of SharePoint. That includes lists, libraries, Web pages, Web sites, and alerts. SharePoint Foundation is licensed as a Windows Server 2008 component. In other words, as part of a properly licensed Windows Server 2008, you also get all the functionality of SharePoint Foundation 2010.

✔ **SharePoint Server 2010** is a set of applications that uses the building blocks of SharePoint Foundation 2010 to deliver all the functionality mentioned earlier. SharePoint Server is licensed as several separate products, each one offering a batch of functionality. When using SharePoint internally, you have at least a standard license that grants you access to use search, portals, social networking, and some content management features. You also need an enterprise license if you intend to use SharePoint's advanced content management, business intelligence, and business application features.

Additional licensing is required to use SharePoint in Internet scenarios. Microsoft offers additional products to enhance the search experience.

I approach SharePoint with the following model:

✔ **Product:** SharePoint is a product with a lot of features, even in SharePoint Foundation. I always explore how SharePoint works without any customization when I'm deciding how to approach a solution.

✔ **Platform:** I like to view SharePoint as a platform. SharePoint provides everything you need to deliver a robust business solution. It provides security, logging, and most of the other "plumbing" required to deliver Web-based solutions.

✔ **Toolkit:** Finally, I view SharePoint as a set of components and controls that I can mix and match to provide a solution. Almost everything you see on a Web page in SharePoint can be reused on the pages you create. I mean everything, even menus and buttons.

From a technical perspective, I view SharePoint as

✔ **Database driven:** SharePoint uses SQL Server to store your content. That means you can get your content out of the database in XML format. Given the flexibility of XML, the sky's the limit in terms of what you can do with that content. Don't be tempted to query the SQL Server directly. SharePoint 2010 provides a set of well-documented services that you can use to query SharePoint.

✔ **ASP.NET:** Everything you may know about ASP.NET applies to SharePoint. SharePoint is essentially a reference architecture.

✔ **A Web application:** Emphasis on *Web*. Everything I know about building solutions for the Web applies to SharePoint.

Who Should Read This Book

This book is intended for power users and site stewards who need to be productive in SharePoint, and also technical users who are looking to get a good introduction to SharePoint.

Others who may benefit from this book include

- **Developers:** This isn't a development book, but the best SharePoint developers are those who understand the product. This book explains just that. I deliver 100 percent of SharePoint solutions without writing any server-side code. I don't think server-side code is bad, but I don't believe it's the place to start when designing a SharePoint solution.

- **IT professionals:** This isn't a book that explains how to stand up a SharePoint server farm. However, this book helps you understand what features your end users may want to see in a SharePoint farm that you architect or support.

- **Managers:** If you manage a department or business unit, you need to understand how to get the most out of SharePoint. If your company has made significant investments in SharePoint deployment, it'd be a shame if you didn't know how to leverage that investment.

How to Use This Book

This book is a *reference:* You don't have to read it cover to cover. Because many of the features in SharePoint are dependent on other features, I point you to related chapters in the book when appropriate.

Foolish Assumptions

Because SharePoint is such a huge topic, I have to make some assumptions about your configuration and starting knowledge, such as

- **You have some version of SharePoint 2010 installed.** Microsoft usually has a pre-built evaluation version of SharePoint available on its download site. To do all the scenarios covered in this book requires an Enterprise Edition license of SharePoint 2010.

- **You're a contributor or ideally, you're a *site collection administrator,* which means you have full control over your site.** Of course, many of the scenarios in this book require only that you be a contributor. So long as you know who your site collection administrator is, you can ask that person for elevated permissions.

✔ **Ideally, you have a sandbox or test environment where you can try different scenarios.** Your company probably has an environment where it can easily stand up a sandbox. Don't be afraid to ask. I don't recommend using your production environment to perform some of the scenarios in this book, such as customizing page layouts.

✔ **Many of the scenarios in this book assume your implementation includes My Site.** Unfortunately, many companies try to avoid using this feature. In SharePoint 2010, My Site is an integral component for many features. I strongly advise utilizing My Site.

How This Book Is Organized

This book groups related SharePoint topics in parts. Each part covers a different aspect of getting the most out of SharePoint.

For the geeks out there:

✔ Parts I and II roughly correlate to SharePoint 2010 Foundation.

✔ Part III and IV map to SharePoint 2010 Standard Edition.

✔ Parts V and VI cover aspects of Foundation, Standard, and Enterprise Edition.

Part 1: Collaborating with Team Sites

This part of the book covers all the basics of using team sites. This material is the foundation to much of SharePoint, so if you don't know how to perform the tasks listed here, start in this part:

✔ Sharing documents and list items (calendars, tasks, and so on)

✔ Creating custom lists

✔ Keeping track of changes in your team site with alerts, feeds, and using SharePoint workspaces for offline access

✔ Using My Site for micro-blogging (think Twitter) and sharing interests with your network (think Facebook)

Part II: Taking Your Team Site to the Next Level

In Part II, I show you how to customize your team site to meet your specific collaboration needs. Like Part I, these tasks are foundational to much of SharePoint, so be sure to spend some time in Part II to see how to

- ✔ Use your team site for document management
- ✔ Apply metadata to your documents
- ✔ Add content other than documents to your team site
- ✔ Secure your team site and create new sites

Part III: Putting On Your Webmaster Hat

In this part, I show you how to use SharePoint to host public-facing Web sites and internal informational portals. Topics include

- ✔ How to use page templates to make it easier for folks to add content
- ✔ How to roll up content to a landing page
- ✔ How to take your site live

Part IV: Putting a Bow on It

Whether you want to change the color scheme of your team site or create a completely branded public Web site, this part covers all the bases for putting the polish on your site.

Part V: Enterprise Services

The features I cover in Part V help you extend your collaboration experience beyond your site. In this part, I explain how to use metadata and search to improve the *findability* of your content. I also introduce the business intelligence features of SharePoint 2010.

Part VI: The Part of Tens

In this part, I share some parting words of wisdom in the form of two chapters:

- ✔ Ten ways to get more information on SharePoint
- ✔ Ten things you need to think about to make sure your SharePoint site's entire installation keeps running smoothly after deployment

Icons Used in This Book

You find a handful of icons in this book, and here's what they mean:

Tips point out a handy shortcut, or they help you understand something important to SharePoint.

This icon marks something to remember, such as how you handle a particularly tricky part of SharePoint configuration.

This icon is my chance to share with you details about the inner workings of SharePoint. Most of the information you find here pertains to some aspect of SharePoint that requires configuration at the server. That means you can point out the stuff beside this icon to IT and ask them to make SharePoint do that.

Although the Warning icon appears rarely, when you need to be wary of a problem or common pitfall, this icon lets you know.

Where to Go from Here

All right, you're all set and ready to jump into this book. You can jump in anywhere you like — the book was written to allow you to do just that. But if you want to get the full story from the beginning, jump to Chapter 1 — that's where all the action starts. (If you already have a SharePoint server up and running, you might want to jump ahead to Chapter 2 where you can get your hands dirty with some site content.)

Part I
Collaborating with Team Sites

The 5th Wave   By Rich Tennant

"The odd thing is he always insists on using the latest version of Office."

In this part . . .

*I*n this part, I kick off your SharePoint 2010 exploration with foundational stuff, such as introducing team sites, explaining what they are and why you might want one, and setting up one. I also show you how to upload documents to SharePoint, use lists to manage documents and other kinds of content, and how to keep an eye on things that interest you by setting alerts on lists and libraries. Finally, I cover My Sites (by which I mean *your* SharePoint My Site).

Chapter 1

Getting to Know Your Team Site

- -

In This Chapter

▶ Requesting a new team site and opening it in the browser

▶ Participating in a team site

▶ Changing your team site's home page

- -

*O*ne of the fundamental kinds of Web sites that SharePoint 2010 allows you to create is a team site. A *team site* is a SharePoint site that you can use to collaborate with your coworkers. If the team site is hosted in your company's extranet or by a public hosting company, you may even be able to collaborate with people outside your organization. In most cases, an administrator will create a team site for you.

Many kinds of teams can use a SharePoint team site to collaborate. For example:

✔ Department members can use document libraries to upload document files and enter meetings in a team calendar.

✔ Project members can use a team site home page to post announcements and track important dates.

✔ Corporate communications can use a team site to store the documents and track the tasks required for preparing the company's annual report.

You need to know your way around some of the basic features of a team site, which is exactly what I show you in this chapter.

Requesting Your Team Site

Most organizations have a process for requesting a team site. I've seen everything from the simple process in which you send an e-mail addressed to someone in your IT department to very detailed wizards that walk you through the site creation process. One company requires that you write a justification for why you want the team site and then submit prototypes.

Whatever you have to do to get your SharePoint 2010 team site, get one. At a minimum, you need to provide your SharePoint administrator with this information to get a team site:

- ✔ **The site name:** The friendly caption that appears in the header of your site and in any site directory where your site may be listed.

- ✔ **The site template:** The template determines what kind of site SharePoint makes for you. SharePoint includes dozens of predefined site templates. Your company may even create its custom site templates. Tell your administrator you want a team site, which is the most popular of all the SharePoint 2010 site templates.

- ✔ **The Web address or URL:** The unique location where your team site is hosted. In most organizations, all team sites are located off the same root Web address. Some examples I've seen include

    ```
    http://intranet.company.com/sites
    http://portal/projectsites
    http://sharepoint/sites
    ```

Your organization may also ask who has permission to access the site. Your site's users must be connected physically to your network or have permission from your network administrator to access your network remotely. Some companies set up a special kind of deployment for SharePoint, or an *extranet,* that provides a secure way for non-employees to log into their SharePoint team sites without actually being on the internal company network.

Setting up SharePoint in an extranet environment can be done in lots of ways and is outside the scope of this book. As I like to say, setting up SharePoint in an extranet environment is a networking problem, not a SharePoint problem. The good news is that a number of third-party companies host SharePoint team sites on the Internet for a small monthly fee. If your IT department can't support an extranet at this time, you might explore the option of using a hosted team site instead. These are usually very secure, and you can usually get your content out of the remote site and into your internal site when that time comes.

All SharePoint team sites have three basic kinds of users:

- ✔ **Visitors** have Read Only permission. They can view your site without making any contributions.

- ✔ **Members** can participate in your team site by uploading and editing documents or adding tasks or other items.

- ✔ **Owners** have Full Control permission to customize the site. As the person requesting the team site, the SharePoint administrator will likely assume that you're the proud owner unless you specifically tell him who owns the site.

Viewing Your Team Site in the Browser

You access your team site using a Web browser, such as Internet Explorer or Mozilla Firefox. You need the Web address or URL of your team site, which you can get from your SharePoint administrator. You also need a network user account with permissions.

In my case, the Web address for my team site is

```
http://myteamsite
```

To access your team site:

1. **Open your Web browser.**

2. **Type the Web address for your team site in the address bar and press Enter.**

Figure 1-1 shows the home page for a SharePoint team site.

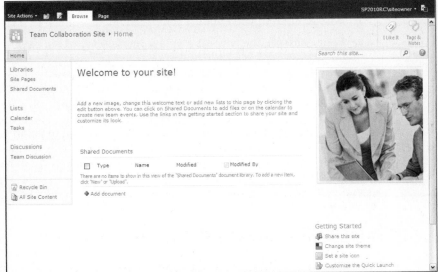

Figure 1-1: A SharePoint team site home page.

All SharePoint team sites have the same features. If you're using a new team site, your site should match the one in Figure 1-1. If your site has been customized, it may look slightly different. Never fear: All the same features are still there. You may just have to hunt a little bit to find them.

Choosing between IE and Firefox

Which browser should you use with SharePoint? Firefox and Internet Explorer browsers have some differences; for instance, some pages look better in Firefox than in Internet Explorer. Because Firefox was designed to be OS-agnostic, it supports Mac users as well as PC users. If any of your SharePoint user audience uses Macs, I recommend developing your SharePoint sites to display in Firefox. (The Microsoft SharePoint development team even uses Firefox to check how their sites look!)

You can think of the SharePoint page as having the following the major sections:

- ✔ **Header:** The header spans the entire top of the page. You can think of the header in a SharePoint page like the menu in a traditional Windows application, such as Microsoft Word. SharePoint 2010 even features the Ribbon in the page header, similar to how the Ribbon appears in the top of many Office applications.

- ✔ **Left navigation pane:** The navigation pane provides quick access to the site's document libraries, lists, and discussion boards. You can even add links to content you create, such as documents and Web pages.

- ✔ **Page content:** The content displays in the body of the page.

Generally speaking, the header and left navigation pane stay fairly consistent, whereas the body of the page changes to display the content for the Web page. This is very similar to how most Web sites work.

 Microsoft has spent a lot of money on usability research to determine how best to lay out the pages in SharePoint. That's why I usually encourage my clients to use the layouts provided by Microsoft instead of creating their own custom layouts.

Contributing to a Team Site

One of the main purposes of a team site is to allow its members to collaborate. But collaborate on what? Think of all the stuff that you do with Outlook and e-mail right now — all the documents you send as attachments, contacts you track, and messages you send with announcements. Now imagine doing all those same tasks in a Web site you share with your coworkers or project members.

Now take that one step further. Think about any public Web sites you use to network with other people, such as MySpace, LinkedIn, or Facebook. You can use your team site along with other features in SharePoint to create a community of people that you collaborate with at work.

Uploading documents

Most teams need to share documents. You probably use e-mail to send documents as attachments. With your new SharePoint 2010 team site, you can upload your files to the team site and send your team members a link to the document.

SharePoint 2010 uses a special kind of container — a *document library* — for storing files. Your team site has a document library dubbed Shared Documents where you can put documents you want to share with others. You can create additional document libraries and give them any name you want. See Chapter 2 for more details on working with files and document libraries in SharePoint 2010.

To upload a document to the Shared Documents library in your team site:

1. **Click the Shared Documents link in the left navigation pane of your team site.**

   The Shared Documents library appears.

   You can click the All Site Content link in the left navigation pane to view a list of all the document libraries that you have permission to access.

2. **Click the Upload Document button on the Documents tab of the SharePoint Ribbon.**

   The Upload Document window appears.

3. **Click the Browse button and in the Choose File dialog box, select a file to upload.**

4. **Click OK to upload the file to the document library.**

   When the file is uploaded, SharePoint displays the document's properties in a new window, as shown in Figure 1-2.

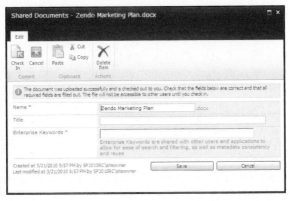

Figure 1-2: SharePoint displays a document's properties in a new window.

5. **Type the filename, title, and any keywords that you want to tag the document with in the Name, Title, and Enterprise Keywords text boxes, respectively.**

   See Chapter 2 for details on working with document properties.

6. **Click the Save button to save the properties you've entered for the document.**

   The uploaded document appears in the document library.

Adding calendar items

SharePoint 2010's team sites provide you with a calendar for tracking your team events. You can access the calendar by clicking the Calendar link in the home page's left navigation pane.

The calendar displays events in the Calendar view. You can use the Ribbon to change the view from month, to week, or day view and to add new events. To add a new event to the team calendar:

1. **Click the Calendar link in the left navigation pane.**

2. **Click the Events tab in the Ribbon and then click the New Event button.**

   A new window appears for you to enter your new calendar item, as shown in Figure 1-3.

3. **Type the information for your event.**

   The Title, Start Time, and End Time fields have asterisks next to them indicating they are required fields.

   To customize the fields that appear on this form, see Chapter 9.

4. **Click the Save button to save the event to the calendar.**

You can add tasks, contacts, announcements, and even new discussion topics just as easily as adding new calendar events. See Chapter 3 for details on this.

Social networking

SharePoint 2010 lets you do some exciting things with *social networking,* which is a fancy way of referring to ways that people can share ideas, insights, and information among groups of users, such as sharing links with your friends on Facebook.

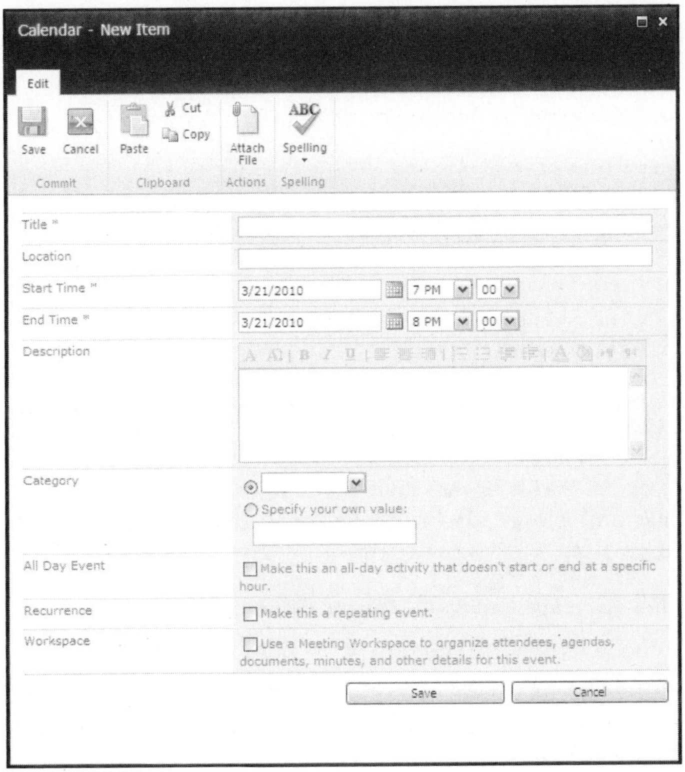

Figure 1-3:
Adding
a new
calendar
event to
your team's
calendar.

For example, SharePoint 2010 lets you tag things so that you can find them later and that people with whom you share your tags and notes also can see them. So for example, if you find a document that you like and want to encourage others in your network to read, you can apply a tag to the document and then that tag is associated with you so others viewing your profile can see the tag.

Don't panic: SharePoint 2010 tags and notes can be made private so that only you can see them, and you can also delete your tags whenever you want.

To tag a document:

1. **Browse to the library containing the document and then select the document using the check box in the list view, as shown in Figure 1-4.**

Figure 1-4:
Select a
document
to tag.

2. **Click the I Like It button on the Document tab, as shown in Figure 1-5.**

   SharePoint briefly displays the Add Tag confirmation message, and the item is saved to your tags and notes, visible to your colleagues in your profile Tags and Notes tab.

Figure 1-5:
Click the
I Like It
button.

To view your tags and notes:

1. **Click the arrow beside your name in the upper-right corner of the page and choose My Profile from the drop-down list.**

   Your profile page displays.

2. **Click the Tags and Notes tab, as shown in Figure 1-6.**

   In the Activities For: section of the page, you see an entry for the tag you just entered.

3. **Select the Make Private check box beside any activity so that only you can see it.**

Now only you can see the item you marked as private.

SharePoint 2010 has other social networking features in addition to tags; you can see some of them by exploring your profile, and I talk a little more about them in Chapter 7, too.

Why properties?

You may wonder why SharePoint 2010 prompts you to enter properties for your document. The properties that you enter — properties like the filename, title, and keywords — can be used to make it easier for other site users to find your document. SharePoint 2010's search feature indexes these properties so that users can search for them. You can also add new properties to your documents to make them easier to search for. In addition to search, you can use properties to create a list of documents that match a certain property's value. For example, say you have a set of documents with a Sales Territory property. You could display a subset of those documents on your team site's home page that match a certain territory's name.

Figure 1-6:
The Tags
and Notes
profile page.

Customizing Your Team Site

Most teams want to change their team site right away. As the site owner, you'll likely be asked to make these changes. Some of the changes you can make include adding and removing text and images from the home page and adding new lists and libraries. You can even change the site's color scheme and logo, which I discuss how to do in Chapter 19.

For now, stick to changing the home page. Later chapters in this part walk you through the process of working with lists and libraries.

Introducing the Ribbon

The header of the SharePoint 2010 team site page boasts the Ribbon. The Ribbon was introduced in Office 2007 and is a convenient way to display many menu items in a small amount of screen space.

The Ribbon in SharePoint 2010 features menu items that are relevant to the kind of page you're viewing, arranged in tabs. For example, the home page displays three tabs: Browse, Page, and Publish. You find most of the menu commands you need to use on the Ribbon, and some Ribbon buttons contain drop-down lists. Figure 1-7 shows the Ribbon with the Page tab active and the Edit drop-down list displayed.

Document libraries and lists display commands on the Ribbon that provide additional configuration options. These commands are *contextual* because the commands that appear depend on the context of where you are in the site.

Figure 1-7:
Use the
Ribbon to
access
menu com-
mands.

Modifying the home page

A SharePoint 2010 team site creates a home page that you can modify to better meet your team's needs. You can add text or images, or display your announcements, tasks, or calendar items.

You must be logged into your site as a user with permissions to modify the site's pages. That usually means you need to belong to the site's Members group.

The site's Members group has contribute permissions by default, which includes add, edit, and delete. See Chapter 12 for details on managing permissions.

The home page of a team site is a wiki page. Wiki pages provide a richer content editing experience than Web Part pages. I discuss the kinds of Web pages in SharePoint in Chapter 9.

To put the home page in Edit mode:

1. **Browse to the home page of your team site and then click the Page tab in the Ribbon.**

   The Ribbon displays a set of editing options for the Web page.

2. **Click the Edit button in the Edit section of the Ribbon.**

   The page appears in Edit mode.

If you want to lock the page so no one else can edit it at the same time, click the Check Out button in the Edit section of the Ribbon before placing the page in Edit mode.

With the page in Edit mode, you can place your cursor anywhere inside the rectangular boxes in the page's body to edit the content. For example, to change the default text that appears on the home page, with your page in Edit mode, do the following:

1. **Place your cursor in front of the Welcome . . . text.**

2. **Delete the placeholder text and type your new text.**

3. **Use the formatting options displayed in the Ribbon's Format Text tab to apply changes to your text, such as changing the font and adding bullet points.**

   You can even apply styles, as shown in Figure 1-8.

Figure 1-8: Apply formatting changes to your text with the Ribbon.

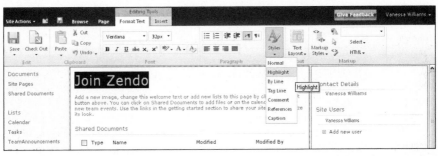

 SharePoint 2010 provides tools for formatting and editing your text in the browser. See Chapter 16 for details on using and customizing these tools.

4. **Click the Stop Editing button to save your changes.**

 If you have your page checked out, click the Check In button when you're done making changes.

To add a table, image, link, or Web Part to your home page:

1. **Place your page in Edit mode by clicking the Edit button on the Page tab in the Ribbon.**

2. **Click the Insert tab on the Ribbon to display your insert options and then place your cursor on the page where you want to insert an item from the Ribbon.**

   You must place your cursor inside one of the rectangular boxes within the page's body.

3. Click the button for the content item you wish to add (see Figure 1-9):

- *For a table,* click the Table button and then select the number of rows and columns you want in your table.

- *For an image,* click the Image button and then select whether you want to upload the image from your local computer or from another Web address. See Chapter 21 for more details on working with images.

- *For hyperlinked text,* click the Link button to add it to your page.

- *For a Web Part,* click the Web Part button to add it to your page. See Chapter 10 for more details on working with Web Parts.

4. Click the Edit tab and then click the Stop Editing button to save your changes.

Figure 1-9:
Use the
Ribbon to
add links,
images, and
tables.

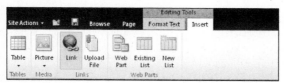

Chapter 2

Sharing Your Documents

. . . .

In This Chapter

▶ Understanding what document libraries are and why they're superior to file shares

▶ Discovering lots of ways to get your documents into document libraries

▶ Working with (and deleting) your documents

▶ Retrieving a document after it has been deleted

. . . .

*Y*ou're probably familiar with *network file shares:* the file systems that let people upload files to a shared network drive so that other people can access and use them. File shares, when they were invented, revolutionized the ability of organizations to keep files in relatively secure locations and manage who had access. But SharePoint has done the file share one (okay, a whole bunch) better.

SharePoint document libraries let you store and share files securely, and they also add features that help you manage things like *document workflow* (the processes that let people edit, comment on, and approve documents) and *version histories* (what happened to a file, and who did what). And although file shares give you one path through folders to your document, SharePoint document libraries give you other paths to expose content. You can access documents directly through the browser, you can bubble them up in Web Parts, and you can sort and filter them with their metadata and content types. And with document libraries, you can expose files by their title, not just their filename.

Document libraries give you multiple choices about how the documents get into them, too. You can save a document with the document library's URL, but you can also e-mail documents to document libraries or drag and drop from Windows Explorer. And you can create documents directly in their document libraries.

If you do a search on a file share, you potentially retrieve hits on documents that you don't have the permissions to open; SharePoint, on the other hand, allows results to be security trimmed so that if you can't access it, you can't even see it in your search results.

Defining Document Libraries

As I discuss in Chapter 3, everything in SharePoint is a list. That can be confusing at first, but for now, you just need to know that a *document library* is just a special kind of list. Although most other SharePoint lists are organized around things that are defined primarily by their metadata, document libraries are organized around files that exist separately and are described by their metadata.

A document library doesn't just have to contain Microsoft Word files. Document libraries can contain many file types, including Excel, PDF, and Visio files. Even Web pages are stored in document libraries.

Document libraries add the ability to find your documents. Unlike a file share, which treats files as separate objects, document libraries treat documents as content and let you associate certain information *(metadata)* with the sets of documents in them. This means that documents can be found based on the similarities described by metadata, and not just by the search options you have on a file share.

You might wonder why leaving your documents on a shared network drive isn't easier than using a document library in SharePoint 2010. The most compelling reason why is that SharePoint offers many ways to organize your documents, such as

- ✔ **Document libraries provide a unique Web address for accessing a group of documents.** Document libraries make it possible to apply security to groups of related documents, and through security trimming, they prevent unauthorized users from seeing them in search results. (See Chapter 12 for more on security.)

- ✔ **Document properties make it possible to create many views of the same documents.**

- ✔ **Folders make it possible to group a subset of documents based on permission requirements.**

Getting Your Documents into a Library

SharePoint 2010 gives you many ways to get your files into document libraries. In this section, I show you how to upload your documents one at a time or a whole bunch at once with the browser, with the familiar Windows Explorer interface, and with Office applications. With all these options, you have no excuse to keep your files on your hard drive!

Uploading a single document

When you have a single document to upload to a document library, you can do so easily through the browser. The process for uploading a document to a library is the same for any kind of library you use, whether it's the Shared Documents library that's created with your team site or another library created by the site owner.

I walk you through the process of uploading a single document to a library in Chapter 1. The steps are similar to uploading multiple documents, which I discuss in the following section.

You can also send documents to a document library via e-mail. If your SharePoint farm administrator has configured SharePoint 2010 to accept incoming e-mail, individual document libraries can be given their own e-mail address. When someone sends a document as an attachment to that e-mail address, it's uploaded to the document library. This approach works well when you need to allow people outside your organization to place documents in a document library. I recommend using one document library to accept incoming documents and then assign someone in your team to move the documents to another document library.

Uploading multiple documents

There may be times when you have multiple documents to upload. SharePoint 2010 allows you to select multiple documents and upload them all at once. This approach saves you time; however, you can't batch-upload for properties. So even though you save time uploading the files, you still have to manually edit the properties on each file.

These steps work only in Internet Explorer.

To upload multiple documents to the same document library:

1. **Browse to the document library where you want to upload your files.**

   For example, click the Shared Documents link in the left navigation pane to go to that document library.

2. **Click the down arrow on the Upload Document button on the Documents tab of the Ribbon and choose Upload Multiple Documents.**

   The Upload Multiple Documents window appears, as shown in Figure 2-1.

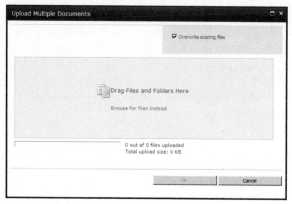

Figure 2-1:
You can
upload
multiple
documents
to a single
document
library.

3. **Drag and drop files from your file system into the Upload Multiple Documents window.**

   Alternatively, click Browse For Files Instead to browse for the files you wish to upload.

   The files appear in the SharePoint Upload Document window, as shown in Figure 2-2.

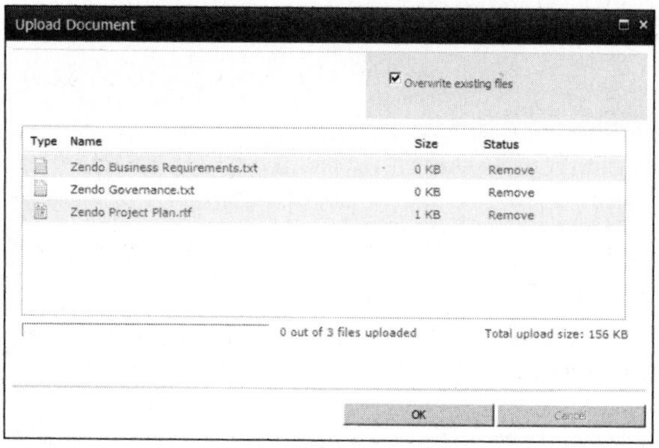

Figure 2-2:
Drag and
drop the
files you
want to
upload.

4. **Click OK to upload the files to the document library.**

   The Upload Document window presents an upload progress bar while the files upload and then a message indicating your files were uploaded.

5. **Click Done to return to the document library.**

An icon with the word New appears in the document library next to the name of each of the files you just uploaded. By default, this icon appears on all newly uploaded files for a period of three days.

Your SharePoint farm administrator can block certain file types, such as executable files. You can upload files from productivity suites, such as Microsoft Office and Open Office.

You may have noticed that SharePoint didn't prompt you to enter the properties for the files that you uploaded. When you perform a multiple upload, you aren't prompted the way you are for a single upload, even for properties that are required (so you have to go back and add those properties later). So uploading multiple files isn't a good approach when you need to capture properties.

If you must manually update the properties for many files at once, you can use the Datasheet view of the library. The Datasheet view works similarly to a spreadsheet. To manually update properties using the Datasheet view in the same document library where you uploaded your files:

1. **Click the Library tab on the SharePoint Ribbon and then click the Datasheet View button.**

   You must have Excel installed on your computer for the Datasheet view to work.

2. **Place your cursor in the field you want to update and make changes, as shown in Figure 2-3.**

3. **Move your cursor off the row you updated and then SharePoint 2010 saves your updates.**

See Chapter 5 for more details on working with Datasheet views.

Figure 2-3:
Use
Datasheet
view to
update
document
properties.

Uploading documents with Windows Explorer

You can also use the familiar Windows Explorer to copy and paste documents into a document library. To access the Windows Explorer folder of a
document library:

1. **Browse to the document library using Internet Explorer.**

2. **Click the Library tab on the SharePoint Ribbon and then click the
   Open with Explorer button in the Connect & Export group.**

   You may be prompted for your username and password. If so, enter
   your credentials and click OK. The library opens in a Windows Explorer
   folder view, as shown in Figure 2-4.

3. **Copy and paste your documents into the folder and then refresh your
   browser window to see your documents.**

This process doesn't prompt you to enter properties or bulk check-in your
documents.

Moving documents in and around SharePoint

Just because you uploaded your document into one document library doesn't mean it's stuck there forever. Sometimes you want to move documents to a different document library. You can use the Windows Explorer view to quickly move documents from one document library into another. But unfortunately, Windows Explorer moves the files only, and not any associated metadata. So for that reason, investigate the copy and move function of the Manage Content and Structure tool. (I discuss this tool in Chapter 15.)

Windows Explorer is great if you need to upload a lot of documents into a document library. But resist the urge to take all the files from your shared drives and to copy them into libraries with Windows Explorer. That's usually a recipe for disaster because most people store files in folders and recreating that folder structure in a SharePoint library makes it very hard to find files. (Although folders have some uses in SharePoint, navigation isn't one of them.) Instead, consider the other options — libraries, tagging, and content types — when moving files into SharePoint.

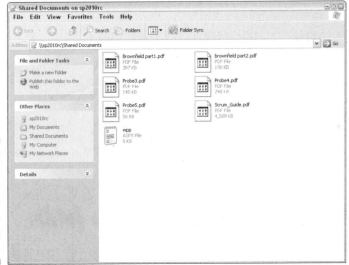

Figure 2-4:
Copy and paste your documents with Windows Explorer.

Why folders in SharePoint are evil

Resist the urge to use folders in your document libraries; this file share paradigm generally causes nothing but problems in document libraries.

One reason to use SharePoint instead of a file share to begin with is so that you can add properties to describe your documents. Properties allow you to view your documents in different ways. If you dump your files in folders just like they were arranged on the file share, ignoring properties, you probably won't be very satisfied with your SharePoint experience.

As well, nested folders in SharePoint are just as hard to navigate as nested folders in file shares (and nested URLs in folders inside doc libs get pretty unwieldy pretty fast). Instead of replicating your file structure in SharePoint, I recommend that you flatten the folder hierarchies by replacing them with views.

When you need to separate a group of documents to give them separate permissions is the only reason to use a folder in a document library. For pretty much everything else, I recommend that you use properties to organize your documents. (See Chapter 8 for details on properties.)

If you're using a browser other than Internet Explorer, you can still access your libraries using Windows Explorer. In Windows Vista, add the Web address of your SharePoint 2010 team site or document library as a new network location in the Computer folder. For Windows XP users, add a new network place to access your library using Windows Explorer.

SharePoint 2010 uses a number of protocols to allow you to access libraries as folders with Windows Explorer. In my experience, this feature either works or it doesn't. If it doesn't, most organizations aren't willing to spend any energy to figure out why.

Uploading documents into a folder

You can use folders within your document libraries as a means to organize your documents. I show you how to create a folder and upload files into it, but I urge you to first read the sidebar, "Why folders in SharePoint are evil."

Okay, so maybe you have a document library and you have a subset of files that only supervisors should see. You could put those files in a separate document library and set the permissions on that library. But say you already have one library set up the way you like and it seems silly to create another one. Instead, you can use a folder to separate the restricted files from the rest of the files in the library.

To create a folder within a document library:

1. **Browse to your document library where you want to create the folder.**

2. **Click the New Folder button in the Documents tab of the SharePoint Ribbon.**

   The New Folder window appears. If you don't see the New Folder button, folders are disabled for the library. Use the Advanced Settings option in Library Settings to enable or disable folders in your library.

3. **Type the name of the folder in the Name field and click the Save button.**

   The folder appears in the document library.

To upload files into the folder:

1. **Click the folder name to navigate inside it and then click the Upload Document button on the Document tab of the Ribbon.**

   The Upload Document window appears.

2. **Browse to the document you want to upload to the folder.**

3. **Make sure the Folder field lists the folder where you want to upload the document, as shown in Figure 2-5.**

   If the folder is incorrect, click the Choose Folder button to select the right folder.

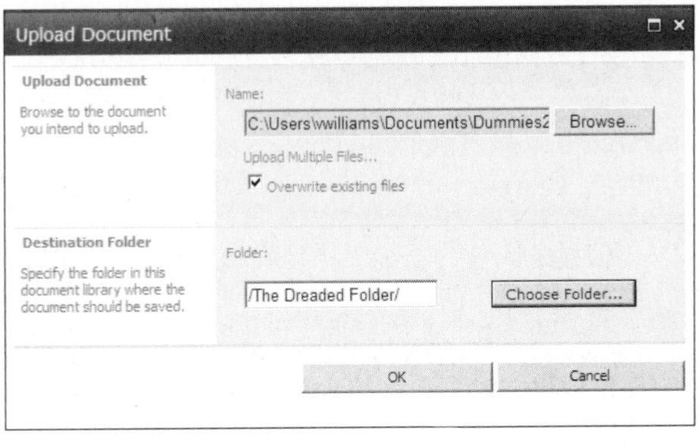

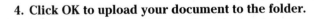

Figure 2-5:
You can
upload a
document
into a folder.

4. **Click OK to upload your document to the folder.**

You can work with folders the same way as you work with documents. That is, the rules about working with properties and the Ribbon also apply to folders.

To restrict access to your folder so that only certain groups can access it:

1. **Click the drop-down arrow on the folder name and choose Manage Permissions, as shown in Figure 2-6.**

   The Permissions page appears.

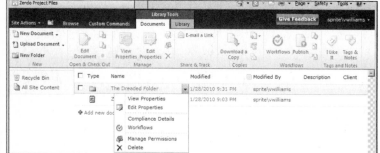

Figure 2-6: Setting permissions on a folder.

2. **Click the Stop Inheriting Permissions button and then click OK on the dialog box warning you that you're creating unique permissions for this folder.**

3. **Set the desired permissions for the folder.**

   I discuss permissions management in detail in Chapter 12.

Working with Documents

After you upload your documents to a library, you need to be able to work with your documents. This includes adding descriptive properties and letting other teammates know where the documents are stored.

SharePoint 2010 provides two methods for working with documents. Each document has an Edit menu that you can use to take some action on that document, such as checking it out for editing. The Ribbon also displays a set of actions that can be taken on individual documents or a group of selected documents.

Using the Edit menu

Accessing the Edit menu is a little tricky because it isn't visible immediately. You see the Edit menu when you hover your mouse pointer over the Name property of your document. When you see a little arrow appear, you can click the arrow to display the Edit menu, as shown in Figure 2-7.

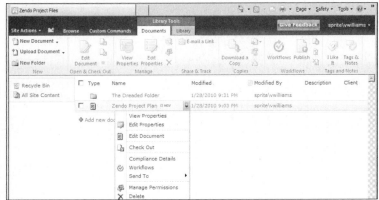

Figure 2-7:
Display the
Edit menu
to work
with your
document.

With the Edit menu, you can view and edit properties. (If SharePoint recognizes the file type, it displays the default application that can be used to edit the document, for example, Edit in Microsoft Word.)

Some options in the Edit menu depend on how your document library has been configured. For example, if versioning is enabled for the document library, you see a Version History item in the Edit menu. (See Chapter 8 for more details on customizing your document library.)

Your organization can add custom menu items to the Edit menu, so don't be surprised if your Edit menu looks different than the one shown in Figure 2-7. The point is that you can use the Edit menu to access a list of actions that you can take on the selected document.

Editing a document's properties

You can use a document's Edit menu or the Ribbon to view and edit a document's properties. By default, SharePoint 2010 asks only for these three properties:

- ✔ **Name:** The filename. For example, if you upload a `myspreadsheet. xlsx` file, that's the value you see in the filename.

- ✔ **Title:** A caption that describes the document. If a title exists already in the document, SharePoint uses that. Otherwise, you can enter your own descriptive title.

- ✔ **Enterprise Keywords:** Terms you use to tag documents and are then added (automatically by SharePoint) to a separate keyword set dubbed the Managed Term Store. The Managed Term Store (it's actually a database) can be used to enable some groovy functions like tag clouds (see Chapter 7).

Your site owner can add more properties to describe the document. For example, the owner might add a Category property that allows you to apply a category to the document. Properties are actually just new columns that you add to your document library. I describe the process of adding new columns in Chapter 4.

The easiest way to view a document's properties is to use the Ribbon:

1. **Click the document in the document library so it's highlighted.**

2. **Click the View Properties button on the Documents tab of the Ribbon.**

   The Display Form window appears.

Figure 2-8 shows the Display Form window for a document. This window includes its own version of the Ribbon that provides commands for editing the document's properties or deleting the document. Simply click the Edit Item button on the Ribbon to edit the form fields.

You can customize the appearance of the display form, and its cousin, the edit form. Each list and library has its own set of these forms (lists also have a new form) you can customize to suit your requirements for displaying and editing a document's properties using SharePoint Designer 2010.

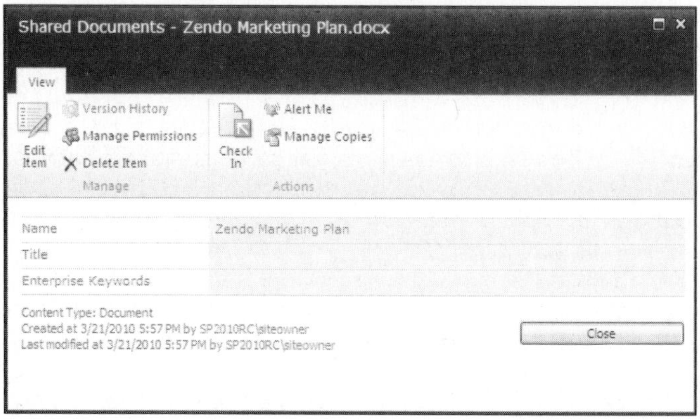

Figure 2-8:
Use the
Display
Form
window to
view or edit
properties.

Shared Documents - Zendo Marketing Plan.docx

View

Edit Item | Version History | Manage Permissions | Delete Item | Check In | Alert Me | Manage Copies

Manage | Actions

Name | Zendo Marketing Plan

Title

Enterprise Keywords

Content Type: Document
Created at 3/21/2010 5:57 PM by SP2010RC\siteowner
Last modified at 3/21/2010 5:57 PM by SP2010RC\siteowner

Close

Checking documents in and out

The Ribbon displays many of the same document actions as the Edit menu. One of the advantages of using the Ribbon is that you can use it to take actions on multiple documents at once. For example, say you want to check out three documents at one time. Here's how you can do it with the Ribbon:

1. **In your document library, select the check box next to each document you want to check out.**

2. **Click the Check Out button on the Documents tab of the SharePoint Ribbon.**

3. **Click OK at the confirmation prompt.**

   The documents are checked out.

Alternatively, you can use a document's Edit menu to access the Check Out menu command.

You may be thinking, "That's great, but why would I want to check out a document?" To me, checking out — and its counterpart, checking in — is just good document library etiquette. What better way to let others know that you're making changes to a document than by checking it out? Checking out a document sets the Checked Out flag to Yes and stores the name of the person who checked out the document.

Generally speaking, I suggest that you check out any document that you intend to edit for a period of longer than five minutes. In other words, if you need to do more than just change a misspelled word or update the date in a footer, check out the document. Of course, always remember to check in documents when your edits are complete.

To tell the truth, I'm horrible about remembering to check documents in and out. That's one reason I like to use SharePoint Workspace (formerly known as Microsoft Groove) for accessing documents in SharePoint document libraries. I can work with documents offline, make changes, and then synchronize those changes. It's much easier for me to remember to synchronize SharePoint Workspace at the beginning and end of each day than it is to remember to check out and check in documents that I've used that day.

When you check out a single document at a time, SharePoint 2010 prompts you to save the document in your local drafts folder. Don't believe me? Follow these steps to see for yourself:

1. **In a document library, hover over the Name column for the document you wish to check out.**

2. **When the arrow appears, click it to display the document's Edit menu and choose Check Out.**

   SharePoint displays the check out prompt, as shown in Figure 2-9.

Figure 2-9:
Check out
a docu-
ment using
local drafts
folder.

3. **Accept the default value to Use My Local Draft Folder by clicking OK.**

   The document is checked out and downloaded to your local hard drive.

   Unless your administrator has changed the location, your local drafts folder can be found at `C:\users\%username%\documents\ sharepoint drafts`.

To open the document you just checked out and downloaded, you must browse to your local drafts folder with Windows Explorer and then open the file. Because most people don't want to bother with this extra step, I don't think very many people bother with using this folder.

When you check out a document, if it's in some Windows-compatible applica-tion (such as Word), you'll receive a message letting you specify whether to check out the document to your local drafts folder. Generally, you want to select the Use My local drafts Folder option because it creates a temporary file on your hard drive and will let you edit the checked-out file even when you're offline.

By choosing not to use your local drafts folder, the file will open from the SharePoint server. This can cause your system to hang and appear unrespon-sive because it has to wait for your changes to travel back and forth across the network to the server. If you lose your network connection, you could lose changes to your document. I always recommend downloading a local copy of the file when making changes. You can use your local drafts folder as I describe here, SharePoint Workspace, or manually download the file and upload it again when you're done making changes.

Documents that are checked out show an arrow in the document type icon. As shown in Figure 2-10, the bottom item is checked out, whereas the top two aren't.

If you want to see who has a document checked out, you have to display the Checked Out To column in the document library. (I discuss working with views in Chapter 5.)

Figure 2-10:
The bottom
document
is checked
out.

To check in a document after you're done making your changes, you can
repeat the steps you followed earlier in this section to check out the document, only in Step 2, choose the Check In option from the document's Edit
menu or click the button on the Document tab of the Ribbon.

If you change your mind and want to pretend that the check-out never happened, you can click the Discard Check Out button instead of checking in
the document. This can be useful if you accidentally checked out the wrong
document.

Sending a link to your document

To share your document with others, they must know where to find the document. One way to do so is to send them the Web address of the team site or
the document library. You can also send them a link directly to the document
itself.

To send a link to a document:

1. **Hover your mouse over the document's filename.**

   Don't click the filename or else the document will open.

2. **Right-click the document link and choose Copy Shortcut from the
   menu.**

   In Firefox, choose Copy Link Location. The link to the document is
   copied to your clipboard.

3. **Paste the link into your e-mail message.**

As long as your team members have network access and permissions to your
document library, they can click the link and open the file.

SharePoint 2010 also provides a menu option you can use to send a link to the document. On the Edit menu, choose Send To⇨E-mail a Link. This opens an e-mail message in your default e-mail program and pastes a link to your document. (I don't like to use this option because I don't like to let one program open another program.)

Recovering Deleted Documents

I often say that SharePoint delivers on the promise that software has been making for years to make us more productive. Although that's not always true, one feature of SharePoint that truly delivers is the Recycle Bin. When you delete a document from a document library, it isn't gone forever. Nope. The document just moves to a holding place in your site — the Recycle Bin.

Go ahead and try it. Go to a document library and delete a document. You can use the Edit menu or the Manage group on the Ribbon to access the Delete command. Either way, you're prompted to confirm the deletion, and then your document appears in the Recycle Bin.

The Recycle Bin works for list items also.

To restore a document from the Recycle Bin to its original location:

1. **Go to the Recycle Bin by clicking the Recycle Bin link in the site's left navigation pane.**

   You must click the Recycle Bin link in the same site where you deleted the file. Otherwise, the file won't appear.

2. **Place a check mark next to any files you wish to restore.**

3. **Click the Restore Selection link, as shown in Figure 2-11.**

   The file is restored to the document library.

You can click the Delete Selection link in the Recycle Bin to remove the file from your Recycle Bin. Doing so, however, doesn't permanently delete the file. Instead, the file is moved to another Recycle Bin that can be accessed by the site collection administrator.

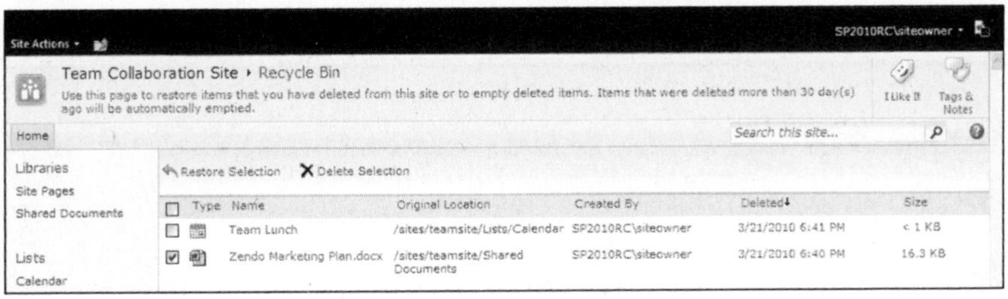

Figure 2-11:
Restoring a
document
from the
Recycle Bin.

If you're the site collection administrator, you can follow these steps to access the administrator's Recycle Bin:

1. **Log into the site as the site collection administrator.**

   Your SharePoint administrator in IT can look up this account information.

2. **Click the Site Actions menu above the Ribbon and select Site Settings.**

   The Site Settings page appears.

3. **In the Site Collection Administration section, click the Recycle Bin link.**

4. **In the Recycle Bin's left navigation pane, click the Deleted from End User Recycle Bin link.**

5. **Click the items you wish to restore and click Restore Selection.**

   The items are restored.

Files remain in the site collection Recycle Bin for a period of 30 days or until they're deleted by the administrator, whichever comes first. When removed from the Recycle Bin, the fate of your documents depends on your company's business continuity management plan. That's a fancy way to say, do they back up their data? SharePoint stores your documents in databases. An administrator can connect to a backed-up copy of the database and select individual documents to restore.

Chapter 3

Working with Lists

- -

In This Chapter

▶ Creating new SharePoint lists

▶ Adding, editing, and viewing list items

▶ Adding Web Parts to default list forms

▶ Using SharePoint Workspace 2010 to work with lists offline

- -

SharePoint 2010 provides many kinds of lists that you can use to track information. A *list* is similar to an Excel spreadsheet or a table in an Access database. Unlike a spreadsheet that is blank when you first create it, SharePoint provides several predefined lists. These lists have columns and forms that make it possible for you to track everything from contacts to tasks.

SharePoint provides three basic kinds of lists:

- ✔ **Communications lists** are used to track announcements, contacts, and discussion boards.

- ✔ **Tracking lists** are used to track information such as links, calendars, tasks, issues, and surveys.

- ✔ **Custom lists** provide a starting template that you can build on to create a list with the exact columns you need.

This chapter discusses communications and tracking lists, and Chapter 4 covers custom lists.

The types of lists you can create with SharePoint 2010 depend on the product edition that your company has installed. You may have more or fewer options.

Libraries are a special kind of SharePoint list. They're a list that is used to store files in addition to tracking items. The items that you track in a library are the files themselves. Everything you know about lists also applies to libraries.

Getting to Know SharePoint's Lists

Determining which type of SharePoint list to use can be confusing at first. Do you need a Contact list or a custom list? Although all lists perform the same basic function of tracking information, some lists offer additional columns or menu commands that are unique to that kind of list.

I know some people who always start with a custom list because they figure they know exactly what they want their list to look like. However, with that approach, you never get an understanding of the features and limitations of the other list types. Don't be afraid to create lists, use them for a while, and then discard them. This process is *prototyping,* and professionals do it all the time. There's no one "right" list.

All the lists in SharePoint 2010 use the Ribbon to display access to all list commands; check the "Using the Ribbon to manage lists" section for more.

In Table 3-1, I provide a comparison of some of the SharePoint list types. This is by no means an exhaustive list. The list types in the table appear in the same order they are shown when you create a new list.

Table 3-1	Comparison of SharePoint's List Types	
Type of List	*When to Use It*	*What Makes It Special*
Announcements	To display brief announcements on your site's home page.	You can enter expiration dates for announcements.
Contacts	To track contacts, especially if you want to use Outlook for data entry.	You can remove columns that you don't need.
Discussion Board	To create a discussion forum where people can post messages and reply to them.	Evaluate third-party add-ons if you want a robust discussion forum.
Links	To track hyperlinks.	Uses a Hyperlink column that automatically formats entered text as HTML anchor links.
Calendar	To track calendar items.	Can synchronize with Outlook and knows how to handle recurring events.

Type of List	When to Use It	What Makes It Special
Tasks	To track tasks.	Can synchronize with Outlook; Tasks lists can be grouped with summary tasks.
Project Tasks	To track work items for a project.	Can display as a Gantt chart. Many people consider this SharePoint's Project Lite offering.
Issue Tracking	To track trouble tickets.	Works well with issues that have three states — open, closed, and resolved.
Survey	To take a poll.	Allows you to create a set of questions that users must walk through.
Custom	To create a list with columns that you define.	Allows you to create a list specific to your content and can for example act on certain content in special ways.
KPI (Key Performance Indicator)	To display graphical status indicators.	Lets you evaluate selected business data against specified goals and display that information in various formats such as scorecards and dashboards.
Import Spreadsheet	To create a list based on an existing spreadsheet.	Lets you use an existing Excel spreadsheet as the basis of the list; can help avoid rework and repeated effort entering data.
External	To create a list based on a data source outside SharePoint.	Lets you display data from other (non-SharePoint) databases or Web services.

The lists in Table 3-1 are intended primarily for tracking information for a team, such as a department calendar or a project issues log. The lists here just scratch the surface of what you can do with lists in SharePoint. Lists can be used similar to how tables are used in databases to store the data for an application.

Although lists have columns and rows like a database table, they aren't database tables. In fact, the lists from your team site are stored in a single table in SharePoint's content database.

Creating a new list

A SharePoint 2010 team site has a few lists created for you — Announcements, Tasks, and Discussion Board. You usually want to create your own list to match the needs of your team.

To create a new list in your team site, you need to have the Manage Lists permission. This permission is usually granted with the Hierarchy Managers SharePoint group. (See Chapter 12 for more details on managing permissions.)

Regardless of the kind of list you want to create, the steps are the same. These steps are the same for creating new libraries also. To create a new list in your SharePoint 2010 team site, follow these steps:

1. **In your SharePoint site, choose Site Actions⇨More Options. (See Figure 3-1.)**

   The Create page appears.

   You can also access the Create page by clicking the Create button from the View All Site Content page.

   Figure 3-1 shows the Site Actions menu that is typically seen in a team site. Other kinds of SharePoint sites will have different menu options.

2. **On the Create page, click the List link in the Filter By section.**

   A list of icons appears for each kind of list you can create in SharePoint. Click a list category to further filter to display.

3. **Click the icon for the kind of list you want to create.**

   For example, click the Announcements icon to create a new list to store announcements.

4. **Type a name for your list in the text box that appears, as shown in Figure 3-2.**

   I recommend creating your list names without any spaces. The list name is used as part of the Web address. You can change the list name to a friendlier name after the list is created.

5. **Click the Create button.**

   SharePoint creates the list and displays it in the browser.

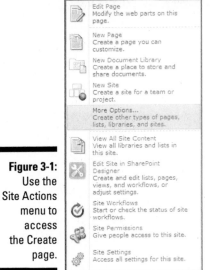

Figure 3-1:
Use the
Site Actions
menu to
access
the Create
page.

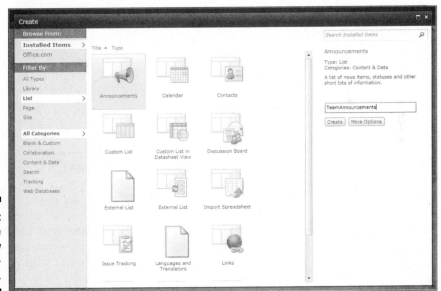

Figure 3-2:
Create
a new
Announce-
ments list.

If you set the list's Web address in Step 5 of the preceding list, you may want to change the list's name to something friendlier after the list is created. With the list you created open in the browser, do the following:

1. **Click the List tab in the SharePoint Ribbon.**

2. **In the Settings group, click the List Settings button that appears on the far right of the Ribbon.**

   The List Settings page appears.

3. **Under General Settings, click the Title, Description and Navigation link.**

4. **In the List General Settings page that appears, update the name and description (you can leave Navigation alone).**

   The Name field changes the caption used for the list, but the Web address remains the same.

5. **If you want to add or remove the list from the site's left navigation pane, you can change your selection to the question, Display This List On the Quick Launch?**

6. **Click the Save button to update your list.**

   The name, description, and navigation of your list updates to match your changes. Because the Web address doesn't change, any links to your list will continue to work.

Instead of using a SharePoint predefined list template, sometimes you have a very specific set of columns you want to track in your list. That's when a custom list comes in handy. Because creating custom lists requires you to add new columns to your list, I cover that topic in Chapter 4.

Using the Ribbon to manage lists

All SharePoint lists display the Ribbon at the top of the list. You can use the SharePoint Ribbon to access the common tasks used for working with lists. These include creating new items, editing existing items, and viewing items. Additional tasks include deleting items and viewing an item's version history. You can also use the Ribbon's List tab to make configuration changes to the list, such as changing which columns appear in the list. I explain how to do this in Chapter 4.

The menu commands you see in the Ribbon depend on the kind of list you're viewing. Usually the Ribbon displays list commands in one of two tabs under List Tools, as shown in Figure 3-3:

✔ **Items** displays all the commands you need for working with items. I discuss several of these options in the following section.

✔ **List** displays commands for managing and customizing the entire list, such as creating views and exporting the list to Excel.

A more thorough explanation of list and library commands can be found in Chapter 8.

Figure 3-3:
Use the
Ribbon to
manage
your list.

Entering Data in SharePoint Lists

Some primary tasks you perform in SharePoint are entering, editing, and viewing your data in a SharePoint list. The kind of list you're using doesn't matter; the steps for performing the tasks are the same.

To perform the tasks that I describe in this section, you must have the Add Items, Edit Items, and View Items permissions. These permissions are usually granted with the Contributor permissions level, which is usually granted via the *Site* Members SharePoint group.

Follow these steps to add, edit, or view list data, such as a Tasks list in your SharePoint 2010 team site:

1. **Browse to your Tasks lists either by clicking the Tasks link in the left navigation pane of the team site or by entering the Web address in the browser.**

2. **In the Ribbon, click the Items tab, and then click the New Item button to add a new item to the list.**

    The New Item form appears in a dialog box, as shown in Figure 3-4.

3. **Click the Save button to add your item to the list.**

    The item appears in the list.

4. **To select an item in the list to edit or view, select the check box for the row you wish to edit or view.**

    The row is highlighted, as shown in Figure 3-5.

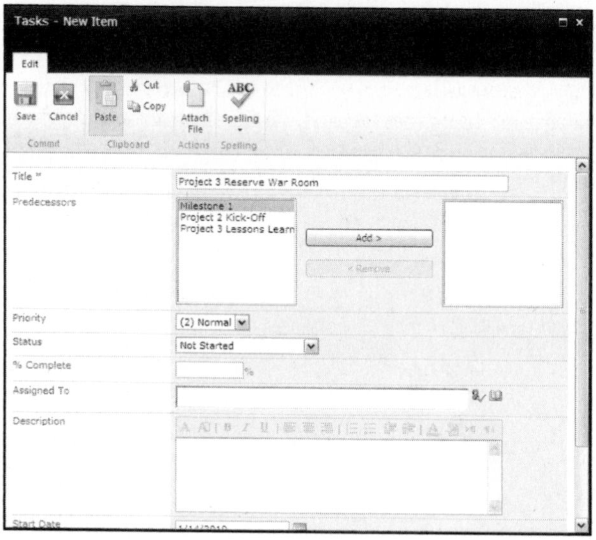

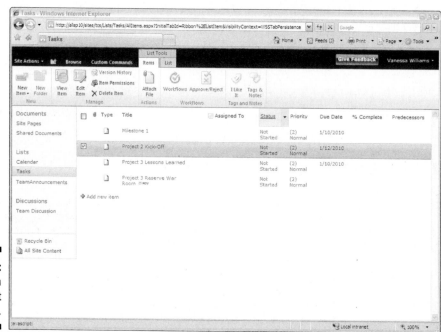

Figure 3-4:
Add news
tasks to
your list.

Figure 3-5:
Select an
item to edit
or view.

5. **To edit the item, click the Edit Item button in the Items tab of the Ribbon.**

   The Edit Item window appears. Make your changes to the item in the window and click the Save button. The updates are saved to the list.

   You can also use the Edit menu to edit a list item, as I describe in Chapter 2. Figure 3-6 shows the additional menu items that allow you to manage permissions, set alerts, or check compliance policies on the item you're viewing.

6. **To view an item in the list, select the row you wish to view and click the View Item button.**

   The Display Form window allows you to view the values for a list, but also access additional commands for working with the list item.

   You can also edit list items using an inline form, which makes it easy to edit items without opening each item individually. See Chapter 5 for details.

Figure 3-6:
View an item to access more menu commands.

Customizing List Forms

When you add, edit, and view items in your SharePoint list, the items display in a set of Web forms. Each list automatically creates one list form for each of these tasks — a New Form, Edit Form, and Display Form. You can edit these forms in the browser to add additional Web Parts to the form when it's displayed.

To customize list forms with the browser:

1. **In the list where you want to customize forms, click the List tab in the Ribbon and then click the Form Web Parts button in the Customize List group.**

   A drop-down list appears.

2. **Click the Web Part that corresponds to the list form you want to edit — Default New Form, Default Display Form, or Default Edit Form, as shown in Figure 3-7.**

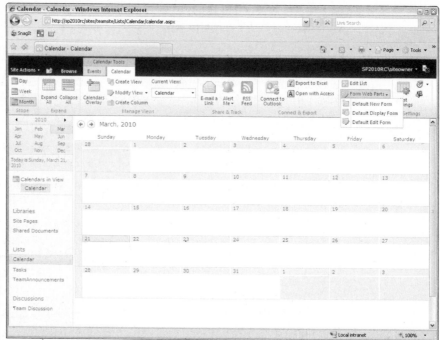

Figure 3-7:
Select a list
form to
customize.

3. **In the Ribbon, add Web Parts to the form or modify the Web Part for the list form.**

   I discuss working with Web Parts in detail in Chapter 9.

4. **To save your changes, click the Page tab of the Ribbon and then click the Stop Editing button.**

You can use SharePoint Designer 2010 to make more extensive changes to list forms.

Taking Lists Offline

You may not always find it convenient or possible to work with SharePoint lists in the browser. Sometimes you aren't connected to the network. Sometimes working in the browser is just a pain. To work with your SharePoint lists (and libraries) offline, you can choose from using Microsoft Outlook 2010 or SharePoint Workspace 2010. (SharePoint Workspace is the product formerly known as Groove.)

You could always work offline with libraries using Outlook 2007 and Groove 2007. The Office 2010 versions of these products allow you to work with both lists and libraries offline. That means you can view, edit, and add new documents without being connected to SharePoint. You can also edit and update your lists.

To access your SharePoint lists offline using SharePoint Workspace 2010:

1. **Launch SharePoint Workspace 2010 and then click the New SharePoint Workspace button to create a new workspace to connect to SharePoint.**

   If your company has its own internal server for managing SharePoint Workspace accounts, log into that server. Otherwise, you can follow the instructions to create an account using Microsoft's server. There's no charge, and the server doesn't store any of your files or other data.

2. **Type the Web address of your SharePoint 2010 site in the Location box and click OK.**

   SharePoint Workspace 2010 attempts to connect to your SharePoint site.

   Assuming a successful connection is established, Workspace downloads the lists and libraries from your site. If you can't connect, seek assistance from your help desk.

3. **With the Workspace Explorer, click through your lists and view, edit, and add new list items, as shown in Figure 3-8.**

4. **To synchronize your changes with your SharePoint site, click the Sync button.**

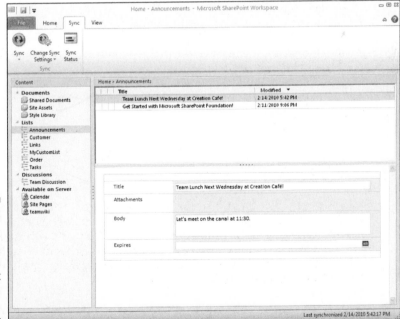

Figure 3-8: You can work with lists in SharePoint Workspace 2010.

Chapter 4

Creating Custom Lists

· ·

In This Chapter

▶ Planning, creating, and importing a custom list

▶ Adding new columns to lists

▶ Renaming and hiding the Title column

▶ Importing your spreadsheet as a list

▶ Creating calculated and lookup columns

· ·

*O*ne of the neat features about SharePoint is the ability to add columns to the predefined lists and libraries as well as make entirely new custom lists. Custom lists make it possible for you to create a Web site unique to your tasks and responsibilities. You can build your custom list from scratch or import a spreadsheet.

Think about all the spreadsheets you have for tracking and simple mathematics, like adding inventory! Creating or importing custom lists gives you a centralized location for this information and an easy-to-use form interface for data entry and display. Plus, if you use the supporting lists SharePoint provides — Links, Announcements, Issue Tracking, and Tasks — your team is a lean, mean, productivity machine!

In Chapter 3, you can read about the lists included with SharePoint and how to use them. Even if you're ready to jump into building your own custom list, don't forget about the templates SharePoint provides — several come with special, premade Web Part views (Announcements and Links, for example) that take extra effort for you to create for a custom list.

The process for adding columns is the same in libraries and lists. However, in a library, your columns capture information about a *file,* such as its category or author. Lists generally are all data columns and are used for tracking and communication.

Planning Your Custom List

A long time ago I worked at the distribution center for a company that makes private-label baby wipes. Each trailer of baby wipes that left the company dock was sealed with a metal seal. Each seal had a unique identifier that was entered on the bill of lading and written manually on a paper log. Once a month, I typed the log with a manual typewriter and sent the typewritten log to the corporate headquarters in New York. I'm not making this up; it's all true.

When I automated that process, I used a Lotus 1-2-3 spreadsheet. Fast-forward 20 years; assume this company still has no way of tracking seal numbers with their orders and must use an Excel spreadsheet. Here I show you how to do this with a custom SharePoint list. I want to track the shipment's date (date), bill of lading number (text), order number (text), trailer number (text), and the seal number (text). Note in this example, all these numbers are used as text, not mathematical values.

Do the same for your custom list — identify the columns you need and think about the type of data that each column contains. Planning a custom list is similar to starting a new spreadsheet in Excel or a table in Access. In all cases, a little preplanning saves time in the long run. What order do you want the columns to be in? What options do you want in your drop-down lists?

Already have a spreadsheet that you think would make a good list in SharePoint? Make sure you check out the section "Importing a Spreadsheet as a List," later in this chapter. That section can save you a lot of effort, and you'll have a custom list in no time.

Columns can also be called *fields* (for those used to database terminology). When these columns are used to describe files (usually documents in a document library), they're also referred to as *metadata* or *properties*.

Creating Custom Lists

You create a custom list using the same steps described for creating pre-defined lists from templates in Chapter 3. On the SharePoint Create page, you see a Custom List category, as shown in Figure 4-1. The list categories on the Create page include

 - **Custom List:** A list with a Title column.

 - **Custom List in Datasheet View:** A list with a Title column that displays in datasheet or spreadsheet view by default.

✓ **Import Spreadsheet:** A dialog box opens that allows you to import a spreadsheet into a SharePoint list.

✓ **External List:** A list that displays information from an external data source, such as a database. I discuss external lists in Chapter 22.

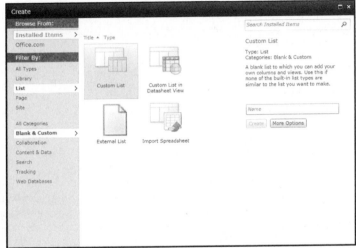

Figure 4-1:
Create page
choices.

Follow these steps to create your custom list:

1. Select one of the four custom templates on the Create page, which I describe in the preceding list, and then enter a name for your list.

The name you type here is used in the list's Web address. Avoid using spaces in the name when you create the list. You can change the list's name to a friendlier name after you create it.

2. Click the Create button.

SharePoint creates your new custom list and generously adds a single Title column to it. See the section "Adding Columns to Your List" later in this chapter for details on working with columns.

Choose the Custom List in Datasheet View template when you know users will use the datasheet (or spreadsheet) view as the default. This view is good for bulk-editing and copying/pasting as you would in Excel. In reality, all roads lead to Rome — regardless of which custom list template you choose, creating new columns is the same, and you can easily add or switch the view(s) of the list. (Chapter 5 discusses Datasheet views in more detail.)

Adding Columns to Your List

A new custom list displays a single text Title column. The list also contains several behind-the-scenes columns that you can't see, such as ID and Version. To make the custom list your own, you have to add columns to the list.

Columns are like fields in a database table. When you add a column to your list, a data entry field appears in the list's New Form to give you a place to enter data into that column.

A little planning goes a long way. You created a plan for your custom list, right? Because now is when you start adding the columns to your list that you listed in your plan.

You can also add columns to the predefined SharePoint lists that I discuss in Chapter 3.

Here's a quick overview to add columns to your custom list:

1. **With your list open in the browser, click the List tab on the Ribbon and then click the Create Column button (see Figure 4-2) in the Manage Views group.**

   The Create Column window appears.

   You can also add new columns with the List Settings page.

Figure 4-2:
Add a new
column to
your list.

2. **Type a name for your new column in the Column Name field.**

   The name you type is what users will see, so pick a name that's concise but meaningful. I don't recommend using spaces in your column names when you first create them. You can always add spaces later.

   Spaces entered in a column name become a permanent part of that column's *internal name* in SharePoint. Some of these internal names can get quite lengthy and downright nonsensical, which makes referencing them a real pain.

3. **Select the type of information you want to store in the column.**

   The options given here are fairly intuitive — Single Line of Text, Number, Date and Time, and so on. See the section "Getting to know column types" later in this chapter for details on selecting the column type.

Try to determine what kind of data you have when you first create the column. Changing the data type later may result in loss of data or you may not have as many options when you change the type.

4. **In the Additional Column Settings section, select the options that further define your column's type.**

   The column type you select in Step 3 determines what options you have available for configuring the column.

5. **(Optional) If you want SharePoint to test the values entered into your column, use the Column Validation section to enter your formula.**

6. **Click OK.**

   SharePoint adds the column to your custom list.

You can change the column properties later and rearrange the order of the columns by using the List Settings page.

When you first create a custom list, use the List Settings page, where you have all the commands at your fingertips to power through the column creation — you can pick site columns, create your own, and rearrange them, as shown in Figure 4-3. After your list has been created and you need to add additional columns, the Create Column button on the list page is a handy way to add one or two columns without leaving the list page.

Columns

A column stores information about each item in the list. The following columns are currently available in this list:

Column (click to edit)	Type	Required
Inventory Item Name	Single line of text	✓
PreferredSupplierName	Choice	
CatalogItemNumber	Single line of text	
Created By	Person or Group	
Modified By	Person or Group	

Create column
Add from existing site columns
Column ordering
Indexed columns

Figure 4-3: Columns section of the List Settings page.

Getting to know column types

Columns are used to store data, and unlike a spreadsheet, you need to define the *type* of column as you create it, as in Figure 4-4. For those that work with databases, this is a familiar concept. By defining the type of column, you gain extra functionality based on that type, and you help to control the type of information that can be entered into the column and how that information is presented onscreen. For example, users can enter only a number in a Number column; they can't add miscellaneous text.

Reusing columns in other lists

SharePoint actually has two kinds of columns — list columns and site columns. I show you how to create a *list column* (a column that's associated with one and only one list) in the "Adding Columns to Your List" section, earlier in this chapter. What if you like a column so much you want to reuse it on more than one list? That's when you create a *site column.* You define a site column once and then associate it with as many lists as you want. SharePoint comes with a set of *predefined* site columns — those are the columns that are used in SharePoint's predefined lists. You can reuse any of those columns in your lists also. I discuss site columns in more detail in Chapter 22.

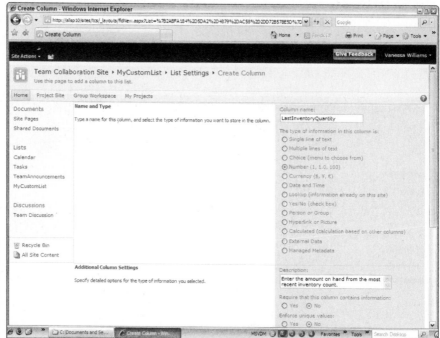

Figure 4-4:
Create
Column
page show-
ing choices.

SharePoint provides a number of built-in column types that you can select for your lists, such as columns that know how to handle dates and URLs. Third-party companies and developers in your organization can also create custom column types that can be added to SharePoint. For example, if your company needs a column that handles a zip code plus four values, a developer could create it for you.

Table 4-1 lists common SharePoint column types and what they're used for.

Table 4-1	SharePoint Column Data Types	
Column Data Type*	**What It's Used For**	**Display on Form**
Single Line of Text	Display text and numbers (such as phone or course numbers, or zip code) up to 255 characters.	Single line text box (The text box may not show all 255 characters.)
Multiple Lines of Text	Display multiple lines of text.	Select from Plain Text, Rich Text, or Enhanced Rich Text. Depending on the number of lines you select, this option shows as a text area of that size with additional toolbars to format text.**
Choice***	A defined list of choices; for example, categories or departments.	Drop-down list is the default and most common.
Number	Numerical values that can be used for calculations.	You can identify a min/max value number with a choice of decimal options.
Currency	Numerical values that represent money.	You can identify a min/max value currency. Includes options for decimal places and currency format.
Date and Time	Dates and times.	Date and/or Time-Calendar Picker.
Lookup	Values from another list — for example, categories could be stored in a lookup list for document metadata.	Drop-down list populated based on values from other list.
Yes/No	Boolean value of Yes or No.	Check box.
Person or Group	Directory listing information from SharePoint.	The person or group is shown as a hyperlink and can include presence information.
Hyperlink or Picture	Hyperlink (internal or external) or an image.	Hyperlink or picture.
Calculated	Data that can be calculated by formula.	Result of calculation; can be text or numerical.
External Data	Data stored in a data source; for example, a table or view in an enterprise database.	Text.
Managed Metadata	Provides a common set of keywords and terms that can be used across the organization.	Text.

* Most columns also include property options for Required, Allow Duplicates, Default Values, and Add to the Default View.

** Gotcha: Although you may set a number of lines for editing, this isn't a defined limit. Users can type or cut/paste a large amount of text into this control. You may want to use column validation to restrict the length.

*** Choice can also be shown on the form as radio buttons for a single choice or check boxes for multiple choices.

In addition to the column data types in Table 4-1, other data types, such as Publishing HTML (an even richer form of text), can be selected when creating site columns. I discuss these additional column types in Chapter 14.

When you're creating columns for your custom list, you can change the order of the columns as they're shown in the Columns section of the List Settings page. Changing the column ordering in this section helps with organizing the list flow for owners and how they display on the lists form. However, changing the order on the List Settings page doesn't change the order of columns in the default view — you must modify the view separately, which I discuss in Chapter 5.

Don't underestimate descriptions! Creators of lists often carry a lot of information in their heads about the content in the list. Users aren't mind readers. Type descriptions to help them understand the intent of the column and the data expected.

Validating data entry

Column validation options are new to SharePoint 2010 lists and allow you to define additional limits and constraints for your data. For example, you may want to ensure that a value in one Date column occurs after another Date column. (So for example, column validation can ensure that the date in the Date Finished column can't be earlier than the date in the Date Started column — you can't finish a project before it's begun!)

To use column validation on your list:

1. **In your list where you want to validate data entry, click the List Settings button on the List tab.**

2. **Under General Settings, click the Validation Settings link.**

3. **Type a formula in the Formula text box, as shown in Figure 4-5.**

   The result of the formula must evaluate to TRUE to pass validation. The formula syntax is the same as calculated columns, which is similar to Excel syntax.

4. **Enter a user message that you want to appear when the validation formula fails.**

   The message should give the user an idea of how the formula works and how to fix the problem.

5. **Click the Save button.**

When users enter data into your form, the validation formula is evaluated. If the formula evaluates to FALSE, your user message appears on the form, as shown in Figure 4-6.

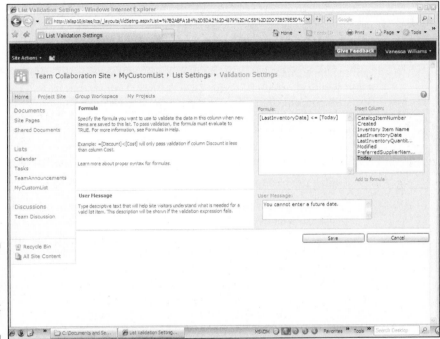

Figure 4-5:
Entering a formula for list validation.

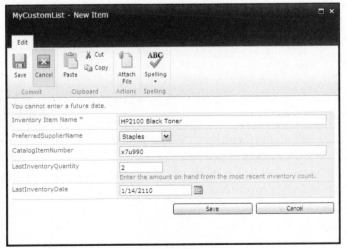

Figure 4-6:
User message appears when validation formula equals FALSE.

You can add column validation to columns created at the list or site level. Validation created for site-level columns applies everywhere that column is used, although the formula can be overridden at the list where the site-level column is used.

Working with the Title Column

Unlike SharePoint's predefined lists, your custom list has only one column when you first create it — the Title column. Unfortunately, you can't delete the Title column or change its data type, but you can rename or hide it.

To rename the Title column:

1. **Select the List Settings button on the List tab on the Ribbon.**

2. **Under the Columns heading, click the Title hyperlink.**

3. **Replace *Title* with your own title and make modifications to the other properties as desired.**

The Title column is used by the list as a means to access the data entry forms to view and edit the list item, as I discuss in Chapter 3. You can opt to hide the Title column so that it doesn't appear on any of the list forms.

To hide the Title column:

1. **In your list, click the List Settings button on the List tab.**

2. **If the Content Types section isn't visible, enable management of content types by following these steps:**

    a. *Click the Advanced Settings link on the List Settings page.*

    b. *Select the Yes radio button under Allow Management of Content Types? and then click OK. The Content Types section will be visible on the List Settings page.*

3. **In the Content Types section of the List Settings page, click the Item content type.**

    The List Content Type Information appears.

    If you want to change the Title column in a document library, you click the Document content type. The Item content type applies to custom lists only. In a predefined list, such as a Tasks list, you click the Task content type.

4. **Click the Title column.**

    The Title column's properties appear.

5. **Under Column Settings, select the Hidden (Will Not Appear in Forms) radio button, as shown in Figure 4-7, and click OK.**

The Title column doesn't appear on forms.

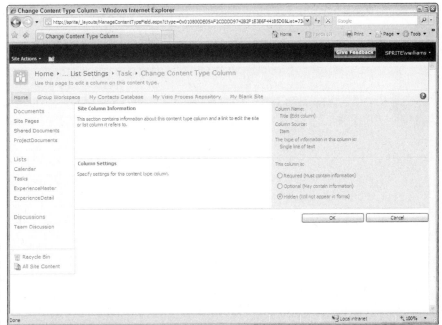

Figure 4-7:
Hide the
Title
column.

Importing a Spreadsheet as a List

Already have data in a spreadsheet that you want to be a SharePoint list? You're halfway there! Before you start, make sure you do the following:

- ✔ **Clean the list.** Make sure your list looks like a table, with no blank columns or rows.

- ✔ **Make sure your list has headers.** All columns should have a column title.

- ✔ **Make sure your column data is consistent.** For example, if a column has a comment in what would otherwise be a Date column, remove the text.

- ✔ **Make sure your first row is representative of the rest of the data.** SharePoint reads that first row and makes assumptions about the information in that column. Figure 4-8 shows an example of a clean spreadsheet ready for importing.

Figure 4-8:
Cleaned
spreadsheet
ready for
import into
SharePoint.

	A	B	C	D	E	F	G
1	Employee Name	Department	Telephone Number	Supervisor	Volunteer Project	Data Scheduled	Complete
2	John Jones	Marketing	317-555-1212	Ann Taylor	West Park Cleanup	6/6/2010	
3	Sarah Smith	Accounting	317-555-1213	Joe Johnson	Meals on Wheels	9/1/2020	
4	Jenny Williams	Accounting	317-555-1214	Joe Johnson	Humane Society	7/4/2010	
5							
6							

SharePoint looks for what it believes is the first text column and uses it as the pseudo-title field (the primary field in the list that has the Edit menu attached to it). Therefore, try to place a text field with unique data in the first column position. Unfortunately, if your unique field is a number, such as a serial number, this can cause issues. To work around the problem, create the list and copy and paste the data from the spreadsheet.

A good example of a first column is a unique name of a person or an item, such as Event Name.

A bad example of a first column is the category of an item or a department of an employee.

To import your spreadsheet into a custom list:

1. **Choose Site Actions⇨View All Site Content.**

   Other options include View All Site Content Link on the Quick Launch toolbar or the Create Option Link on the Site Actions menu.

2. **Select the Create command and then select the Import Spreadsheet option from the List category and click the Create button.**

3. **In the Name text box, enter a name for your list.**

   Follow the naming conventions I outline for list names: Keep them short and eliminate spaces.

4. **(Optional) In the Description text box, enter a description of the list.**

5. **Click the Browse button, browse to your spreadsheet, select it, and click the Import button.**

   A dialog box appears that asks how your range is designated. The default is Table Range, but other options are Named Range or Range of Cells. If you haven't named your range in Excel or set as a table, select the Range of Cells option.

6. **If you chose the Range of Cells option, click the Select Range field in the dialog box, and then click your spreadsheet and highlight the desired range.**

7. **Click the Import button in the dialog box.**

After you import your spreadsheet, verify the column types SharePoint chose for you. Generally SharePoint assumes text, number, and dates. You may want to change some text fields to Choice, Yes/No, and so forth.

Don't have the patience to create all your custom columns one by one — but you don't have a current list in another format either? Create a spreadsheet with your column headers and at least one row of data, and then import this spreadsheet and modify the column properties as necessary.

Taking Your List to the Next Level: Calculated and Lookup Columns

Calculated columns are especially powerful for automatically generating data. Don't be intimidated, the Web is full of great formula examples for SharePoint calculated columns. Some common uses include

- ✔ Adding days to a date column to calculate an expired or due date column.

- ✔ Adding Number or Currency columns to get a total.

- ✔ Using the Me function to automatically add the username to a field.

Creating a calculated column

To create a calculated column, follow these steps:

1. **Select the Calculated column type in the Name and Type options in the Create Column dialog box.**

   The Additional Column Settings area changes to support entering a calculation (see Figure 4-9) and specifying column options.

2. **Type your formula using the proper syntax in the Formula text box.**

   If you're basing your calculation on another field in the list, you can reference that field using the square brackets reference syntax.

   For example, to calculate a Shipping Deadline, you might want to add five days to the Order Date value in another column by entering **[Order Date]+5** in the Formula text box.

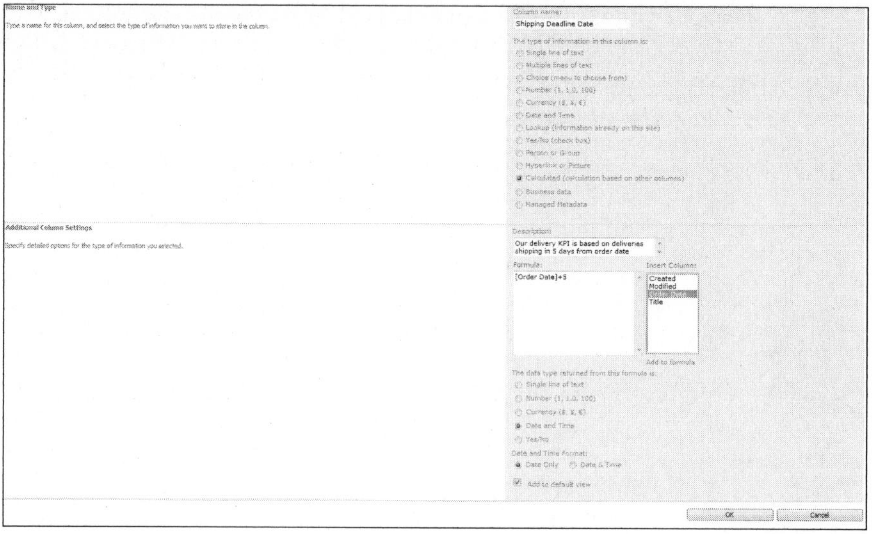

Figure 4-9:
Column settings for a calculated column.

3. **Select the proper data type for the returned value and other data type property options, if available, from the Additional Column Settings section of the page.**

   Not all return values are of the same data type as the input columns. You subtract one date from another, but your returned value is a number (the number of days difference between the two dates).

   Other examples include

   - Adding the current username to a field. Simply type the constant **[Me]** in the Formula text box.

   - Using today as a date in a calculation to create a new date by entering **[Today]+7** in the Formula text box.

Using a lookup column

Maintaining all your options in a Choice field can be cumbersome and prone to error. SharePoint uses a similar model to relational databases by separating the *lookup* information from the *transaction* list. Think of all the lookup data that could be maintained in separate lists. For example, computer hardware inventory lookup lists could include hardware type, maintenance contract, and department location. These lists can be maintained independently of the *transaction list* — the inventory itself.

In the following example, I create a Department custom list with a single field — Title — and populate it with the names of departments in my organization. I build the Volunteer Projects transaction list (where I track employees working on volunteer projects), and Departments is a column in this list. Rather than build a Choice field, I use the Lookup data type to connect to my Departments list and use the Title field as data for the Department column in the Volunteer Projects list.

You can also add other columns from the lookup list to the drop-down list to help users select the proper choice. When a user selects the value from the drop-down list, values for the additional columns also display. Figure 4-10 shows a scenario that uses a lookup column to display a customer's sales territory. The customer's name and sales territory are stored in one list and displayed in another list using a lookup column. Figure 4-10 also shows the use of inline editing in a Web Part, which is discussed in Chapter 5.

For users familiar with databases and referential integrity, SharePoint 2010 now adds additional options to support this implementation. Lookup columns can also be used to create a chain of joined lists that can be used to query and display values from additional columns.

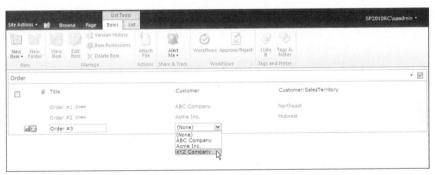

Figure 4-10: Selecting a value from a lookup column.

Chapter 5

Getting a New View

In This Chapter

▶ Knowing when to create a view

▶ Understanding view formats

▶ Working with various views

▶ Managing views that already exist

▶ Displaying views by using Web Parts

As I explain in Chapters 3 and 4, SharePoint creates Web pages that you use to create and edit list items, such as tasks and calendar events. SharePoint also lets you create additional pages, or *views,* that you can use to customize the display of your information. In Excel, you might hide rows and/or columns to create a new view of the data. In a database, you may query only certain fields and use criteria to create a specific snapshot of data. The concept is similar here.

Common reasons for creating new views include showing only active items, only tasks associated with a certain person, only documents in a certain category, and so on. These views help users find or focus on certain data in the list without having to see everything, all the time.

In this chapter, I explain your options for creating views and how to modify existing views.

Viewing the View

Each SharePoint list comes with at least one view, the *All Items view,* which is a public view available to list users. Certain lists come with several more predefined views, such as the Discussion Board list, which has special views for showing threaded discussions.

You use the SharePoint Ribbon to access the options for changing a list's or library's views. Figure 5-1 shows the List tab under List Tools (use the Library tab under Library tools in libraries), where you can see the commands that are available for changing the current views or creating new views.

Figure 5-1:
Use the
Ribbon to
change
the current
view.

Anyone with Design and Full Control permissions (Designer and Owners) can make Public and Personal views for the list. However, *Site* Members (Contributors) can create Personal views for their own use.

Use a view instead of folders. When you organized files on your network, folders were the predominant method of subdividing your content. In SharePoint, you gain great power in using columns in combination with views to hide/show what users need to see. Folders take extra effort for the user to drill down and then navigate back up to look for other content. Views coupled with built-in sorting and filtering header options allow the user to easily and quickly find different content by toggling back and forth.

Getting to Know Your View Formats

SharePoint provides five predefined formats for creating new views. These formats jump-start your view creation experience by determining how information appears on the Web page:

- ✔ **Standard:** This is the default view when you first access a library or list. The document or title item is in hyperlink format with an Edit menu for accessing properties and other options, and the rest of the list resembles a table without borders.

- ✔ **Datasheet:** An editable spreadsheet format. Although any list has the option to Edit in Datasheet format, certain views may make sense to be created in this format if users will edit multiple items at a time.

- ✔ **Calendar:** As you would expect, this view displays as a Calendar. You need at least one date field in your list to create a Calendar view.

- ✔ **Gantt:** If you are familiar with project management charts, you will recognize the Gantt view as showing tasks along a time line. This view makes it possible to do simple project-management tracking using a SharePoint list.

- ✔ **Access View:** This view creates an Access database with a linked table to your SharePoint list so that you can create a form or report in Access based on your SharePoint list. Lookup tables and a user list are also linked as tables in this option.

✔ **Custom View In SharePoint Designer:** If you have SharePoint Designer 2010 installed on your computer, you have the option to use it to create custom views.

You may not see all the view formats listed above. Your options are dependent on which client software, such as Excel, Access, and SharePoint Designer, is installed on your computer.

In the rest of the chapter, I walk you through creating a view using each of these view formats.

Creating a Standard View

The most common kind of view you create in a SharePoint list or library is a public, Standard view. A public view can be used by anyone to view the contents of a list or library.

Standards views have the following traits:

✔ They're accessible by all browsers, including Firefox.

✔ They have the most configuration options, such as filtering, grouping, and editing options.

✔ They're available for all lists and libraries.

✔ They don't require any special columns for configuring the view. Other view formats, such as a Calendar view, require date columns.

To create a new Standard view:

1. **Browse to the list or library where you want to create the new view.**

2. **Click the List tab on the Ribbon to access options for managing the list's views.**

   In a calendar list, click the Calendar tab to manage the list's views.

3. **Click the Create View button.**

   A list of view format options appears.

4. **Click the Standard View link to create a view that looks like a Web page.**

   After selecting your view format, the next page displays your options for creating the new view. I call this page the View Definition page for clarity throughout the chapter.

5. **In the View Name field, type the name you want to call this view.**

   The View Name field has two purposes:

   - It provides the friendly name that can be selected to display the view.

   - It provides the filename for the Web page, which is part of the Web address.

   I suggest giving the page a name that's easy to remember. For example, if your view will group by department, entering the name **GroupByDepartment** will create a Web page named `GroupByDepartment.aspx`. You can change the friendly name after the filename has been created.

6. **To set this view as the default view for the list or library, select the Make This the Default View check box.**

   If this isn't the default view, users can select the view from a drop-down list on the Ribbon.

7. **In the View Audience field, select the Create a Public View radio button.**

   Optionally, you can create a private view that only you can see. You must have at least Designer or Owner permissions to create a public view.

8. **In the Columns section of the page, place a check in the Display column next to any columns you wish to display, as shown in Figure 5-2.**

   You can also indicate the relative order that columns appear on the screen using the Position from Left column. See more on choosing columns in the "Choosing columns for your view" section, later in this chapter.

9. **(Optional) In the Sort section, use the drop-down lists to select the first column you want to sort by and then select the second column to sort by.**

   The default sort option is ID, which means that items will be sorted by the order they were entered in the list.

10. **Select the remaining options to configure your view, such as the columns you want to filter or group on.**

    Some of the options you can choose from are

    - *Select Tabular View* to include check boxes next to items for bulk operations.

    - *Select Inline Editing* to allow your users to add a new item directly in the Standard view rather than opening a new window.

    - *In the Totals section,* select which columns to aggregate using Count or Sum functions.

    - *In the Folder section,* specify whether items should appear inside folders or flat as if the folders don't exist.

    - *Item Limit* allows you to limit the items that are displayed on a single page. This can improve the performance of the view.

    I discuss additional options in more detail in the "Filtering lists with views" and "Grouping results" sections, later in this chapter.

⊟ Columns

Select or clear the check box next to each column you want to show or hide in this view of this page. To specify the order of the columns, select a number in the **Position from left** box.

Display	Column Name	Position from Left
☑	Attachments	1 ▾
☑	Last Name (linked to item with edit menu)	2 ▾
☑	First Name	3 ▾
☑	Company	4 ▾
☑	Business Phone	5 ▾
☑	Home Phone	6 ▾
☑	E-mail Address	7 ▾
☐	Address	8 ▾
☐	City	9 ▾
☐	Company Phonetic	10 ▾
☐	Content Type	11 ▾
☐	Country/Region	12 ▾
☐	Created	13 ▾
☐	Created By	14 ▾
☐	Edit (link to edit item)	15 ▾
☐	Fax Number	16 ▾
☐	First Name Phonetic	17 ▾
☐	Folder Child Count	18 ▾
☐	Full Name	19 ▾
☐	ID	20 ▾

Figure 5-2:
Create a new view and select the columns you want to show.

11. Click OK to create the view.

The new view appears in the browser.

If you created a public view, SharePoint creates a new Web page using the name you specified in Step 5. Users can select this view from the drop-down list in the Manage Views Section of the Ribbon.

Experimenting with all these options is the best way to discover what works for your site. Item Limits, for example, is great for List View Web Parts where you want to control the amount of space the list view takes up on a page.

Choosing columns for your view

When you choose the columns to display in your view, you see many columns that are usually behind the scenes, including Edit menu options. These include

✔ **Edit (Linked to Edit Item):** Displays an icon that a user can click to edit the item. This column is useful when you don't want to display the Title column.

✔ **Title (Linked to Item):** Displays the Title column with a hyperlink to the list item or document. When a user clicks the hyperlinked title, a Web page opens and displays the list item or opens the document.

✔ **Title (Linked to Edit with Edit Menu):** When a user hovers her mouse over this column, the Edit menu appears.

I may want Edit menu columns on my list page for a member to modify items, but I generally don't want them in my List View Web Parts on home pages and publishing pages (in that case, I just want users to click a link to open a document or only view the list as a table).

Other columns you may have available to add to your view include

- ✔ **ID** displays the identity number of the item. The ID number is used to display the item's values in a form.

- ✔ **Version** displays the version number of the item or document. This allows you to easily see what the latest version of a document is.

- ✔ **Checked Out** shows who has the document checked out.

- ✔ **Folder Item Count** displays the number of folders contained within a folder.

- ✔ **Child Item Count** displays the number of items contained with a folder.

- ✔ **Content Type** displays the content type associated with the list item or document. When this column is displayed in Datasheet view, you can change the content type associated with the item (read more about content types in Chapter 22).

When you create a view, you often realize that you want to display a column that's based on a value calculated from another column. For example, if your list displays an anniversary date, you may want to calculate years of service. You can do that by creating a new column and then displaying it in your view. (See Chapter 4 for details on working with calculated columns.)

Filtering lists with views

You can use the filtering options of views to limit the items displayed. You can choose which columns to filter on and how to apply the filter. You can use filters to display lists where a certain column is equal to some value or not equal to some value, or where an item was created between a certain date range.

You can create filters using columns that are based on String, Number, Currency, or Choice data types. However, you can't filter on lookup columns or multiline text fields.

Building a filter is like writing an equation; for example, $x > y$. In this case, x is the column you want to filter on, and y is the value you want to test the column contents against. The operator in between determines what the test evaluates. This test gives the system a TRUE or FALSE response to your equation.

Available operators are

- ✔ **Equality:** Is Equal To or Is Not Equal To
- ✔ **Comparison:** Is Greater Than or Is Less Than
- ✔ **Substring:** Contains or Begins With

The filtering equation is evaluated for each item in your list. If the equation is TRUE, the item is included in the list; otherwise, it's excluded.

If you don't see the results you expect to see in your view, your filter is probably evaluating to FALSE.

For numerical values, you usually use the Equality or Comparison operators. When you create filtered views based on string (text) values, you want to be familiar with your data before trying to create the filter. For example, if you want to filter a Contact list to display only those contacts in the U.K., you have to ask how the value for the U.K. has been entered in the list. Is it U.K., United Kingdom, or both? You can use a Datasheet view to quickly scan the data to determine the range of possible values.

One way to get around this problem is by validating your data when it's being inputted. You can use Choice columns to do that or use SharePoint 2010's validation features. (See Chapter 4 for details.)

Say you discover that your data includes both values — U.K. and United Kingdom. You could go through and make all the data consistent. Or you could filter for both values using the Or option, as shown in Figure 5-3.

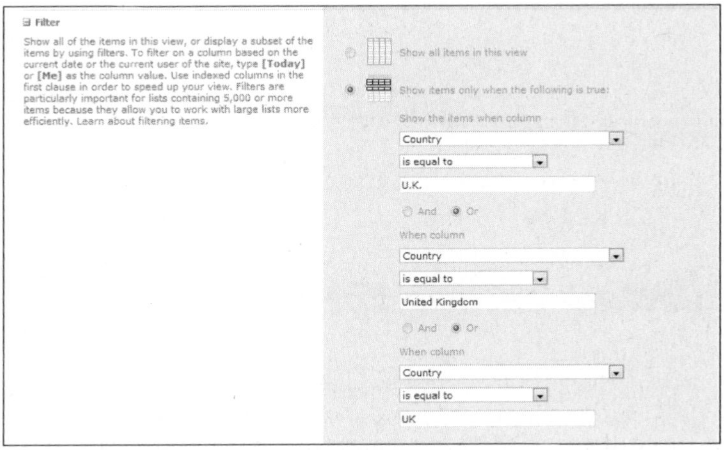

Figure 5-3:
Select the column to filter the view.

You can also use the constants Today and Me to filter your columns. (See Chapter 4 for details on using these constants.)

Grouping results

You can configure your view to group together items based on a common value in a column. For example, you can group a list of contacts that all share the same department or company.

Figure 5-4 shows the grouping options. You can indicate whether to automatically collapse or expand grouped items and how many items to display per page.

Figure 5-5 shows a list of contacts grouped by department. Use the plus and minus signs to expand or contract the grouped items.

Don't forget the Totals option! Often when grouping data, you want to create totals. For example, grouping on Inventory by Category and totaling the Qty will create subtotals for the Category grouping as well as an overall total for the list.

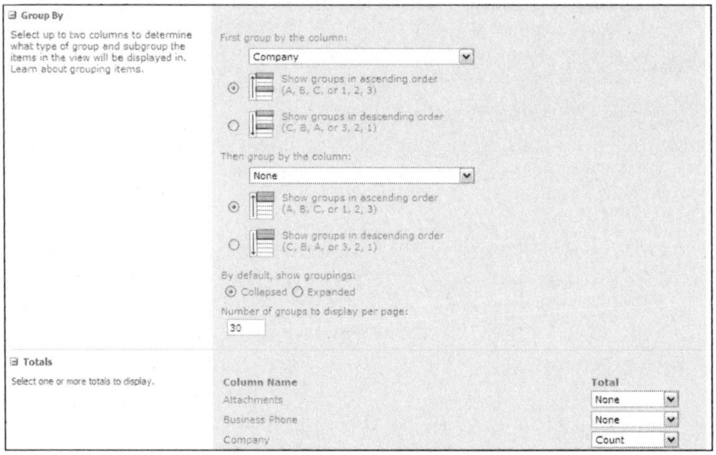

Figure 5-4:
You can group items based on a shared value.

Allowing editing options

You can configure your views so that they aren't just views — they can be used for data entry as well. SharePoint 2010 has added new options to improve the data entry experience. The two options that make that possible are inline editing and Tabular view, as shown in Figure 5-6.

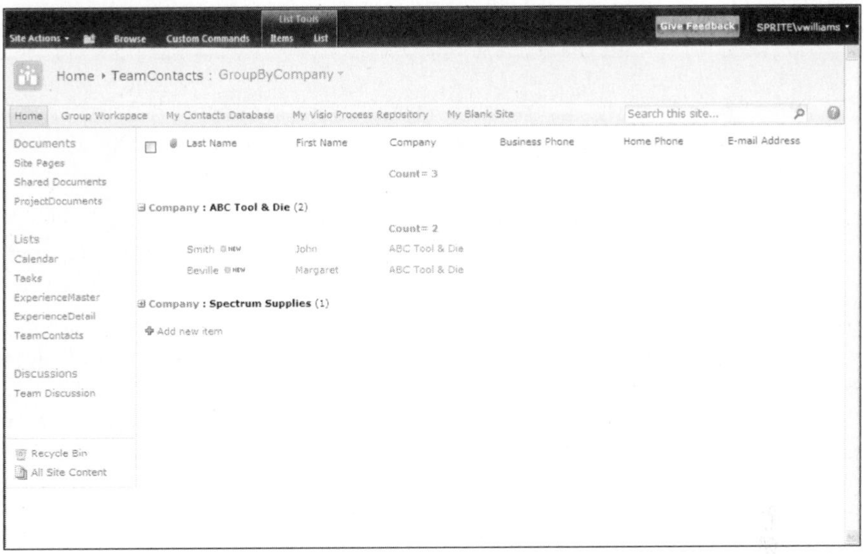

Figure 5-5:
Expand or
contract
grouped
items.

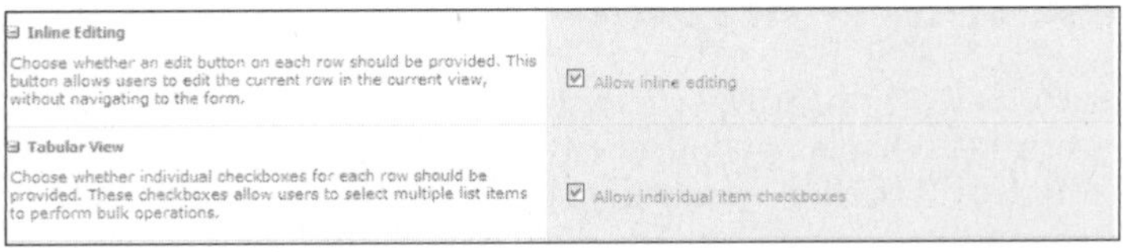

Figure 5-6:
Use these
options to
extend your
views.

Inline editing displays a form in your view that allows users to enter a new item or edit existing items. To use the form, a user with permission to edit the list can click an icon to create a new list item or click any item to edit it. Figure 5-7 shows an item being edited inline. The icon below the item being edited can be used to add a new item to the list.

Having the option to edit and add items inline is valuable for creating data entry applications. You can use the inline editing option in a Web Part so that users can add or edit items right on the home page of your team site. (See Chapter 10 for details on working with Web Parts.)

Tabular view displays check boxes next to each item in the view. By clicking one or several check boxes, a user can use the Ribbon to perform actions, such as checking in, on the selected items.

Figure 5-7:
You can edit
items inline
in your view.

Choosing a display style

SharePoint 2010 provides several preformatted view styles that you can use to control the display of your view. The default view style displays your list data in rows. You can use several additional styles. Many of these are especially helpful in configuring List View Web Parts:

- ✔ **Basic Table** displays lists in a simple table.

- ✔ **Boxed** and **Boxed, No Labels** displays list items as a series of cards, with or without column labels. This display is similar to the Address Card view in Outlook.

- ✔ **Newsletter** and **Newsletter, No Lines** displays a table with a streamlined format.

- ✔ **Shaded** displays items in rows, with each alternate row shaded.

- ✔ **Preview Pane** displays a list of items on the left and previews the details on the right. This is a great way to display a lot of information in a compact display.

Many users overlook these effective display styles. Again, experimenting is the best way to find out how a display style can improve a user's experience with the data.

Figure 5-8 shows the style options you can choose from when configuring your view.

⊟ Style

Choose a style for this view from the list on the right.

View Style:

Basic Table
Boxed, no labels
Boxed
Newsletter
Newsletter, no lines
Shaded
Preview Pane
Default

Managing List Data in a Datasheet View

Datasheet views are great for performing bulk updates on list items and document properties in a library. A Datasheet view displays a list in a spreadsheet. Datasheet views work only in Internet Explorer browsers.

With Datasheet views, you can

- ✔ Support most column types including Text, Choice, Date, Number, and lookup columns. Datasheet views don't work with Rich HTML columns. Additionally, not all column features work as expected in a Datasheet view. In short, when Datasheet views work, they work great. You just have to test your column types before getting overly ambitious.

- ✔ Use the arrow keys to move around in the view like a spreadsheet.

- ✔ Copy and paste values, which is another great way to make bulk updates to a list. I often use this approach instead of importing a spreadsheet as a custom list, which I discuss in Chapter 4.

- ✔ Right-click a column heading to display additional options, such as hiding the column or setting the column's width.

- ✔ Create a Datasheet view on the fly from any Standard view by clicking the Datasheet View button in the List tab on the SharePoint Ribbon.

- ✔ Drag and drop the columns in a Datasheet view to reorder them.

A Datasheet view is a great way to quickly change the content type of a list item or document. Just add the content type column to your Datasheet view. (I explain how to attach multiple content types to a single list or library in Chapter 22.)

You create a Datasheet view just like you create a Standard view, although you have fewer configuration options. You can sort, filter, display totals, and set the item limit on Datasheet views.

Figure 5-9 shows a Contact list in a Datasheet view. If a column can't be edited because of the column's data type, the message Read-Only appears in the lower-right corner of the datasheet. The message Pending Changes appears in the lower-left corner when updates are made to the database.

Depending on which Office applications you have installed, you may be able to access additional options for managing list data in Datasheet view. You can access these options by clicking the task pane in the far right of the Datasheet view. This pane shows options for working with the list in Microsoft Access and Excel, as shown in Figure 5-10.

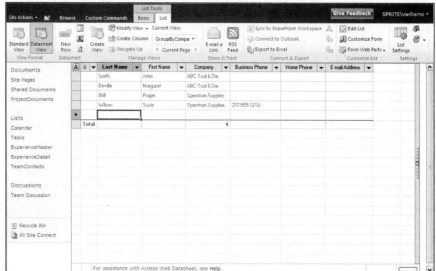

Figure 5-9:
Use a
Datasheet
view to
update data.

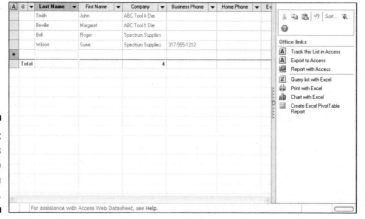

Figure 5-10:
Use Access
and Excel to
work with
your list.

Using Ad Hoc Views

Users can make Ad Hoc views in any Standard or Datasheet views by using the headers of the columns to sort and filter the data on-the-fly. These ad hoc changes aren't saved with the list the way defined views are. Helping your users be productive by using these ad hoc options may involve training tips or help support. Follow these steps to create an ad hoc view:

1. **Click a view heading in Standard or Datasheet view.**

   A drop-down list appears on the column header cell.

2. **Click the drop-down list and select whether you want to sort ascending or descending, or to filter the list based on data in that column.**

   Clicking the column header also toggles the sort order between ascending and descending.

   Filtering options appear as distinct data from the values in the column (for example, if Marketing appears ten times in the column, it appears only once as a filter choice).

3. **Select a value from the Filter list.**

   Filtering hides rows that don't contain that value.

   A Filter icon appears in the column header to indicate a filter is applied.

4. **To remove the filter, click the drop-down list again and select Clear Filter from *[Column Name]*.**

If you want to access your Ad Hoc view again, simply save it as a favorite in your Web browser. You can even copy the Web address from the address bar in your browser and send it to other people.

Creating a Calendar View

To create a Calendar view, you must have at least one Date field in your list. The predefined SharePoint Calendar list, not surprisingly, uses this view as its default. A Calendar view helps users visually organize their date-driven work and events.

To create a Calendar view, start as you'd begin to create a Standard view (refer to the earlier section, "Creating a Standard View"), but in Step 4, select the Calendar View. Like the Gantt view (which I describe in the following section), you see new options on the View Definition page. You have a section for Time Interval, where you select the date column to use as the Begin and End fields for the view.

You also have selections to make for Calendar columns including Month/Week/Day Titles and Week/Day Sub Heading Titles (optional). Choose the column of data you want visible on those days in the different calendar layouts.

There is also a scope option for the default display — Month, Day, or Week. As expected, several options aren't available for Calendar views including sorting, totals, item limits, and styles; however, filtering choices are important and often used with Calendar views.

Displaying Tasks in a Gantt View

To create a Gantt view, your list needs to contain task/project management information relative to that view format. The predefined SharePoint Tasks list contains these types of columns, including Title (task title), Start Date, Due Date, % Complete, and Predecessors (optional).

The View Definition page includes Gantt view options not seen in other views based on the five columns mentioned previously.

The Gantt view is a *split view* (see Figure 5-11), where you see a spreadsheet of data on the left and the Gantt chart on the right. A split bar between the two views can be moved by users to see more or less of one side. Unlike Standard or Datasheet views, the column headers don't allow you to sort or filter the data but do allow you to hide or configure the columns shown. You can create a custom list or modify the Tasks list to add more columns for this spreadsheet side if you wish.

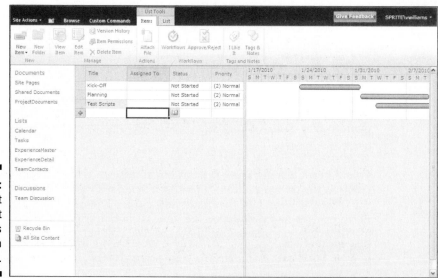

Figure 5-11: The Gantt chart columns available in Gantt view.

Managing Existing Views

Chances are you'll want to modify your views over time. In the following sections, I explain how to modify your views and set one as the default view that users see when they browse to your list or library. SharePoint also provides a couple of built-in views that you may want to customize.

Modifying your views

After creating your fabulous new view, you'll quickly realize that you need to change it. Maybe you forgot a column, it doesn't sort the way you want it to, or the grouping is just all wrong.

To modify a view, follow these steps:

1. **Browse to the list or library where you want to modify the view.**

2. **Display the view you want to modify.**

   To change the view that is currently displayed:

   a. Click the Library or List tab on the Ribbon.

   b. In the Manage Views section, click the Change View drop-down list and select the view you want to modify.

3. **Click the Modify This View button in the Manage Views section of the Ribbon.**

   A View Properties page similar to the Create View page appears, enabling you to edit the view's properties.

4. **Make your desired changes to the view, such as selecting or removing columns, or setting sorting or filtering options as described earlier in this chapter.**

5. **Click OK to save your changes to the view.**

Setting the default view

To change the default view, select the Make This the Default View check box when you create or modify a view. This removes the default view property from the current default view and makes the view you're working with the new default.

Most libraries or lists have only one default view, the exception being the Discussion Board list, which has both subjects and replies as default views. Keep in mind that if you make a view a default view, it must be a public view.

Other SharePoint built-in views

In addition to the other view formats we discuss earlier in this chapter, two other options fall under the *view* discussion:

- ✔ **Mobile:** Simplified, text-only views of your libraries and lists for use on a mobile device. Mobile is actually a section on the View Definition page. You can enable a view to be a Mobile view or set it as the default Mobile view. (Mobile views must be public.)

  You can also set the number of items to display for Mobile views. If you don't see the Mobile section in your View Definition page, this type of view can't be displayed in Mobile format.

- ✔ **RSS:** SharePoint generates RSS feeds for libraries and lists. (See Chapter 6 for more on how users subscribe and view SharePoint RSS feeds.)

Displaying Views via Web Parts

Throughout this chapter, I make references to List View Web Parts to point out what view properties are helpful and applicable to this type of view.

You want to display your list with other text and Web Parts in multiple locations, such as team site home pages, Web Part pages, or publishing pages. In these situations, you don't want your users to interact with the list page itself with all the editing options. You just want them to see several columns to access a document or view a list item.

Chapter 10 goes into detail about using Web Parts, including linked Web Parts, connections, and master/detail settings. However, you need to know that each list generates a List View Web Part that can be used on Web Part pages and publishing pages, in multiple locations if necessary. Each of these Web Parts has a Properties panel that allows you to change the view in that instance of the Web Part.

Predefined SharePoint lists may have specific views that are defaults for Web Parts (for example, Announcements has a special default view that can't be recreated in the browser for other lists). Custom lists generally show all columns when first generated.

After selecting the Modify Shared Web Part command on the Web Part, you can use the Selected View drop-down list in the Web Part Properties panel to apply another view, or you can also click the Edit the Current View hyperlink to modify the view on-the-fly. Depending on the complexity of your choices, creating a view first to apply to the Web Part(s) may be a better long-term maintenance strategy.

Figure 5-12 shows the List Views options in a List View Web Part for a Tasks list.

Figure 5-12:
Change the
view in a
List View
Web Part.

What I've been calling the List View Web Part is technically the XSLT List View Web Part, or XLV. In the browser, this Web Part behaves very similar to how it behaved in previous versions of SharePoint. Crack open a view in SharePoint Designer 2010, however, and it's a whole new world. These Web Parts still use Collaborative Application Markup Language (CAML) to specify queries. However, CAML is no longer used for specifying the display. Instead, the industry standard Extensible Stylesheet Language, the XSLT in the name of the Web Part, is used to specify the display of the list's content.

Chapter 6

Subscribing to Feeds and Alerts

In This Chapter

▶ Viewing RSS news feeds of your SharePoint lists

▶ Displaying RSS feeds from Outlook

▶ Viewing RSS feeds of other sites

▶ Subscribing and managing alerts

*N*owadays, virtually all Web sites publish a syndication feed, or *RSS feed,* of their site's content. SharePoint 2010 sites are no different. In fact, every list and library in SharePoint can publish an RSS feed. You can even create RSS feeds based on views, which means you can filter what gets published to it. If you subscribe to the feed, you're *pulling* the information. However, you can also subscribe to alerts to make SharePoint *push* updates to you.

Viewing RSS Feeds

RSS feeds are a popular way for people to keep track of updates to a Web site without visiting that site. All the lists and libraries in your SharePoint 2010 team site can display an RSS feed.

To use RSS feeds, they must be enabled for your list. To see whether RSS feeds are enabled, you should see the standard RSS button enabled in the list's Ribbon. If RSS is disabled, the button appears in the Ribbon but is disabled, as shown Figure 6-1.

To enable RSS feeds for your list or library:

1. **In your list, click the List tab, and then in the Settings group, click the List Settings button.**

   The List Settings page appears.

   If you're in a library, click the Library Settings button on the Ribbon.

2. **In the Communications section, click the RSS Settings link.**

Figure 6-1:
The
disabled
RSS button.

If you don't see the RSS Settings link, RSS isn't enabled for your site. You can enable RSS settings for your site by clicking the RSS link in the Site Administration section of the Site Settings page. RSS must also be enabled for your Web application by the SharePoint farm administrator.

3. **On the Modify RSS Settings page, select the Yes radio button under the Allow RSS for This List option.**

   You can also use this page to configure the settings for the list's default RSS feed, such as the feed's title, columns, and item limit.

4. **After you finish configuring the default settings for your list's feed, click OK to save your changes.**

Each list and library has its own RSS feed. Therefore, you must configure RSS for each list where you want to use RSS.

After you enable RSS for your list or library, you can view the RSS feed as follows:

1. **Browse to the list or library where you want to view the RSS feed and then click the RSS Feed button on the Share & Track tab of the Ribbon.**

   Most browsers display the feed using a built-in style sheet for formatting. Figure 6-2 shows an RSS feed for a SharePoint Tasks list in Firefox.

2. **Subscribe to the feed using your browser as a reader or paste the Web address for the feed in the feed reader of your choice (see the section, "Reading Feeds with Outlook," later in this chapter, for instructions).**

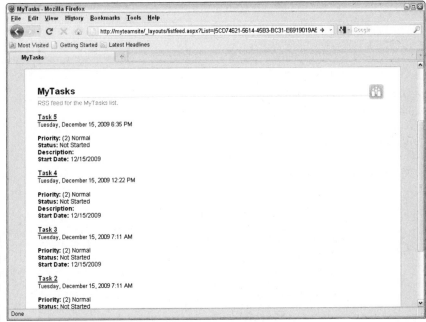

Figure 6-2:
Viewing an
RSS feed in
the browser.

You can also view the RSS feed for a specific view in a list or library. (See
Chapter 5 for details on creating a view.)

RSS must be enabled for the farm, site, and list. In other words, you can't use
RSS feeds if they aren't turned on. You can also turn off RSS feeds for a given list
or site if you don't want people to use them. The default option is to allow RSS
feeds. At the site level, RSS feeds are enabled in the Site Settings page. The
RSS settings for an individual list or library are managed in the List Settings or
Library Settings page for that list or library, respectively.

Reading Feeds with Outlook

Your e-mail application, and specifically in terms of SharePoint integration,
Microsoft Outlook, is still the bedrock of online communication for most
business users. As in the past, you can still integrate Outlook with SharePoint
calendars, contacts, and tasks, but here I give the steps for reading your RSS
feeds in Outlook.

To add an RSS feed through the Microsoft Office Outlook 2007 Account Settings dialog box:

1. **Choose Tools⇨Account Settings.**

2. **On the RSS Feeds tab, click New.**

   The New RSS Feed dialog box appears.

3. **Type the URL of the RSS feed (or press Ctrl+V to paste it), such as** `http://server/site/list/main.xml.`

4. **Click the Add button.**

   The feed is added to the list of subscribed feeds on the RSS Feeds tab.

Displaying RSS Feeds of Other Sites

SharePoint 2010 includes an RSS Viewer Web Part that allows you to display RSS feeds from SharePoint lists and libraries and public Web sites in your team site. To use this Web Part, do the following:

1. **Browse to the page where you want to add the RSS feed, click the Page tab on the Ribbon, and then click the Edit button.**

   The page is in Edit mode.

2. **Click the Add a Web Part button in the zone where you want the Web Part to appear.**

   The Insert tab appears on the Ribbon.

3. **In the Categories section of the Insert tab, click the Content Rollup category.**

   A list of Web Parts appears.

4. **Click the RSS Viewer Web Part.**

   A description of the Web Part appears.

   The SharePoint Server Standard Site Collection Features must be activated to see the RSS Viewer Web Part. If you don't see the Web Part, activate this feature. See Chapter 22 for details.

5. **Click the Add button to add the Web Part to the page, as shown in Figure 6-3.**

   The Web Part appears on the page awaiting configuration.

Figure 6-3:
Add the RSS
Viewer Web
Part to your
page.

To complete the configuration of the Web Part, you need to have the Web address or URL for a feed you want to display in the Web Part. I use the CNN Top Stories RSS feed Web address in these steps:

1. **With your Web Part on the page, place a check mark in the upper-right corner of the Web Part.**

2. **Click the Web Part Tools Options tab in the Ribbon; then click the Web Part Properties button.**

   The Web Part's properties appear as a tool pane on the right side of the screen.

3. **In the RSS Properties tab of the tool pane, enter the Web address of the RSS feed you want to display in the RSS Feed URL text box, as shown in Figure 6-4.**

4. **Click OK, and your feed appears in the Web page.**

You can click a headline in your Web Part to display the item's details, as shown in Figure 6-5. You can also click the More link to open the items from the RSS feed.

You can modify the default XSLT (Extensible Stylesheet Transformations) template that the RSS Viewer Web Part uses if you want to change the output display. The XSL template can be accessed from the Web Part's properties pane. For example, you can change the template so that the headline links to the article instead of displaying the item's details. You can use any XSLT programming or text editor to modify the XSL template, including SharePoint Designer 2010.

Figure 6-4:
Enter
the RSS
feed Web
address.

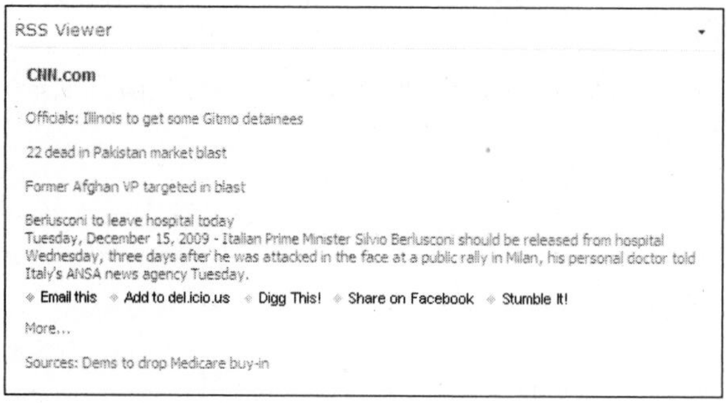

Figure 6-5:
Click the
headline to
view details.

Alert Me

If RSS isn't your thing, you can opt to receive e-mail notifications when lists or libraries change by creating an alert. *Alerts* are a great way to keep track of the changes your teammates make to documents and lists.

You need the Create Alerts permission to create alerts. This permission is granted usually with the out-of-the-box configuration of the *Site* Members SharePoint group. (See Chapter 12 for details on working with permissions.)

To create an alert to a list or library, follow these steps:

1. **Browse to the list or library where you want to subscribe to an alert and then click the Alert button in the Share & Track tab of the Ribbon.**

   The New Alert window appears.

   You can subscribe to an alert for a list item or document by choosing Alert Me on the item's Edit menu.

2. **In the Alert Title box, enter a name for the alert.**

   I suggest making the name something meaningful to you in your inbox.

3. **In the Send Alerts To box, enter the names of people in addition to you who should receive the alert.**

   That's right, you can subscribe other people to an alert!

   Organizations and site owners may want to subscribe multiple users to an alert to make sure they get important updates, as well as encourage them to contribute to a discussion board, blog, or wiki. Users can still opt out by modifying settings in their Alert settings.

4. **In the Delivery Methods box, indicate whether to receive alerts via e-mail or text message to your cellular phone.**

5. **In the Send Alerts for These Changes section, choose when to receive alerts.**

   The options you see here vary based on the kind of list you're working with. For example, a Tasks list allows you to receive an alert when a task is marked Complete or anytime a high-priority task changes.

   Any time users say they need a workflow to receive notification, try an alert first. You'd be surprised at how often alerts provide the options that are needed.

6. **In the When to Send Alerts section, choose the frequency of your alert delivery.**

   You can receive them immediately, once a day, or once a week. I like to receive a daily summary; otherwise, I get too many e-mails.

7. **Click OK to create your alert.**

Figure 6-6 shows an example of an alert.

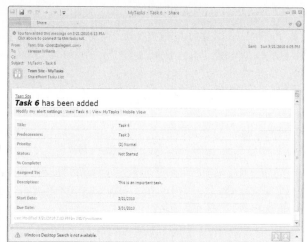

Figure 6-6:
Receive
an e-mail
when a list
changes.

You can manage all your alerts from a single page instead of navigating to each list. To manage all the alerts you have on a given site and modify or delete them, follow these steps:

1. **Browse to a list or library where you currently subscribe to an alert.**

2. **On the Share & Track tab of the Ribbon, choose Alert⇨Manage All Alerts.**

   Alternatively, you can click the My Settings option in the Welcome menu (usually in the upper-right corner of the page, as shown in Figure 6-7). You can manage your alerts and regional time zone defaults from this page.

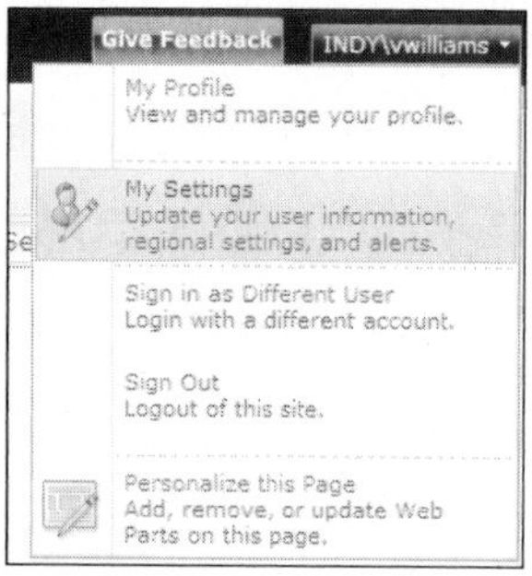

Figure 6-7:
Use the My
Settings link
to manage
alerts.

3. **Select the proper alert name link.**

   The Manage Alert page appears with all the options you viewed when you first created the alert. Change the settings as desired.

   Didn't set the alert to begin with? You can still read through the settings and change the choices (see the preceding steps list). Your changes don't affect the Alert settings for others if the alert was created for multiple users at the same time.

4. **Click OK to modify the alert with your new settings or Delete to delete the alert.**

   Deleting an alert that was created for you doesn't delete the alert from other users who are in the group the alert was created for.

If you're the site administrator, you can manage the alerts of everyone on the site by clicking the User Alerts link on the Site Administration section of the Site Settings page.

When the event occurs that matches your alert — say, for example, the time or location of a calendar event change — you receive an e-mail in your inbox. The e-mail notification you receive is based on a template. These templates can be modified by your administrator, so they can provide for more detail. Instructions for modifying these templates can be found in the SharePoint Server Foundation 2010 SDK (Software Development Kit) in the Microsoft MSDN (Microsoft Developer Network) site; search Google using the phrase *SharePoint Server Foundation 2010 SDK* to find the latest URL.

Chapter 7

Yours, Mine, and Ours: Social Networking

In This Chapter

▶ Using the Ribbon to share and track sites

▶ Tagging in SharePoint

▶ Making it your own with My Site, My Profile, and My Tags and Notes

▶ Talking on blogs, wikis, and discussion boards

*T*he folks at Microsoft got to thinking how SharePoint is a lot like social networking communities on the Web. *Social networking* services build online communities of people who share interests and/or activities, and consist of services and sites such as instant messaging (IM), discussion boards, blogs, wikis, bookmarking sites, Facebook, MySpace, Flickr, Twitter, and so on (and on).

Let me tell you, I have a family member who uses them all. I just can't. And neither should you feel like you have to use all the social networking options in SharePoint. Focus on picking the right tool(s) for you and your team. You can still be cool (and productive!) using just a few. There are good and specific reasons for using discussion boards, blogs, and wikis, and even more reasons for using alerts, feeds, and tagging. And SharePoint even has a What's Happening feature similar to the on-the-fly updates of Twitter.

SharePoint offers other social networking features that all site visitors can use, and some features (such as blogs, wikis, and discussion boards) that a site owner must set up for a team to use. SharePoint also offers social networking features with My Site.

In this chapter, I discuss social networking tools that let individuals and groups communicate and collaborate, and I cover My Site features that let you tag and share content. Depending on the culture of your organization and the projects you work on, these tools may find greater or lesser use; I encourage you to experiment with them all. Organizations generally experience some anxiety and growing pains around the less structured communications that social networking facilitates, but after a period of adjustment, I often find that those who were initially most reluctant become social networking advocates as they discover the value these tools can bring to productivity, collaboration, and morale.

Sharing and Tracking Using the Ribbon

The Ribbon in SharePoint 2010 features a Share & Track group that consolidates several common tasks for keeping track of useful SharePoint resources and sharing them with others. Figure 7-1 shows the Share & Track group.

Share & Track has three command buttons:

- ✔ **E-Mail a Link** uses Outlook to send a link to a page to someone else.

- ✔ **Alert Me** allows you to set and manage your alerts to lists or libraries so that an e-mail is sent to you when changes are made.

- ✔ **RSS Feed** enables you to subscribe to an RSS feed. Each list and library in SharePoint 2010 publishes an RSS feed that you can subscribe to and view in your favorite RSS viewer.

Figure 7-1: The Share & Track group in the Ribbon.

Tagging for Yourself and Others

Tags are keywords that you assign to content. Tagging pages to share with others is *social bookmarking,* and it's very popular on the Web. If you've ever used a site like Delicious (`http://delicious.com`), you already know how social bookmarking works.

As more people assign the same tags, tags become a way to navigate to similar content. The Tags and Notes group on the Ribbon has two buttons that let you tag items:

- ✔ **The I Like It button** is a single-click way to tag items you like; think of this as a recommendation, viewable to others.

✔ **The Tag & Notes button** lets you type your own tag keywords, so you can mark content with terms that are meaningful to you. This button also lets you access the *Note Board,* which you can use to leave publicly viewable comments on a document or page.

Your company can add more buttons to the Ribbon that map to other specific tags.

The emphasis is on *keyword* in tagging. SharePoint doesn't prevent you from typing longer tags, but I recommend you use, and train others to use, single words or very short phrases as tags. Otherwise, you defeat the purpose in using tagging as a fast, concise way to categorize information. If you need to make longer remarks, use the Note Board.

To tag content in SharePoint:

1. **Browse to the page you want to tag.**

   To tag individual list items or documents, you must browse to the list or library and then click the row you want to tag.

2. **Locate the Tags and Notes group in the Ribbon to see your tagging options.**

3. **To apply a predefined tag, click the I Like It button.**

   SharePoint applies the tag to your content and briefly displays a notification confirming your tag.

4. **To apply your own tags, click the Tags and Notes button.**

   The Tags and Notes Board window, as shown in Figure 7-2, appears, populated with recent tags you've applied.

5. **In the My Tags box, click an existing tag and/or type the tags you want to apply to the content.**

   Use a semicolon to separate tags.

6. **(Optional) To mark your tags as private so others can't see them, select the Private check box.**

7. **Click the Save button to save your tags.**

   When you save your tag, it appears in the Suggested Tags section of the page. You can click any of the tags in this section to view the Tags Profile page, which I discuss later in this chapter.

8. **To add a note to the item, click the Note Board tab and type your note in the text box.**

   Unlike tags, notes entered with the Note Board can't be marked private and therefore are viewable by anyone else with the same access; choose your words carefully.

Figure 7-2:
The Tags
and Note
Board
window.

9. **Click the Post button to post the note.**

The note appears in the window along with any other notes that have been entered. You can scroll through all the posts entered for this content using the Next and Previous buttons, as shown in Figure 7-3.

10. **To close the window, click the X in the upper-right corner of the window.**

Figure 7-3:
Scroll
through
notes.

"My" Site and Other "My" Stuff

Before I get into using all the My things in SharePoint, I want to describe how your My Site information is arranged. Previous versions of SharePoint included My Site. The contents of your personal My Site, as well as new social tagging functions, have been consolidated in SharePoint 2010 into *My Site,* accessible by choosing Welcome➪My Site.

The home page of your My Site, as shown in Figure 7-4, has main sections for My Newsfeed, My Content, and My Profile, which are described here:

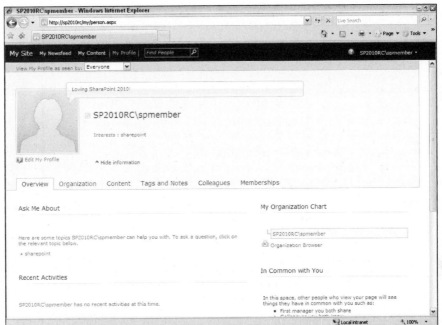

Figure 7-4:
The My
Profile page.

✔ **My Newsfeed** allows you to configure what social networking activities you wish to track. Examples include other people's new blog posts, ratings, and updated status messages. If you've ever used the social networking site Facebook, setting these options should sound familiar.

✔ **My Content** opens your personal My Site. This site is your very own SharePoint team site of which you are the complete boss. Use this site to store all your documents, slides, and other files. I use my personal My Site site to store all my data files, so I can easily access my files anywhere.

✔ **My Profile** lets you edit your profile and see how it's displayed compared to others. In addition to a Twitter-like function that lets you enter brief remarks on the fly, My Profile includes the following tabs:

- *Overview:* A quick look at your recent social networking activities, the Organization Chart you fit on, and a list of colleagues, memberships, and managers you have in common with others.

  The intended audience for this page is other people in your company. The information displayed here is what other people see about you when they visit your profile.

- *Organization:* Access to your profile and those of others in your organization in a scrollable Silverlight interface.

- *Content:* Access to your personal My Site where you can store shared documents, pictures, and recent blog posts.

- *Tags and Notes:* The tags and notes you've entered, organized by month.

- *Colleagues:* A list you can maintain of links to your colleagues and friends who also have SharePoint profiles.

  This list is one way you define your social network in My Site.

- *Memberships:* Distribution lists to which you've been subscribed as well as groups to which you've been added.

Access to the Content tab and your personal My Site is permission-based. It's possible to use all the other social networking features mentioned in this chapter without using your personal My Site. These permissions are configured by the SharePoint 2010 administrator responsible for the User Profile Service Application.

So how is My Profile different from your personal My Site? Think of your My Profile as the public face of your personal site information in a standardized format, whereas your personal My Site is a complete SharePoint site collection for your own use with much of the functionality that I describe in this book. You can set permissions within your personal My Site, libraries, and lists as you see fit, but the individual's My Profile pages will share some consistency across the organization.

Whew, having said all that, it will take some getting used to the new layout of My Site and My Profile, especially for users of past SharePoint versions.

The site that you're viewing when you click My Site or My Profile is called the *My Site Host.* The My Site Host is usually in a separate Web application with its own URL. It is a site collection with a set of Web Part pages and navigation menus that create the user experience known as My Site and My Profile. An administrator in your company can log into the My Site Host with full control permissions and make changes to the site's navigation and Web Parts so that the My Site experience matches your business requirements. In other words, there's nothing magical about My Site and My Profile. It's just another site that can be designed and modified using the techniques described in this book.

Using Your Tags and Notes Page

Your Tags and Notes page is a separate page in your My Site showing all your tagging and commenting activities. See Figure 7-5 for an example of this page.

The Tags and Notes page is divided into two columns. The right column shows a list of all your tags and notes, which are referred to in SharePoint as *activities*. In the left column, you have a few Web Parts that allow you to refine the list of activities displayed in the right column. For example, if you click Notes in the Refine by Type section, only activities of the type Note appear in the right.

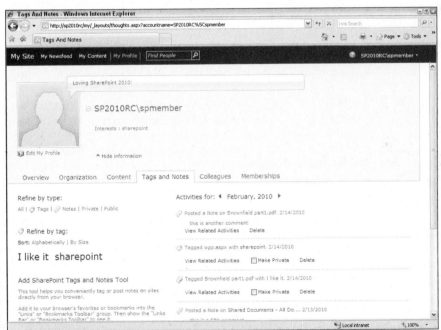

Figure 7-5:
The Tags and Notes page.

The Tags and Notes page in your My Profile shows both types of tagging, Country and Western — I mean Tags and Notes, which has a variety of sections to help you sort and find your tagged content. To view and arrange your Tags and Notes:

1. **Click the Tags and Notes tab in your My Site.**

2. **Use the headings on the page, such as Refine By and Activities For, to view and arrange your Tags and Notes:**

    - *To Refine by Type,* select Tags, Notes, Public, Private (the default is All).

    - *To Refine by Tag,* select Alphabetically or Size (Alphabetically is the default). Size is judged by the quantity of tags with that label. The more tags that have that label, the larger the size (and text display). Click a specific tag to view that tag's activities in the right column.

    - *Use the Activities for Month* (choosing from the month picker) to scroll to the tags for a specific prior month.

    - *Use the links and check marks under the Activities For section* to view related content and modify the properties of your tags and notes.

One of the great things about reviewing your Tags and Notes page is the ability to change tags to private or vice versa, to delete/edit notes, or to find related activities in a single location. See Figure 7-5 for an example of this page.

The Add SharePoint Tags and Notes Tool option that appears below the tag refinement options on the left lets you tag pages that are external to SharePoint. This is similar to the social bookmarking site, Delicious. Tagging an external site allows people in your social network to see what sites or articles you find useful. This option replaces the My Links feature in previous versions of SharePoint.

My Site includes several social network Web Parts that you can use for tracking tags and activities. For example, Recent Activities and Ask Me About are two Web Parts that are displayed in your My Site profile. Another interesting Web Part is the Tag Cloud Web Part, which displays your tags so that more frequently occurring tags appear in a larger font. See Chapter 10 for details on working with Web Parts.

Information Sharing with Blogs and Wikis

Blogs are intended to be mainly one-way communication: An individual or group with an opinion or expertise creates posts that others read and subscribe to. Granted, readers can comment on the posts, but the blog posts themselves aren't collaborative. You'll often see executives in an organization maintaining blogs to communicate to employees, or IT departments creating a blog with helpful posts that address FAQs.

Wikis, on the other hand, are specifically collaborative efforts: information is added to, and maintained by, a network of users. Perhaps the most well-known wiki is *Wikipedia* (www.wikipedia.com), a Web encyclopedia of information about any topic imaginable, editable by anyone in the Wikipedia community. A wiki is a very flexible and democratic way for individuals to work together to share, refine, and collect information.

Good candidates for wikis include corporate encyclopedias, dictionaries, and training manuals because many individuals can add their knowledge and examples.

Lone voice in the corporate wilderness? Creating a blog site

To create a blog in SharePoint, you create a new site/subsite. Take the time to consider where this blog will be located in your site hierarchy.

Although you can change permissions at any level, it may make more sense to have your President's blog away from the root site of your SharePoint intranet (and open to all users of the site hierarchy), but perhaps your Manager's blog should be created as a subsite of your team site (so that permissions can be inherited from the team site). See Figure 7-6 for an example of a blog site.

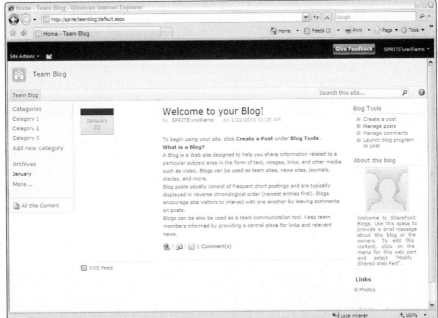

Figure 7-6: A SharePoint blog site.

To create a blog site:

1. **Navigate to the Create page by choosing Site Actions➪New Site.**

   The Type browser displays.

2. **Scroll until you see the Blog icon and click it.**

3. **Type a name and a URL for the site in the Name and URL fields, respectively.**

   If you click the More Options button, you can enter a blog description and manage permissions and navigation here as well (although you don't have to). You may want to read Chapters 12 and 13 on permissions and navigation to help with these selections, but if you're experimenting with a blog site, you can leave the defaults and change them later.

4. **Click the Create button.**

   You see a message that SharePoint is working and then your new blog displays.

5. **Click the Create a Post button to add a new entry to your blog.**

   The home page of the blog site shows a Welcome to Your Blog default post, a list of Blog tools for posting, a Content Editor Web Part dubbed About This Blog with text and a placeholder image, and a Links list.

   The site content includes a Photos picture library as well as lists called Categories, Comments, Links, and Posts.

Posting to a blog

Creating a blog post and commenting on a post are pretty straightforward. A user with permissions to post can click the Create a Post link under Blog Tools and type or copy their post using a text editor (which is similar to the text editor for discussion boards). The dialog box also allows for adding one or more category labels to the posts. By default, the site is configured so that the post must be approved before appearing to the users of the site.

Comments (if any) are displayed below the blog post to which they apply. The Comments link and the Add Comment field allow users to comment on a post by titling their comment (optional) and adding body text. The Comments link also shows the current number of comments. Other icons allow you to create a permanent hyperlink to the post and/or e-mail a hyper-link to the post.

Other features of the Blog Site template are predefined links on the Quick Launch menu for post categories, making it easy to see a filtered list of posts in one category.

The whole is greater than the sum of its parts: Using wikis to collaborate and coauthor

A *wiki* is a library of pages that can be edited by any member (Contributor) of your site. As I say earlier, encyclopedias, dictionaries, and training manuals are all good examples of wikis for an organization. These examples are entities that provide structure to what is being accomplished, but benefit by input of a group.

One of the marketing mantras of SharePoint 2010 is *wikis everywhere*. A SharePoint 2010 team site is essentially a wiki with the capabilities to add additional kinds of libraries and lists. SharePoint 2010 includes a new site template called the Enterprise Wiki which is intended for collaborative content creation among larger groups of people, such as a division. The steps discussed in this section apply to wikis anywhere — that is, it doesn't matter where you encounter wikis in SharePoint.

Creating a wiki

A wiki in SharePoint is a library of wiki pages. Create the wiki the way you would any other list or library, which I describe in Chapter 3, by selecting Wiki Page Library as the type.

Adding pages to a wiki

Two pages are created by default in your new wiki library, Home and How to Use This Wiki Library. Both provide predefined instructions that may be helpful when you first create the wiki. Most users change the home page content before launching the wiki, but you can keep the How to Use This Wiki Library page or delete it, depending on its usefulness.

To add other pages to your wiki, follow these steps:

1. **Navigate to the home page of the wiki library by using the link on the Quick Launch menu, if available.**

   You can also navigate to the All Site Content page and open the library.

2. **Select the Edit tab on the Ribbon and then click the View All Pages button.**

   You see the list of pages.

   The Library Tools tab appears in the Ribbon and contains two other tabs — Documents and Library.

3. **Click the Documents tab under Library Tools and then click the New Document button.**

   The New Wiki Page dialog box appears.

4. **Type your new page name in the New Page Name field and then click the Create button.**

   The new page appears, ready for editing. Just click in the page and then the Text Editing toolbar appears.

   You can edit now or repeat the steps here to create multiple pages before editing.

Alternatively, you can choose Site Actions➪New Page from an existing wiki page to add a new page to the same wiki library.

Another easy way to create pages is to create a link to them first in a wiki page and then click that link. The new page is created automatically with the name found in the link.

For example, type **[[My New Page]]** to create a link to the My New Page page. The link to an uncreated page appears underlined with dashes. If users click the link, the page is created for editing and the link turns into a normal hyperlink.

To create a link to a page and have the name be different than the wording of the link, type a pipe character (|) after the page name and then type the display text. For example, type **[[Resources|Resources for You]]** to create the Resources link that points to the Resources for You page.

Editing a wiki page

When you first create a wiki page, you're in Edit mode (as shown in Figure 7-7). When you want to edit later:

1. **Access the page from the Quick Launch menu or Wiki Library Page list.**

2. **Click the Edit tab on the Ribbon and then click the Edit button.**

Like other documents, check out the page if you don't want others to be able to edit at the same time and perhaps overwrite your work. See Chapter 2 for details.

Editing a wiki page is very easy, like working in a word processor. You can type or copy text, indent, make bullets, bold and italicize words, and insert all other types of content such as tables and images. To stop editing, click the Stop Editing button on the Edit tab of the Ribbon. You need to check in your wiki as a separate step if you checked it out.

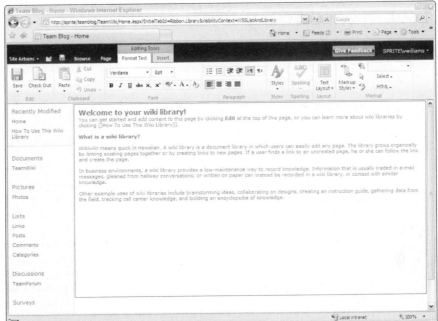

Figure 7-7:
A Wiki
page in Edit
mode.

You can also define your page layout. By default, page layout is one column (full-page wide), but you can change the layout by choosing one you like from the Text Layout drop-down list on the Format Text tab. (***Note:*** You must be in Edit mode to see the Format Text tab.) Now you may have multiple text containers to work with.

You can switch layouts at any point. But be careful — if you switch to a layout with fewer containers than your current layout, SharePoint combines content in one container with content in another. You won't lose the content, but you'll probably have to make some edits to fix the combined content.

Changing the text layout of a wiki page isn't the same as changing the layout on a Web Part page or the page layout on a publishing page. Wiki pages, Web Part pages, and publishing pages all behave slightly differently and have different purposes. See Chapter 9 for a more thorough discussion on SharePoint's Web pages. By the way, if you can articulate the difference between these three kinds of SharePoint pages, consider a career as a SharePoint consultant.

Communicating with Discussion Boards

Discussion boards, along with alerts, are the granddaddies of social networking services. Discussion boards have been around since before the World Wide Web and consist of text postings by individuals with others posting replies to the original subject or to other replies. A discussion board post and the responses to it are one *thread.*

One of the benefits of a discussion board (versus a long e-mail chain, and you know what I'm talking about) is the ability to find and search posts easily for information. Threads provide a useful history of the comments on a topic. Users generally have various levels of expertise in organizing and searching their e-mail, but SharePoint discussion views and search make it easy for users to both find and read posts.

One of the benefits of a team discussion board (should be) the less formal approach in posting questions and answers — a discussion board exchange resembles a true discussion. Blogs and wikis are more formal, so discussion boards are generally where team members can ask questions and share thoughts.

SharePoint discussion boards are a special list type. Rather than using the default list configuration, I recommend that site owners consider enhancing discussion boards to improve users' experiences. Experiment with discussion board views and using a List View Web Part on a page instead of having the posters interact within the list itself.

Creating a discussion board

A team site is created with a Team Discussion list. You can use this one, delete it and create a new one, or create multiple new discussion boards for your team to contain the discussions to more defined areas.

If you prefer a more specific name for the predefined discussion board, you can rename it, or delete the predefined list and create a new one. The advantage to creating a new one is that the URL matches the list name.

To create a new discussion board, follow these steps:

1. **Choose Site Actions⇨More Create Options, or click the All Site Content link on the Quick Actions menu and then click the Create button.**

   In either case, the Create page appears.

2. **Click the Discussion Board link under List and then enter a name for your discussion board in the Name field.**

   I recommend not using spaces in your list names.

3. **Click the More Options button to add a description in the Description field.**

4. **Select the Yes or No radio button to determine whether you want to show the discussion board on the Quick Launch menu.**

5. **Click the Create button.**

   You see the list page of your discussion board. *Note:* In the Current View section, discussion boards are arranged by subject.

Posting and replying to a subject

Unlike other lists, discussion boards have two levels of list items. A new subject is actually a folder, whereas replies (messages) are items in those folders. This allows for the replies to be contained within the original subject in the various views that are available in discussion boards.

To create a new subject in a discussion board, follow these steps:

1. **Browse to your discussion list.**

2. **Click the New Item button and choose Discussion on the Items tab in the Ribbon.**

   The New Item dialog box appears.

3. **In the New Item dialog box, type a subject for the new discussion in the Subject field.**

   This needs to be a short phrase that teammates can relate to as a topic.

4. **Type the detail of your post in the Body field.**

   You have all the editing options of Rich HTML in this area. Use the Editing tools to format your text with the toolbar and styles, as well as insert tables, images, and links. You can upload files using the Insert tab.

   You also have spell checker in this dialog box!

5. **When you're finished with your post, click the Save button on the Edit tab.**

   Your subject post appears in the Subject view and shows the subject title, who created it, the amount of replies, and when it was updated last.

Of course, the site owner can modify this view. In fact, you may find it helpful to add columns, such as the Reply column, to the view so users don't have to open the subject to reply.

To reply to a subject or another reply, follow these steps:

1. **Click the *Subject Title* link in your discussion list.**

   The subject appears in Flat view with a Reply button.

2. **Click the Reply button.**

   If your site owner has added a Reply button to the Subject view, you can click the Reply button there.

   The Reply dialog box appears. By default, the Reply dialog box shows only a Body field with the creator, date, and body of the original subject copied into this text area. You can delete the original post when typing your reply; otherwise, SharePoint nicely hides it in your post as a Show Quoted Messages link that users can click if they wish.

3. **Add your reply using the Rich HTML features (as I describe in the preceding list).**

   Remember you can attach files, upload files, and add all sorts of text formatting.

4. **When you're finished with your reply, click the Save button.**

Viewing discussions

When first navigating to a discussion board (for this example, say you clicked a link on the Quick Launch menu and navigated to the Team Discussion list), you first see the Subject view of a discussion board. The following list helps you understand the different view options:

- ✔ **The Subject view** shows a list of subjects (also called *topics* or *discussions*) with the creator of the subject, number of replies, and last updated columns.

- ✔ **The Flat view** is visible when you click a Subject link. In this view, you can see all discussions posted in chronological order. This view also has a Reply button for replying to the original subject post or any other reply in the thread.

- ✔ **The Threaded view** (see Figure 7-8) is an option from the View drop-down list in the Current View section of the List tab. When users switch to this view, they see posts and replies in the hierarchy they were created. In the Flat view, all posts are shown as the same level, but in a Threaded view, replies to replies are shown grouped and indented.

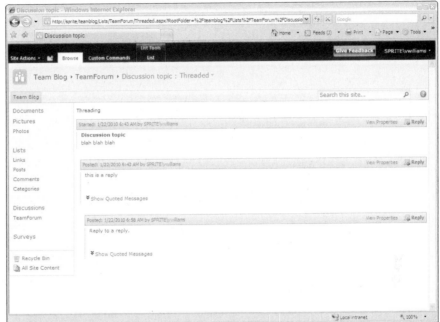

Figure 7-8:
A Threaded
view of a
discussion
subject and
replies.

Part II
Taking Your Team Site to the Next Level

The 5th Wave   By Rich Tennant

"The funny thing is he's spent 9 hours organizing his site directory."

In this part . . .

The options I cover in this part show you how to customize your team site to your team's specifications and to help make sure the right people have access to the right things (and don't trip over each other).

I also cover adding refinements to your document libraries/lists to make things easier to manage and keep track of, including version-management solutions. I cover ways to add more advanced settings, such as validation and audience targeting as well, to enforce document and list management policies. And I also discuss setting permissions and workflows. I explain the different kinds of Web pages in SharePoint and show you how to add functionality to your pages using Web Parts.

Chapter 8

Configuring Libraries and Lists

. . . .

In This Chapter

▶ Finding list settings

▶ Configuring General settings for lists and libraries

▶ Setting unique permissions at the library/list and document level

▶ Configuring standard workflows

. . . .

I introduce document libraries and lists in Chapters 2 and 3, respectively. In Chapter 4, I show you how to create your own custom lists. In this chapter, I show you how to control when documents are visible to others, who can edit another user's list items, how to add workflow options, and even how to limit site visitors' access to a specific library. These are all examples of configuration options in a library or list.

SharePoint 2010 has expanded on the library/list configuration options available previously. I remember learning all the new 2007 settings that I now use every day! So I'm ready for even more — Validation settings, Ratings settings, and Forms settings (for lists) are some of the new configuration options in 2010.

You need to be a site owner to perform the configuration options that I describe in this chapter. Don't let all that control go to your head, however. Sometimes having a document library that's configured too tightly can make your users find creative ways to get around the restrictions, if they don't deem them beneficial! On the other hand, a well-planned configuration for document management can help your team avoid embarrassing errors and time-consuming corrections while creating and maintaining documents and lists.

You need to have the Manage Lists permission to manage lists, which is usually conferred to the site's designer. See Chapter 12 for more about managing permissions and for details on how to get this permission.

Accessing List Settings

To view or change the configuration settings of your library or list, use the Library Settings or List Settings page (which you may remember from adding columns and creating custom lists in Chapter 4).

Follow these steps to access the Library/List Settings page:

1. **Navigate to your library/list by clicking the *Title* link on the Quick Launch toolbar (if it shows in the Quick Launch).**

   You can also locate the list by clicking the View All Site Content link on the Quick Launch toolbar or choosing Site Actions⇨View All Site Content.

2. **Click the Library or List tab under the Library (or List) Tools tab.**

   Locate the Settings section, which should be on the far right with Library Settings, Create Column, Library Permissions, and Edit Form Web Parts icons.

3. **Click the Library (or List) Settings button, as shown in Figure 8-1.**

   The Library or List Settings page appears. (You may have already accessed this page when completing the steps in other chapters in this book.)

Figure 8-1:
Click the Library Settings button to change your library's configuration.

The Library (or List) Settings page is divided into several sections. Each section contains many configuration choices, as shown in Figure 8-2. I suggest you spend some time browsing this page. Some of the sections you see include:

- *List Information:* Displays the library (or list) name, Web address, and description.

List Information

Name: Site Pages
Web Address: http://allsp10/sites/tcs/SitePages/Forms/AllPages.aspx
Description: Use this library to create and store pages on this site.

General Settings	Permissions and Management	Communications
Title, description and navigation	Delete this document library	RSS settings
Versioning settings	Permissions for this document library	
Advanced settings	Manage files which have no checked in version	
Validation settings		
Column default value settings	Workflow Settings	
Rating settings	Generate file plan report	
Audience targeting settings	Information management policy settings	
Metadata navigation settings		
Per-location view settings		
Form settings		

Columns

A column stores information about each document in the document library. The following columns are currently available in this document library:

Column (click to edit)	Type	Required
Wiki Content	Multiple lines of text	
Managed Keywords	Managed Metadata	
Created By	Person or Group	
Modified By	Person or Group	
Checked Out To	Person or Group	

Create column
Add from existing site columns
Column ordering
Indexed columns

Views

A view of a document library allows you to see a particular selection of items or to see the items sorted in a particular order. Views currently configured for this document library:

View (click to edit)	Default View	Mobile View	Default Mobile View
All Pages	✓	✓	✓
Recent Changes			
Created By Me			
By Author			
By Editor			

Create view

Figure 8-2:
The Library/
List Settings
page.

You can change the list's name and description by clicking the Title, Description and Navigation link in the General Settings column.

The Web address is set to the list's default view. Change the default view by scrolling down to the Views section of the Library (or List) Settings page.

- *General Settings:* Includes Title and Description as well as Versioning, Advanced, and Rating settings. See Table 8-1 for a complete list of General settings.

- *Permissions and Management:* Includes saving the library/list as a template as well as Permission and Workflow settings. See Table 8-1 for a complete list of Permissions and Management settings.

- *Communications:* Configure RSS and incoming e-mail settings for the library or list. See Chapter 6 for details on configuring these options.

- *Content Types:* If you have configured your library/list to allow for content types, a Manage Content Types section appears. Use this section to associate content types with your list or library. With content types, you can reuse columns across sites as well as across lists and libraries. See Chapter 22 for a more thorough discussion of content types.

- *Columns:* View, add, and modify columns for the library or list.

  See Chapter 4 to review column types. You can create your own column for that list only, add a site column from the preconfigured SharePoint site columns, or create a new site column of your choosing that can be added to multiple lists.

- *Views:* Display and modify the library/list views. You can also create new views.

Many site owners never change the default settings options; some simply change the title or delete the list. For others, this level of optional setting detail is what they want to know first! Microsoft supplies descriptions on the how and/or why to use the settings on each of the individual settings pages; however, this chapter may become one of the most dog-eared chapters in the book because there are so many options to remember!

Configuring the General Settings

The General Settings area of the library/list has been expanded in SharePoint 2010 to include multiple new settings, including Validation, Column Default Value (for libraries), Rating, Metadata Navigation, Per-Location View, and Form (for lists). See Table 8-1 for an overview to see what you can do with each of these options.

Table 8-1	General Settings Configuration Options
Setting Name	*What You Can Accomplish*
Title, Description, and Navigation	Just like it sounds! (See the section, "Changing the title, description, and navigation," later in this chapter.)
Versioning	Configure item approval, versioning (major and minor), and require check-out.
Advanced	A plethora of options including allowing for content types, search visibility, allowing for folders, or datasheet view.

Setting Name	What You Can Accomplish
Validation	Allows you to create formulas that compare two or more columns in your library or list.
Column Default Value	Add or edit default values for columns indicated in the library or list Validation settings.
Rating	A Yes or No option that allows items in the library or list to be rated.
Audience Targeting	A Yes or No option that allows the library or list to use audience targeting. Enabling audience targeting creates a Targeting column for this list. Some Web parts can use this data to filter list contents based on whether the user is in the audience.
Metadata Navigation	Allows for a hierarchical management of the library or list in the Navigation Tree View. Hierarchical options can include content types, choice questions, or a managed metadata field.
Per-Location View	Allows you to set the default view that appears when a user browses to a specific location in the list or library. When used with metadata navigation, you can set views for each level in the metadata hierarchy.
Form	Available for lists only. You need InfoPath 14 (2010) to utilize these settings.

Changing the title, description, and navigation

The Title, Description and Navigation Settings page is a simple, self-descriptive settings page. Most of these options are what you configure when you first create the library or list, including whether the list appears on the Quick Launch toolbar.

Changing the title does *not* change the Web address (URL) of the library/list. If having the title match the URL is important, or less confusing, to your team, consider recreating a new library or list with the desired title and deleting the old list. Of course, this works better early in the process, before you upload documents or create list items!

If you already have many items in your library or list, you can copy documents from one library to another, or export an existing list to Excel and re-import into a new list. However, this shouldn't be taken lightly. Some column configuration settings, such as a Choice column, need to be recreated along with all the library/list settings I discuss in this chapter. If you're unsure what you want to name a library or list when you create it, take some time to consider your terminology before creating the library or list.

Versioning settings

The Versioning Settings area contains probably some of the most sought after settings in any library or list. Versioning settings cover most of the document management or content management choices. So your new document/content management mantra is *approval, versioning,* and *check out.* I can say it in my sleep. By default, Approval, Versioning, or Check Out requirement settings are *not* turned on in a team site.

If you want to have these options enabled when your sites are configured, consider using a publishing site instead.

Before selecting these options, make sure you know the business processes of your team. If documents are thoroughly vetted and approved outside the SharePoint process, you may not want or need Approval settings or Check Out enforced. If your documents are images, you may or may not want to apply versioning if the versions don't matter to you and you would not need to revert to an older version.

Consider using multiple document libraries and apply different settings based on need. For example, if you have 100 documents in a library and really only need versioning and approval on 5 of those documents, perhaps they can be placed in a library with extra configuration.

I suggest adding the Versions column to your views so that users can quickly see the version of the document. Otherwise, you end up with users appending versioning information to the document's name or title, such as Employee Handbook v1.0, Employee Handbook v2.0, or my favorite, Client_Proposal_Final_v3.0_FINAL.

Versioning can be one of the most misunderstood features of SharePoint document management. Versioning is a helpful protection mechanism because you can revert to a previous version of the document, if necessary. *Versions* in SharePoint are copies of the same document at different intervals during editing. If you require users to view different versions of a document, maybe for choosing between the two, you need to include a designation in the name (such as *v1.0* in the earlier example) or an additional Metadata column.

Follow these steps to apply or modify Versioning settings:

1. **Click the Versioning Settings link in the Library/List Settings Page.**

   The sections of the Versioning Settings page include Content Approval, Document Version History, Draft Item Security, and Require Check Out (libraries only).

2. **Choose whether to require item approval in the Content Approval section by selecting the Yes or No radio button.**

   If you selected Yes in answer to "Require content approval for submitted items" then individuals with the Approve Items permissions can always see draft items.

   Items that aren't approved yet aren't visible to site members or visitors. You can designate who you want to view drafts in the Draft Item Security section. See Chapter 15 for details on content approval.

3. **In the Document Version History section, select a radio button to indicate whether to use No Versioning, Create Major Versions, Create Major and Minor (Draft) Versions, and (optional) specify the Number of Versions to keep by selecting the appropriate check box and entering a number.**

   The default for a list/library is No Versioning. You can select Major Versions (1.0, 2.0. 3.0, and so on) or Major and Minor Versions (1.0, 1.2. 1.3, 2.0, and so on). Selecting either of the last two options enables you to designate a limit for the number of versions of each type by entering a number up to 10,000.

4. **Choose who can see draft items by selecting a Draft Item Security radio button in the Draft Item Security section.**

   This section is disabled unless you allow for minor (draft) versions of your documents or list items. Here are the three options for who can see draft items — Any User Who Can Read Items, Only Users Who Can Edit Items, or Only Users Who Can Approve (and the Author).

5. **Determine whether to require check out for users editing documents by selecting the Yes or No radio button.**

   Although it can sometimes be a hassle (I have plenty of coworkers who forget they checked out a document, sometimes months ago!), requiring check out is another good safety mechanism that makes sure the other users don't see a document in mid-modification, or have multiple users editing at the same time (last save wins).

   Consider adding the Checked Out To column to your views so that users can quickly see who has an item checked out.

6. **Click OK or Cancel.**

   If you click OK, your Versioning settings are applied. Go try them out!

As I discuss in Chapter 2, an Edit menu appears next to a document's or item's title in the library/list view (see Figure 8-3). This drop-down list allows a document's editor to check out/check in the document, approve, set off a workflow, and so forth. This menu is *contextual* — if approval isn't set on the library or list, Approve doesn't appear on the menu. If a document is checked out, the option to Discard Check Out appears.

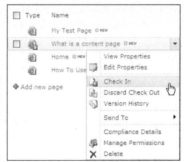

Figure 8-3:
A docu-
ment's edit
menu.

In most cases, team members navigate to the site using a browser to work with lists. However, think about how your team interacts with documents. They may be navigating to a library or a List View Web Part using the browser but they may also be linking from a bookmark, or opening the document directly from the editing application (such as Word, Excel, or PowerPoint). Although current versions of Office support and interact with SharePoint library settings, users may not know where to find these commands.

Avoid frustration by taking a little time to review the settings and options with your team. Training on these document editing and management options is one of my number one recommendations for SharePoint collaboration success, especially for teams with many members/contributors.

Advanced settings

Advanced settings include many powerful configuration options for libraries and lists:

- ✔ **Content Types:** Allows you to add and remove content types associated with the list or library. See Chapter 22 for details on creating your own content types.

- ✔ **Document Template (library only):** Allows you to specify the default template, such as a Word or PowerPoint template, that is used when someone clicks the New button to create a new document.

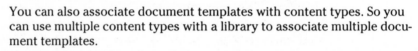

   You can also associate document templates with content types. So you can use multiple content types with a library to associate multiple document templates.

- ✔ **Opening Documents in the Browser (library only):** Allows you to determine the behavior of the browser when someone clicks on a document to open it.

✔ **Custom Send to Destination (library only):** This is a great option that lets you add your own Web address to the Send To menu on a document's Edit menu. Your SharePoint administrator can also add global addresses that appear in the Send To menu in every document library. The Send To command sends a copy of your file to another location, such as another team site where you want to share the document.

✔ **Folders:** Indicates whether users can create new folders in the library. I like to turn this off so people don't go folder crazy. You can always turn it on so you can create folders when necessary and then turn it back off.

✔ **Search:** Specifies whether items in the list or library should appear in search results.

✔ **Offline Client Availability:** Allows you to specify whether users of desktop client software, such as Word and Excel, can browse to the library.

✔ **Site Assets Library (library only):** Allows you to designate the library as a Site Assets library, which makes it easier for users to browse to the library to find multimedia files.

✔ **Datasheet:** Allows you to specify whether users can edit the items in the list or library using the datasheet view.

✔ **Dialogs:** By default, list and library forms launch in a dialog box. This option lets you specify that forms should open in the browser window as a page instead of a dialog box.

In addition, *list* advanced settings include item-level permissions and attachments.

Follow these steps to apply or modify Advanced settings:

1. **Click the Advanced Settings link in the Library/List Settings page.**

   The Advanced Settings page appears, as shown in Figure 8-4.

2. **Choose whether to enable management of content types by selecting the Yes or No radio button.**

   If you select Yes, after applying, your Library/List Settings page will contain a new section for Content Types. The default is No.

3. **Change the document template (library only) by specifying a template URL.**

   Libraries have a default template for new documents. Remember, you can start a new document in a library as well as upload documents that have been created previously. For example, the document template for a document library is the default Word template. You could change this is to an Excel or PowerPoint template. You could also change it to a custom template you created in one of these applications.

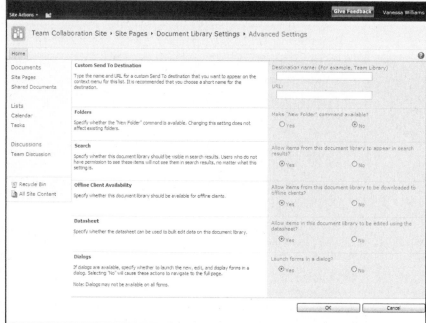

Figure 8-4:
Configuring
Advanced
settings.

If you're working with content types, you can enable a different template for each document type. For example, your library may house contracts and have three content types for different contracts, all with a different template available off the New button.

If you opt for a different document template, upload the template to the Forms folder in document library and change the Template URL in the Document Template section of the Advanced settings.

4. **Choose when to open documents in the browser (library only), the client application, or as the server default by selecting a radio button option in the Opening Documents in the Browser section.**

If the client application is unavailable, the document opens in the browser.

5. **Add a Custom Send To Destination (library only) by entering the name that should display on the Send to menu, and the URL destination.**

Similar to Windows commands (for example, Send to Desktop), you can create an option to appear on the Edit menu for documents in this library to be sent to another SharePoint destination. Supply a short name to appear on the contextual menu and a URL for the destination in the Destination Name and URL text boxes.

6. **Select whether folders can be created in this library/list by selecting the Yes or No radio button in the Folders section.**

   Selecting Yes or No determines whether the New Folder command is available on the New menu. The default is Yes.

   I usually disable folders unless I have a good reason to use them. In my opinion, the only good reason to use folders is when you have a set of documents that require unique permissions but must remain in the same document library. If you leave folders enabled, people will use them.

7. **Determine the search visibility for this library by selecting the Yes or No radio button in the Search section.**

   Selecting No for the Search option can keep the items in the library or lists from being presented in search results, even if the site or library is included in Search settings. The default is Yes.

8. **Enable offline client availability by selecting the Yes or No radio button in the Offline Client Availability section.**

   The Offline Client Availability option determines whether items in the library/list can be downloaded to offline client applications. The default is Yes.

9. **Add library/list location to the Site Assets library (library only) by selecting the Yes or No radio button in the Site Assets Library section.**

   This new Site Assets Library option specifies whether this library appears as a default location when uploading images or other files to a wiki page. This can be especially beneficial for document libraries than contain images or a picture library. This keeps wiki editors from searching all over for the images they should be using. The default is No.

10. **Determine whether library/list can be viewed in datasheet view by selecting the Yes or No radio button in the Datasheet section.**

    This option determines whether the datasheet can be used to bulk-edit data on this library or list. The default is Yes.

11. **Indicate whether forms should launch in a modal dialog box by selecting the Yes or No radio button in the Dialogs section.**

    Modal dialog boxes get old pretty quickly, so I suggest you select the No option on this page quite often.

12. **Click OK or Cancel.**

    If you click OK, your selections are applied.

Other advanced configuration settings available in a list (not library) include a Yes/No option for allowing attachments for a list item (default is Yes) and item-level permissions. The default for item-level permissions in a list is for all members (contributors) to be able to read and modify all items. You can adjust these settings for users to either read only their own items and/or edit only their own items.

Validation settings

Validation settings are new to SharePoint 2010, as is validation for columns that I describe in Chapter 4. *Validation* is a formula or statement that must evaluate to TRUE before the data can be saved. The difference between the two is that column validation compares only the data in that single column to some test, such as

= [Discount] < = .50

This means that the discount entered must be less than 50 percent.

Validation settings in the library/list level compare two or more columns to evaluate to TRUE. So you can set a rule that [Discount] < [Cost] so customers don't get an item for free (or money back!) because they buy an item with a discount.

To use Validation settings, follow these steps:

1. **Click the Validation Settings link in the Library/List Settings page.**

   The Validation Settings page has two sections, Formula and User Message. The Formula section is the test your comparison of the columns must pass for the item to be valid. The User Message section is what the user receives if the test fails. Users can then adjust their values until the test passes.

2. **Create a formula for the validation by entering it in the Formula field.**

   The formula needs to compare (or validate) two columns in your library or list. The Library (or List) Settings page provides an example and a link to learning more about the proper syntax.

   A selection list of columns in your library/list is available for use in your formula.

3. **In the User Message text box, enter a message to be shown to users who enter an invalid list item.**

4. **Click OK or Cancel.**

   If you click OK, your validation is applied to your list.

Validations aren't retroactive. They apply only to new and modified entries on the specified columns.

Rating settings

Rating settings is a simple Yes/No option to allow the items in the library/list to be rated by users. The Rating feature is a much requested feature. When enabled on your list or library, a Rating field appears, as shown in Figure 8-5.

Figure 8-5:
Rating a
document.

Audience Targeting settings

This setting includes one section with a Yes/No option to enable audience targeting for the library/list. Selecting Yes creates a Targeting column for this library/list. Certain Web Parts, such as the Content Query Web Part, can use this column to filter list contents based on the user's inclusion in a specific audience.

Audience targeting isn't the same thing as permissions. A user can still access content even if they aren't included in an audience. Audience targeting is simply a way to filter the presentation of content to certain groups of people.

Metadata Navigation settings

This new SharePoint 2010 configuration option adds navigation options to the Site Hierarchy Tree View. This Metadata Navigation Settings page has three sections:

✔ **Configure Navigation Hierarchy:** The ability to select hierarchy fields that appear under the list in the Tree View. Options include content types, choice fields, and managed metadata fields. Folders is a default selection that can be removed.

✔ **Configure Key Filters:** Select from available Key Filter columns to use as filter input controls on the list views.

✔ **Automatically Manage Indices for Metadata-Driven Navigation:** Settings related to the indexing of the library/list.

These settings give your users another way to filter and navigate to list items. Figure 8-6 shows a screenshot of a library that's using metadata navigation.

Per-Location Views settings

Per-Location Views work hand-in-hand with Metadata Navigation to allow you to specify which views are visible at a selected location. *Location* is a bit misleading in this context. It refers to the hierarchical location within the library's metadata navigation. Folders are also considered a location, so you can specify which views are available when a user navigates to a specific folder. Figure 8-7 shows an example where the GroupedByCampaign view is selected for the Audio metadata filter in the library. When a user clicks Audio in the library's metadata navigation, they will see the GroupedByCampaign view.

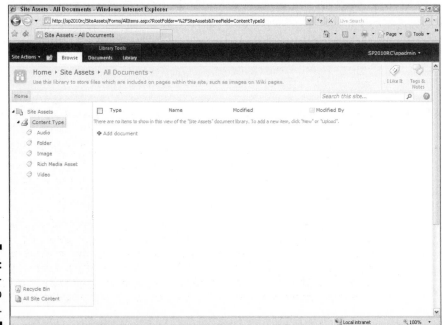

Figure 8-6:
Use meta-
data to
filter lists.

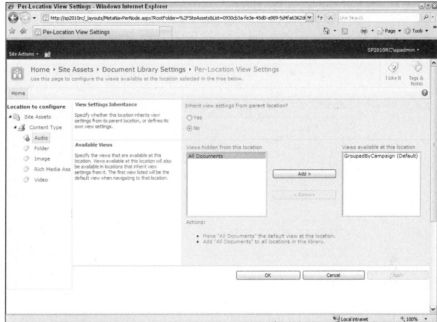

Figure 8-7:
Specify the
default view
for a
location.

Form settings

This option is available only for lists. If InfoPath 2010 is installed on your machine, you can opt to allow customization of the list form using InfoPath by selecting the Customize the current form using Microsoft InfoPath radio button.

Permissions and Management Options

Are you tired yet?! I know all these options can seem daunting, but the good thing is that applying the configurations is easy and located all in one spot. The hard part is deciding what you can do, and hopefully this chapter helps with that!

Permissions and Management options can seem a lot more straightforward than some of the General Settings options. I can remember when I first started using SharePoint, I struggled with the fact that deleting a list was buried in settings and that it was actually easier to delete a site! I now appreciate that the Delete option is in a location that makes you think about whether you want to delete the list (and that's a good thing!).

I don't detail every settings option in the Permissions and Management category. See Table 8-2 for an overview of the settings. In the following sections, I discuss the Permission for This List, Workflow, and the Generate File Plan Report settings.

Table 8-2	Permissions and Management Options
Setting Name	*What You Can Accomplish*
Delete This Document Library (or List)	Just like it sounds!
Save Document Library (or List) as a Template	A way to reuse the library or list columns and settings (with or without content) in your site (or collection).
Permissions for This Library (or List)	An option that allows for different permissions for the library or list versus the entire site.
Workflow	Allows you to enable workflow and specific Workflow settings for this library or list only.
Generate File Plan Report	You can add/edit default values for columns indicated in the library or list Validation settings.
Information Management Policy	Settings to be used in conjunction with a Records Center site or for in place records management.
Enterprise Metadata and Keywords Settings	Adds a managed keywords column to the list/ library and lets you treat those keywords as social tags if desired.

Permissions for This Document Library (or List) setting

To create unique permissions for the library/list (rather than inheriting the site-level permissions), follow these steps:

1. **Choose the Permission for This Document Library (or List) link from the Customize page.**

   You see a message bar below the Ribbon that tells you that the library/ list is inheriting from the parent site. You can stop inheriting to apply unique permissions. If you've already broken inheritance on the list, you can revert to inheriting from the parent again.

2. **Click the Stop Inheriting link.**

   The users and groups that have access to the parent (in this case, the *site*) become available to delete or modify. Make sure that you leave owners with the ability to edit the list!

   Think through this process carefully. Breaking inheritance often causes confusion for both users and site owners. Users who can access everything on a site can be baffled when they're denied access to a certain library or list. Site owners who may have at first liked the idea of granular permissions are suddenly stuck hunting down what's causing access problems. Consider using a subsite with different permissions to contain exclusive libraries or lists.

3. **Use the Permissions Tools tab on the ribbon to modify permissions by clicking the option buttons.**

   One of the common scenarios in this situation is the need to remove certain entire site groups, for example, visitors (readers), and add specific users to the list.

Workflow settings

A *workflow* is an automated version of a business process; it was (and still is) one of the big buzzes around SharePoint. You can associate SharePoint workflows with items and documents so that SharePoint sends notifications or asks users to fill out forms when certain conditions in the process are TRUE or when the item or document reaches a certain step in the process.

At a minimum, your team site should have the *three-state workflow,* which allows you to trigger actions when the state of an item changes. The most obvious use of the three-state workflow is with an Issue Tracking list. Issues automatically have three states — Active, Resolved, and Closed. For example, you could use a three-state workflow to assign a task in SharePoint to a selected user when the status of the issue is changed from Active to Resolved.

If your company has granted you a higher license, you may also use various approval workflows that are intended for managing document approval.

SharePoint Designer 2010 includes a powerful workflow designer that you can use to create custom workflows. I suggest checking out the workflow designer, if there's anything remotely automated you want to do around list items or documents in a library. Unlike previous versions of SharePoint Designer, the custom workflows you create in SharePoint Designer 2010 are reusable throughout your site.

Follow these steps to configure your library or list to use a workflow:

1. **Click the Workflow Settings link under Permissions and Management.**

   You can also access this command using the List or Library tab on the Ribbon.

   If no workflows have been assigned to this list, you see the Add a Workflow form. This form has five sections: Workflow, Name, Task List, History List, and Start Options.

   If other workflows already exist for this library/list, the Settings page for workflows allows you to view/modify settings of existing workflows, add a workflow, remove a workflow, and view workflow reports.

2. **In a library, click the Add A Workflow link to add a new workflow to your library.**

3. **Select a workflow template.**

   Depending on what license your company has given you for SharePoint will determine how many workflow templates you have available. You see a short description of each as you highlight that option:

   - *Disposition approval:* Manages document expiration and retention by allowing participants to decide whether to retain or delete expired documents.

   - *Three-state:* Use this workflow to track items in a list.

   - *Collect signatures:* Gathers digital signatures required for your Microsoft Office document.

   - *Approval:* Routes a document for approval. Approvers can approve or reject the document, reassign the approval task, or request changes to the document.

   - *Collect feedback:* Routes a document for review. Reviewers can provide feedback, which is compiled and sent to the document owner when the workflow has completed.

4. **Type a unique name for the workflow in the Name text box, as Figure 8-8 shows.**

   In naming your workflow, be careful not to name it something similar to the templates I describe in Step 2 (such as *collecting signatures*) to avoid confusion between your workflow and a template.

   You can create as many workflows as you want for a list or library. For example, say you have two kinds of approval processes — a shortened process and a longer process. Just step through the Add a Workflow process twice and select different configuration options to meet your needs.

5. **Select a task list to be used by the workflow by choosing a Select a Task List option.**

   You can select an existing task list or have the system create a new one by selecting New Task list. I suggest creating a new task list for each workflow.

6. **Select a history list for the workflow from Select a History List options.**

   You can select an existing history list or request that a new history list be created. Again, I suggest creating a new history list for each workflow.

7. **Select your Start options by enabling one or more check boxes.**

   Depending on which workflow template you picked, only certain Start options may be enabled. Generally, it's a good idea to allow the workflow to be manually started, although you can also have the workflow start automatically when an item is created or changed.

8. **Click the Next button.**

   You aren't done yet! A new page of options appears.

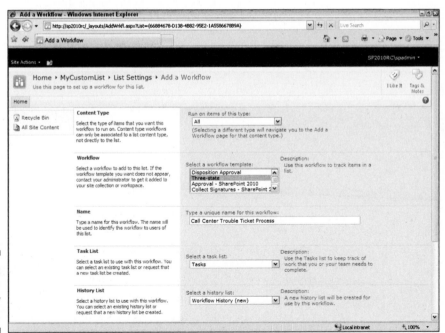

Figure 8-8:
Customize
workflow
options.

Depending on the type of workflow you select, you have different options to choose, including whom the workflow goes to, whether the actions happen in serial or parallel, what the deadline is for the actions, and what happens to the workflow if someone rejects the document or the item changes.

Several improvements have been made to 2010 workflows including having more than one type of stage available (parallel, serial).

9. Click OK or Cancel.

If you click OK, your settings are applied.

Chapter 9

Working with Web Pages

In This Chapter

▶ Choosing between wiki pages and Web Part pages

▶ Creating new wiki pages

▶ Linking to wiki pages

▶ Creating new Web Part pages

*H*ow many times have you heard, "We need the team to get on the same page?" Well, no problem if you're using SharePoint. If you're a facilitator, communicator, and/or have a creative streak, you want this chapter. Although SharePoint gives you a lot of helpful tools to work with content, the ability to communicate effectively with your team, starting with a customizable home page, pulls together everything.

Using Web pages and Web Parts is how you arrange and present information in a collaboration site. Pages can display freeform text, tables, hyperlinks, and images, as well as Web Parts showing library/list content from your site (or other sites!) arranged as you wish. Web Parts can be closed temporarily or moved. You can modify the Web Parts to show only the data you wish from a library or list. You can inform, organize, and focus your team with your pages; something that otherwise would take a lot of effort with e-mails and network shares alone.

In this chapter, I show you how to work with Web pages. In Chapter 10, I go into more detail about working with Web Parts.

Understanding SharePoint Web Pages

Your team site is really just a collection of Web pages. You have two different types of Web pages for displaying your content — *Wiki Content pages* and *Web Part pages.*

If you're familiar already with SharePoint team sites, you've probably worked with Web Part pages. In SharePoint 2010, Wiki Content pages are now the default Web page type. They are stored in a wiki page library dubbed *Site Pages*.

Why wiki pages?

You may be wondering, why wiki pages? A *wiki* is a site that's intended to be modified by many people. Think about the very popular wiki site Wikipedia (www.wikipedia.com). Everyone can contribute to Wikipedia. That also sounds like a SharePoint team site. Team sites use wiki pages to make it easy for everyone on your team to share information.

Only members of your team site's default Members group have permissions to modify wiki pages. If you want some people to be able to read your wiki pages but not edit them, add those users to your site's default Visitors group. See Chapter 12 for more details on managing site access.

A Wiki Content page consists of a very large text page where you place your content. In this large text box, you can place almost any kind of content imaginable — freeform text, tables, hyperlinks, images, even Web Parts. A Wiki Content Page combines the best aspects of a typical wiki page with a Web Part page.

You can create other Wiki Content pages for your site by choosing Site Actions⇨New Page. These new Wiki Content pages are also stored in the Site Pages library.

You can create additional wiki page libraries if you wish to manage a specific wiki topic in your site.

What about Web Part pages?

The traditional type of SharePoint page contains various zones in which to place Web Parts; it doesn't have the same editing experience as the Wiki Content page. The Web Part page, however, has been enhanced to allow for easier text editing and image insertion.

Web Part pages are also saved to libraries. You may want to create a document library to hold your Web Part pages before you create them, unless you want to save them to the Site Pages library.

Many of the system pages that you see in SharePoint team sites are actually Web Part pages. Pages for displaying, editing, and viewing list properties are Web Part pages. These pages are *list forms,* and I discuss customizing them in Chapter 3.

Any Web page that has the path `_layouts` in the Web address is one of SharePoint's application pages and can't be customized.

Throughout this book, if you say, "I need a site that's more like a regular Web site, more informative than collaborative, with lots of formatted text, links, images, and animations," read Part III to find out more about publishing sites. Most everything I cover earlier in this book still applies to publishing sites. Libraries, lists, and views are still the building blocks of content in a publishing site, but you can create many pages in a publishing site, as well as use SharePoint Designer 2010 to create your own master pages, page layouts, and custom styles to create templates and skins.

Choosing a Wiki Content page over a Web Part page or vice versa

For some who have lived through different versions of SharePoint over the years, it may simply be familiarity that keeps you using a Web Part page. Converting previous sites to the new version may be a factor as well. However, the need for creating rich content pages in a collaboration site is now better served by the Wiki Content page.

The following list helps you decide which type of page to create, based on your needs:

- ✔ **Web Part page:** Use when you need mostly Web Parts with little text content. Examples include pages with multiple List View Web Parts, Office application Web Parts, custom search and site directories, and pages that use connected Web Parts. Web Part pages are simple to create without the editor needing skills in rich content editing. Although versioning may be turned on in the library you store your Web Part pages in, the Web Parts themselves don't retain history.

- ✔ **Wiki Content page:** Use when you have a predominance of Rich content; for example, text, tables, links, and images. You can still insert Web Parts, or use no Web Parts at all. The HTML content in wiki pages is also subject to versioning if versioning is turned on in the library.

Prior to SharePoint 2010, the home page was named `default.aspx` and was a Web Part page. SharePoint still includes that `default.aspx`, although it isn't visible by default. You can, however, find this page by navigating to the current home page and replacing `/sitepages/home.aspx` with `/default.aspx` in the browser's address bar.

If you prefer the original `default.aspx` interface, you can use the Page Ribbon to edit the page by clicking the Make Homepage button. The default home pages of many other SharePoint collaboration sites (like the document workspace, meeting workspaces, and blogs) are still Web Part pages in SharePoint 2010.

Another kind of page in SharePoint 2010 is a *publishing page*. Publishing pages are mostly used in portals and public-facing Web sites. They are very versatile and are very useful in situations where you need ultimate control over the look and feel of the site. SharePoint 2010 Standard Edition includes a special kind of publishing page — an *Enterprise Wiki;* it works similarly to a team site wiki page, but it has all the underlying features of a publishing page. (See Part III for a lot more information on how to use publishing pages and Enterprise Wikis.) In theory, you can still create many pages in a collaboration site and style them as well, but the intent between the collaboration sites and publishing sites is very different.

Creating a New Wiki Content Page

If you want additional pages in your site that look and function like the home page, create a new Wiki Content page. Creating a new page of this type is slightly different than creating other content. You can create a new page in multiple ways, including choosing Site Actions⇨New Page, creating a Forward link in a wiki page, and selecting the New Document command in the wiki library.

To create a new Wiki Content page using the New Page option, follow these steps:

1. **Choose Site Actions⇨New Page.**

   This creates a Wiki Content page only, not a Web Part page.

   A dialog box appears asking for the name of your new page and informing you that it'll be created in the Site Pages library.

2. **Type the name for your page and click the Create button.**

   I suggest typing a single word that's a meaningful name, and use the text editors to type any title or other text in the page to communicate its purpose. The name for your page will be part of the page's URL.

   Unfortunately, in a Wiki Content page, you can't follow the tips I share earlier in the book — naming the page without spaces and re-titling it with a user-friendly name.

   Your new page is created and placed in Edit mode. You see other recently modified pages in this wiki library via links on the lower left of the Quick Launch pane.

By default, the page is a single column, but you can change the page's layout to include more columns by clicking the Text Layout button on the Format Text tab of the Ribbon, as shown in Figure 9-1.

Every wiki library is created with a How to Use This Wiki Library page. After you have experience working with wiki libraries, you can choose to delete this page; however, it contains many helpful instructions and tips on working with the wiki functionality.

Your wiki pages are stored in the Site Pages library. You can browse to the Site Pages library using the left navigation pane or by choosing Site Actions➪View All Site Content.

Finding and linking other Wiki Content pages

When you're in Edit mode in a Wiki Content page, you can select the View Pages button in the Library Settings section on the Ribbon to see the list of pages and work with the document pages similar to other libraries.

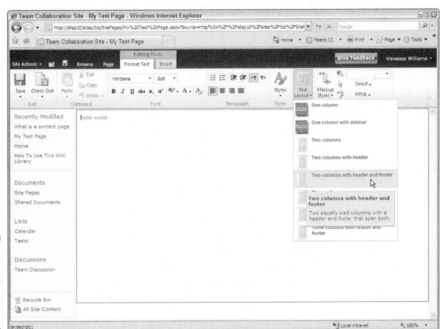

Figure 9-1: Change the layout of your wiki page.

On the bottom left of the Quick Launch menu, when you're on a wiki page, you see a reference to Recently Modified pages in the wiki library. You can use these links to navigate to the listed pages. This section doesn't appear on the Wiki Content home page.

You can link to another page in the same wiki library by enclosing the name of the page in double brackets in the rich content area. For example, type **[[Team Events page]]** to create a link to the Team Events page.

An additional way to create a new Wiki Content page is the Forward link — using the double bracket method to create a link, except that the page you name in the double brackets hasn't been created yet. The name has a dotted underline. The first time you or someone with the proper permissions click the link, SharePoint creates the new page.

Last but not least, you can use the Insert Hyperlink command to add the URL address or browse to either a Wiki Content page or a Web Part page to any other page.

Categorizing your wiki pages

Wikis often include a way to categorize pages, and SharePoint wikis are no different. By default, the wiki includes a Managed Keywords field that allows you to enter freeform keywords or tags on your wiki page. These tags can be displayed in a *tag cloud,* a visual representation of tags that indicates how often they occur in relation to each other and can help users find content they are interested in.

To add a tag to your wiki page:

1. **Browse to your wiki page, click the Page tab on the Ribbon, and then click the Edit Properties button.**

   The Edit Form appears.

2. **Type tags in the Managed Keywords field.**

   For the Managed Keywords field to be active, your site must be configured to use a default keyword store. See Chapter 22 for details.

3. **Click the Save button.**

   The Web page has your keywords associated with it.

Creating a New Web Part Page

I outline reasons earlier in this chapter on why you may need a Web Part or multiple Web Part pages in your collaboration site. A Web Part page can also be set as the home page. You can link back and forth between your Wiki Content pages and Web Part pages by using hyperlinks.

To create a new Web Part page:

1. **Click the View All Site Content link from the Quick Launch menu.**

   You can also use the New Page option on the Site Actions menu, the More Create Options command on a team site Site Actions menu, or the Create link on the All Site Content pages accessible from the View All Site Content command.

2. **Select the Create command from the top of the View All Site Content page.**

3. **Click the Web Part Page link under the Web Pages category.**

   The new Web Part Create page appears with name, layout, and save location choices.

4. **Type a name for your page in the Name field.**

   Follow the naming convention rules I describe in Chapter 21.

5. **Select a layout for the page by choosing an option from the list.**

   Click different options in the list box to see a thumbnail of the layout.

   Layouts for Web Part pages can't be changed after the fact. You don't need to use every zone that appears on your layout, but select a layout that supports the desired design of your page.

6. **Select the document library that will contain this page by selecting an option from the Document Library drop-down list.**

   Web Part pages are stored in libraries, so by default, your only two choices to store a new Web Part page is in the Shared Documents library or the Site Assets library, unless you've created other libraries. Consider creating a new library to contain your Web Part pages.

7. **Click the Create button.**

   Your new Web Part page opens in Edit mode, ready for you to start inserting Web Parts.

 You can change the home page of your site to any Wiki Content page or Web Part page. Simply click the Make Homepage button in the Page Actions area of the Edit tab on the Ribbon while editing the preferred page.

Chapter 10

Working with Web Parts

In This Chapter

▶ Adding Web Parts to your Web pages

▶ Picking the right Web Part

▶ Changing the way your Web Part acts

▶ Using one Web Part to filter another

Web Parts are reusable components that display content on Web pages in SharePoint. They are a fundamental part of the team site experience, so make it a point to get comfortable with them and know what your options are.

In this chapter, I introduce you to Web Parts and show you how to use them on your Web pages.

Adding a Web Part to Your Page

A Web Part is an individual component of content that can be placed on a SharePoint page, in either zone in a Web Part page or in Rich Content areas of the Wiki Content home page. Web Parts can be moved, added and deleted, framed by borders and titles, and closed and reopened depending on your need.

In a team site, you may place List View Web Parts on your home page for your users to read and access items from your libraries/lists, such as announcements, documents, links, calendars, and contacts. You can add text for additional instructions and images to enhance the collaboration experience.

As I mention earlier (more times than you have probably wanted to hear), the Web Parts based on your libraries and lists are *List View Web Parts*. Over the versions of SharePoint, the number and complexity of Web Parts has grown considerably.

Some of these Web Parts can be used only if certain functionality is enabled in your site, such as Business Data Sources to use the Business Data Web Parts. Other categories of Web Parts, such as Content Rollup Web Parts, provide the ability to feed data from lower-level sites to a site higher in the hierarchy, such as the home page of an intranet.

SharePoint 2010 has a new interface for selecting and inserting Web Parts. The Web Part section of the Ribbon on the Page tab first shows a list of Web Part categories and then all the parts contained in that category. When the Web Part name is highlighted, you can see a description as well as an example of each in the About the Web Part section before inserting it.

Follow these steps to insert a Web Part:

1. **Make sure you're in Edit mode of either the Wiki Content page or the Web Part page (choose Site Actions⇨Edit Page).**

   In a Wiki Content page, insert Web Parts into one of the Rich Content containers in the layout. In a Web Part page, insert Web Parts into one of the zones on the page.

2. **In a Web Part page, click in a zone. In a Wiki Content page, click in a Rich Content zone.**

   The Insert tab appears on the Ribbon.

   Because a Web Part page can contain only Web Parts, the Insert tab buttons for text and images actually insert a Content Editor Web Part or an Image View Web Part, respectively, for those selections.

3. **To insert a Web Part, click the Web Part button on the Insert tab.**

   Categories of Web Parts appear in a list box on the far left. As you pick a category, the Web Parts contained in that category appear in the adjoining list box. As you highlight a Web Part name, a description and example appear in the About the Web Part section in the top right.

4. **After you decide on a Web Part, click and drag the Web Part name into the zone or Rich Content area you wish to place it in (see Figure 10-1).**

   In a Wiki Content page, you can also use the Add button under About the Web Part section to insert the Web Part into the Rich Content section your cursor is in.

   In a Web Part page, the About the Web Part section contains a drop-down list containing the names of all the zones on the page. You can select the zone and then click the Add button. In any case, the Web Part is placed on the page.

5. **Modify the Web Part properties by clicking the Edit drop-down list (in the far right of the Web Part title) and choosing Modify Shared Web Part.**

Web Parts can be moved in a Web Part page or a Wiki Content page simply by dragging them from one zone or area to another.

Figure 10-1: Inserting a Web Part in a Web Part page.

Choosing the Right Web Part

The SharePoint 2010 gallery contains more than 75 Web Parts as well as List View Web Parts created for any libraries/lists you've made. In addition, your company may create custom Web Parts or purchase them from third-party vendors.

Besides purchasing or creating additional Web Parts, your company may also choose to not supply you with every Web Part that I describe in the following list. Companies may also modify some Web Parts, such as the Content Editor Web Part, to disallow certain styles or JavaScript content.

With so many choices, how do you decide which Web Part to use? If you're like me, I'm sure you'll find your favorites. I think about Web Parts as being either specialized or generalized in what they do. I tend to use the more general Web Parts, but in a lot of Web sites, I want to control how it appears. When I'm using an internal team site, I tend to use the specialized Web Parts in which I have to think about fewer configuration items.

This list describes the set of the general Web Parts, along with what they do and when you might use them:

   ✔ **Content Rollup Web Parts:** These include the RSS Viewer Web Part and the XML Viewer Web Part, which are useful for displaying RSS and XML, respectively. Because more and more content is available in RSS and XML formats, these Web Parts are especially useful. You use an XSL template to tell the Web Part how to display the RSS or XML content on your Web page.

Another very useful Web Part is the Data Form Web Part. Unfortunately, you can only access it with SharePoint Designer, but it's extremely versatile; in fact, it's often referred to as the *Swiss Army Knife Web Part*. If you need to do something custom (or even interesting) without writing custom code, you can do some very interesting things with the Data Form Web Part.

Team sites with the publishing features enabled can take advantage of additional Content Rollup Web Parts, including the Content Query Web Part, which is similar to the Data Form Web Part but is accessible from the browser. I cover these two Web Parts in more detail in Chapter 17.

✔ **Filter Web Parts:** These Web Parts provide numerous ways to filter the information displayed on the page. For example, you can add the Choice filter to a page and then connect it to a List View Web Part so that the list is filtered by the value selected by the user. Your filter options include filtering by the current user who's visiting the page, date, good old-fashioned text values, or a query string. A *query string* is a value that you pass into the page by using a question mark, such as `mypage.aspx?filter=somevalue`.

✔ **Media and Content Web Parts:** These Web Parts work well when your content needs are simple. Use the Media Web Part to display Windows Media Player on your Web page. The Image Viewer Web Part lets you link to an image and display it on your page. If your company has Silverlight applications, they can be played using the Silverlight Web Part. The Content Editor Web Part is a perennial favorite because it allows you to enter almost any HTML, CSS, or JavaScript you want on your page.

Some of these Web Parts, especially the Content Editor Web Part, can really make it difficult to manage a site's content long-term. Imagine you have a team site with ten Web pages. On each Web page, you've placed three Content Editor Web Parts. That's 30 individual components you have to touch every time you need to change content. Because of the long-term maintenance headaches, I tend to avoid the Content Editor Web Part. Instead, I use publishing fields and Content Rollup Web Parts. These Web Parts allow me to manage my content in lists and library without touching each place their content is presented. See Part III for more about managing pages and content.

✔ **Search and Business Data Web Parts:** Although these Web Parts may seem specialized, they are actually quite powerful. You can use the Search Web Parts to create a custom search results page that is scoped to the content you want to filter. The Business Data Web Parts allow you to display data from external data sources. See Part IV for more information on both these kinds of Web Parts.

SharePoint also provides many specialized Web Parts that are meant to be used in a certain context or to return a certain set of content. Some of these include

- ✔ **Lists and Libraries:** These Web Parts displays items from the lists and libraries on your team site. You can use list views to filter, sort, and group the information presented in the Web Part.

- ✔ **My Information:** If your company uses Exchange Server 2003 or higher for e-mail, you can use these Web Parts to display your inbox, calendar, and other folders on a Web page in SharePoint.

  Your company needs to provide you with a Web address for Exchange that's configured to use Windows Integrated Authentication.

- ✔ **Office Client:** SharePoint 2010 has a lot of integration points with Office clients, and these Web Parts are a testament to that. Here you find Web Parts that let you interact with Excel spreadsheets, Visio models, and Access databases. The cool factor isn't so much that you can interact with your Office files; it's that SharePoint publishes the output to your Web page so that other people can interact with your Office files.

  The Office Client Web Parts are present only if you're licensed to use the Enterprise Edition of SharePoint. Many large companies take a two-tiered approach to SharePoint where only certain users get Enterprise licenses. If you need these Web Parts, ask for a license upgrade. Individual users can be upgraded without upgrading the licensing for the entire company.

- ✔ **People:** These Web Parts are kinda boring, but one really cool one is here — the Note Board. Dropping this Web Part on your page adds a Social Commenting box. So folks can add comments right inside your Web page. Social commenting is part of SharePoint's new social networking features, which I discuss in Chapter 7.

Any configuration or content that you put inside a Web Part isn't version-controlled. In other words, each time you change the Web Part, you write over any previous configuration or content. That's another reason I caution against using the Content Editor Web Parts. Store your content in lists and libraries where the content is subject to version control and retention policies rather than placing it directly in the Web page. You can export your Web Part's configuration using the Export on the Web Part's menu.

Content that you place inside a Rich Content control on a wiki page is version-controlled if versioning is enabled in your library.

Changing Web Part Properties

After you select and insert a Web Part into your page, you may want to modify its properties to fit your needs. The number and type of properties you can modify are based on what type of Web Part you use.

When you select the Edit Web Part command by clicking the Web Part menu (in the far right of the Web Part title), SharePoint opens the Web Part tool pane. In some Web Parts, SharePoint creates a link to this tool pane as part of the placeholder text. Following is a list of properties in the tool pane common to List View Web Parts:

- **Selected View:** The options in the Selected View drop-down list are dependent on the type of library or list, and/or other views you may have created.

  The current view is simply what's showing currently. Unlike views that I describe in Chapter 5, you change view properties on-the-fly using the Edit the Current View link of the tool pane. Your changes are now part of the current view. If you use the Edit in Current View link, you can't revert to a past view.

  The Edit the Current View options are, for the most part, identical to what you see when you create a view in the library or list. Make sure you look at Styles and Item limits when creating a view for a Web Part because these options are overlooked frequently.

  If the changes you need to make to the view are simple and few, the Edit the Current View link is handy. If you need to consistently apply the same view selections for this Web Part, create a view in the library or list you can apply so that you don't lose the options you chose.

- **Toolbar Type:** Depending on the library or list, this drop-down list allows you the options of Full Toolbar, Summary Toolbar, No Toolbar, or Show Toolbar.

  For example, in a document library, choosing Full Toolbar enables users to upload the document, check it out, and so forth.

  The Summary toolbar is somewhat of a misnomer; it adds a link at the bottom of the list for users to add a new document (item).

- **Appearance:** The Appearance section allows you to title the Web Part, fix the height and width as necessary, and determine the chrome type. *Chrome* is another word for the Web Part surround; for example, title and border options.

- **Layout:** In the Layout section, you can change the zone location of the Web Part as well as hide it without closing it.

- **Advanced:** This section contains many of the options you use to allow users with permissions to modify Web Parts, such as Allow Minimize or Allow Close.

✔ **Ajax Options:** This section is new to SharePoint 2010 and gives the owner/admin the choice of enabling *asynchronous behaviors.* This means that the data in the Web Part is sent to the page without causing the Web page to refresh.

✔ **Miscellaneous:** Miscellaneous options including sample data, XSL link, and some caching properties.

Editing Web Part properties is pretty straightforward. Again, experimenting is key. The most commonly used sections are located at the top of the tool pane: Selected View, Toolbar, and Appearance. Many users don't realize how much they can enhance the user experience with the Web Part by the using the options available.

To open the Web Part tool pane and modify Web Part properties, follow these steps:

1. **Click the Web Part menu on the Web Part and choose Edit Web Part.**

   The tool pane opens. You see several of the categories of properties that I describe in the preceding list. You may need to select the plus sign to open certain sections.

   You don't need to be in page Edit mode to modify a Web Part. If the title bar is visible and you have the proper permissions, you see the Edit drop-down list even when the page isn't in Edit mode.

2. **Adjust properties as desired (see Figure 10-2).**

   Make your selections based on the categories and options that I describe in the preceding list or other options available per the specific Web Part.

3. **Click the Apply button to apply your current changes before modifying others, or click OK to finish modifying.**

   Your changes are visible in the Web Part.

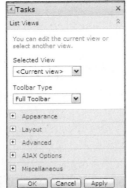

Figure 10-2: Change your Web Part's configuration.

You have two options for removing a Web Part from your page — minimizing or deleting. Closing a Web Part leaves the Web Part on the page so you can enable it again for future use. Deleting the Web Part removes the Web Part from your page (but doesn't delete it from SharePoint).

To close or delete a Web Part from your page, click the Web Part menu, as I describe in the preceding list, and choose Close or Delete.

Every now and then a Web Part misbehaves and prevents your page from opening. If you edit the properties of your page, you find a link to the Web Part Maintenance page. Use this link to close or delete Web Parts that are preventing your page from opening.

Connecting Web Parts

One cool thing you can do with Web Parts is connect them to each other. This allows you to use one Web Part to filter the values of another Web Part. This is a very powerful feature that allows you to create useful, data-driven Web pages in your team site.

Follow this process to connect two Web Parts:

1. **Add both the Web Parts you want to connect to your Web page.**

   For example, you can add two List View Web Parts to your page, and use one List View Web Part to filter the other. If you have an Enterprise license for SharePoint 2010, be sure to check out the cool filter Web Parts designed for filtering other Web Parts using a date or free-form text field.

   If you use a Lookup column to create a relationship between two lists, you can bypass these steps by clicking the Insert Related List button on the Web Part Tools tab in the Ribbon.

2. **Save your page (choose Page⇨Stop Editing).**

   I find that if you don't save your page first, sometimes you can't connect.

3. **Click the Edit button on the Page tab of the Ribbon to place your page in Edit mode.**

4. **Place a check mark in the upper-right corner of the Web Part you want to use as the filter.**

5. **On the Ribbon, click the Web Part Tools Options tab and then click Web Part Properties button.**

   The tool pane appears.

6. **Click the drop-down arrow on the filtering Web Part, choose Connections⇨Send Row of Data To, and then choose the name of the Web Part you want to filter, as shown in Figure 10-3.**

   The Choose Connection dialog box appears. The Choose Connection tab displays the connection type that you selected in this step.

7. **Click the Configure Connection tab and then choose the field name you want to filter on from the Consumer Field Name drop-down list.**

   This is the field that has the set of values you want to match from your filtering Web Part. In this example of filtering a Tasks Web Part with a Date Filter Web Part, I chose the Due Date field, as shown in Figure 10-4.

8. **Click the Finish button.**

   The connection is established. As you select values in one Web Part, the connected Web Part is filtered accordingly, as shown in Figure 10-5.

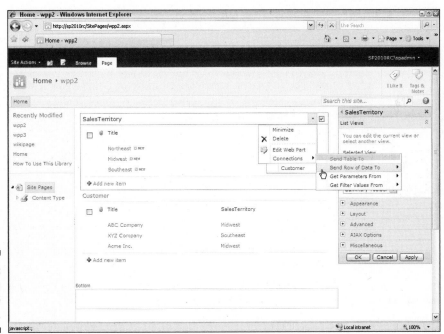

Figure 10-3: Choosing which Web Part to filter.

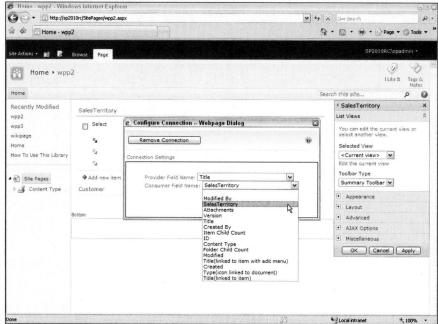

Figure 10-4:
Select the
field that
contains
your filter
values.

Figure 10-4:
Select the
field that
contains
your filter
values.

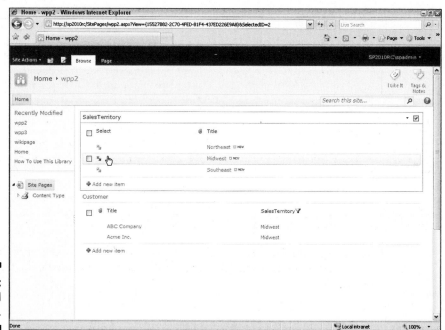

Figure 10-5:
A filtered
Web Part.

Chapter 11

Finding Your Way around a Team Site

In This Chapter

▶ Getting comfortable with navigating SharePoint

▶ Using the Quick Launch bar

▶ Navigating to administrative tasks

All good Web sites have navigation menus that site visitors can use to access the site's resources. Keeping navigation menus consistent throughout the site makes it easy for site visitors to get from one area of your site to another.

Your SharePoint team site provides a standard set of navigation menus. Some of these menus can be customized to suit the navigational needs of your site. Other menus are provided by SharePoint and can't be customized via the browser. In this chapter, I walk you through configuring the navigation in your team site.

This chapter addresses the navigation options for team sites. Although this material also applies to publishing sites, those sites have additional navigation options. See Chapter 18 for details on navigation options for publishing sites.

Navigating Your Team Site

All team sites have a common set of global navigational elements that appear at the top of the site's pages. Some of the navigational elements you encounter include

✔ **Ribbon:** The Ribbon displays a set of commands that are available for the currently displayed page.

✔ **Top Link bar:** A set of tabs that displays links to page and subsites.

✔ **Breadcrumb navigation:** Displays a set of hyperlinks that you can use to navigate up to the site's home page.

✔ **Portal navigation:** A link that lets you navigate to another site that's higher than the current team site.

Figure 11-1 shows these navigational elements.

The image in Figure 11-1 shows the out-of-the-box layout of these navigational elements. Your site may look different if it's been customized. See Chapter 25 for details on customizing the layout of navigation.

Top Link bar

Ribbon

Breadcrumbs

Portal navigation

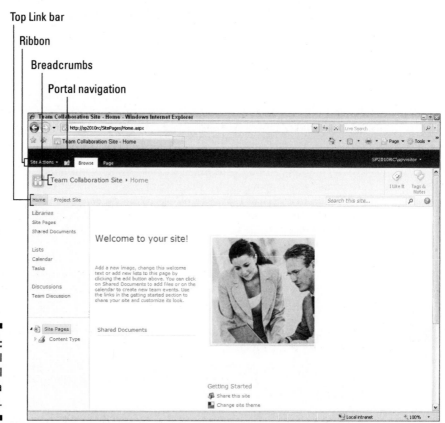

Figure 11-1:
Global
navigational
options in a
team site.

Getting acquainted with the Ribbon

The Ribbon organizes commands using tabs. On each tab is a group where command buttons appear. The Ribbon can grow and shrink based on your browser resolution, so commands may appear as buttons or text. Figure 11-2 shows the Ribbon with the Page tab displayed. On this tab, you can see command groups, such as Edit and Manage. The commands are *security trimmed* — you can access only the commands that you have permission to see.

You can customize the Ribbon by adding custom actions with SharePoint Designer 2010 or deploying an XML file that contains your configuration options.

Figure 11-2:
Some commands on the Ribbon.

Going global with the Top Link bar

Each team site has its own *Top Link bar* — a common navigational element used to provide access to resources across the entire site.

The Top Link bar is a series of tabs that sit in the header on a page in the SharePoint site. The tabs that appear in the Top Link bar display the hyperlinked titles to a subsite or page in the site. Tabs may also expand to display content from within the site.

By default, the Top Link bar displays links to resources on the top-level site of the site collection. You can customize the bar so it shows only the resources for the current site and its subsites.

These steps apply only to team sites. See Chapter 18 for details on configuring navigation for publishing sites.

You manage the Top Link bar with the Top Link Bar page. To access the page, follow these steps:

1. **Browse to the site where you wish to modify navigation and choose Site Actions⊅Site Settings.**

   The Site Settings page appears.

2. **In the Look and Feel section, click the Top Link Bar link.**

    The Top Link Bar page appears. You must have at least Design permissions to access this page.

3. **Click the New Navigation Link link and then enter the URL and name for the link you want to appear in the tab in the Type the Web Address and Type the Description text boxes.**

4. **Click OK.**

    The link appears in the Top Link bar.

To remove or modify an existing tab in the Top Link bar:

1. **Navigate to the Top Link Bar page, as I describe in Steps 1–2 in the preceding list.**

2. **Click the Edit button next to the item you wish to modify.**

3. **Edit the entry or click the Delete button to remove the tab altogether.**

Using the Welcome menu

Team sites display a Welcome menu in the upper-right corner of the page that provides access to common user tasks. Chances are you may not even be aware of this menu because it's so nondescript. In fact, this menu just shows your name as it appears in your user profile in SharePoint. But when you click it, a menu of commands opens.

Figure 11-3 shows the Welcome drop-down list. The links are as follows:

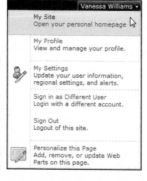

Figure 11-3:
SharePoint's Welcome drop-down list.

✔ **My Site:** Links you to the My Site host where you can access your user profile and your personal My Site, if you have one.

✔ **My Profile:** Opens your user profile.

✔ **My Settings:** Allows the user to manage account details and regional settings, such as time zone and alerts.

✔ **Sign In as Different User:** Prompts for a set of different user credentials.

✔ **Sign Out:** Logs out the user from the site.

✔ **Personalize This Page:** Opens the page in Design view so you can create a personalized view of the page. This option is visible only on Web Part pages when the user has the proper permissions.

✔ **Request Access:** Allows the user to send the site administrator an e-mail to access a resource. This option is visible only if the site administrator has enabled access requests for the site.

Don't be surprised if your Welcome drop-down list doesn't include items for My Site. Your company may not have that feature enabled.

If you've used previous versions of SharePoint, you may be looking for the My Links command. Technically, My Links is no longer part of SharePoint; it still exists, but Microsoft would prefer you not use it. Instead, Microsoft wants you to use social bookmarks, which you can access through the Tags and Notes tab in your profile.

You can still access your My Links by browsing to the page `_layouts/ myquicklinks.aspx` in your My Site host.

Tracking back with breadcrumbs

SharePoint uses breadcrumb navigation to let users keep track of where they are. For those who remember the story of *Hansel and Gretel,* a breadcrumb is what you'd use to mark a trail back out of the deep, dark forest. In Web site terms, *breadcrumbs* are site paths created to mark your progress as you navigate through the site — and they also show how to navigate back to where you started from. (Site-path breadcrumbs also have the advantage of not attracting forest animals that tend to gobble up real breadcrumb trails. Just ask Hansel and Gretel.)

Breadcrumbs in SharePoint look like this by default:

```
Team Site > Project Site > Shared Documents
```

In this example, you're sitting in the Shared Documents document library. You can backtrack to the project site or team site simply by clicking the link to follow the breadcrumb.

The headings displayed in the breadcrumb come from the site's title. You can change the heading by changing the site's title using the Site Settings page.

SharePoint has two kinds of breadcrumbs:

- **Hierarchical Folder breadcrumb:** Breadcrumb that appears at the very top of the page and looks like a folder. This breadcrumb allows you to navigate to higher levels of site collections and portals.

- **Site breadcrumb:** Breadcrumb that appears in the site's Ribbon that shows where you are in the present site, as shown in Figure 11-4.

You can expand a site collection's global navigation by connecting the site collection to a higher-level site collection or portal site. This is useful if you need to attach a divisional site to a company portal. You must be a site collection administrator to perform this task.

To connect to a higher-level site, follow these steps:

1. **Browse to the site collection's top-level site by clicking the farthest left link (usually Home) in the global navigation breadcrumb.**

2. **Choose Site Actions⇨Site Settings⇨Modify All Site Settings.**

   In a Web Part page, choose Site Actions⇨Site Settings.

   The Site Settings page appears.

3. **Click the Portal Site Connection link in the Site Collection Administration section.**

   The Portal Site Connection page appears.

4. **Select the Connect to Portal Site radio button.**

5. **Type or paste the URL for the portal or site collection in the Portal Web Address field.**

   For example, if the URL for the server you wish to connect to is http://intranet, type that value.

6. **Type the name you want to appear in the global navigation bread-crumb in the Portal Name field.**

   The name you type doesn't have to match the name of the portal or site collection. For example, you could type **Corporate Home** instead of the actual name given to the top-level portal. The portal appears in the hierarchical folder, as shown in Figure 11-5.

7. **Click OK.**

You can use the Portal Site Connection feature to create a hierarchy of site collections and portals. This feature isn't limited to SharePoint Server 2010, so you could connect SharePoint Foundation 2010 sites.

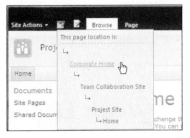

Figure 11-5: Navigate up from your site.

Getting specific with the search box

A big SharePoint feature is the ability to search the SharePoint sites, lists, and libraries to find information and documents. All pages in SharePoint include a search box by default (see Figure 11-6). The search box has the following features:

- ✔ **Search Scope drop-down list:** Widen or narrow the search scope to encompass the current site or list.
- ✔ **Search term:** Type a search term in the text box.

Figure 11-6: The search box.

SharePoint 2010 includes a link for conducting advanced searches and the ability to search more sources, including people and business data. See Chapter 23 to discover more about using SharePoint search.

Finding other sites

A common navigational challenge is finding other SharePoint sites. SharePoint 2010 doesn't provide any kind of site directory. Instead, you can use search to help you find other sites.

Another option is to apply managed metadata to your site. Your users could then view all the sites that have a certain metadata value.

Getting help

Users can access SharePoint's Help and how-to resources by clicking the Help icon in the upper-right corner of the page. The Help and how-to documentation is a combination of local and online resources displayed in a browser window.

Staying Local with the Quick Launch bar

Most pages in SharePoint display a list of navigation links on the Quick Launch bar along the left side of the page, as shown in Figure 11-7. The Quick Launch bar displays links to featured site content such as lists, libraries, sites, and publishing pages. The Quick Launch bar includes two very important links:

✔ **All Site Content link:** The All Site Content link is important because it lets you quickly view all the lists, libraries, and sites that you have permission to access. Users with the Create Subsites permissions can access the Create button on the All Site Content page.

You can append the text **_layouts/viewlsts.aspx** to the Web address of any SharePoint site to access the All Site Content link.

✔ **Recycle Bin:** A link to the Recycle Bin appears at the bottom of the Quick Launch bar. Content deleted by users is saved to the Recycle Bin, where it can be restored.

For some reason, site designers like to remove the Recycle Bin link. I can't figure out why. The Recycle Bin is a completely harmless feature that can actually be quite helpful. If you don't see this link on your sites, ask somebody why not.

The Quick Launch bar appears on all site pages except those related to completing administrative tasks, such as adding new users. You can disable the Quick Launch bar for a site or control what appears on the bar.

Figure 11-7:
The Quick
Launch bar.

You can manage the Quick Launch bar very similarly to the Top Link bar; however, the Quick Launch bar doesn't inherit from the parent site. Instead, the items that appear in the Quick Launch bar are determined by the settings in the site template you use when you create a site. Each list or library contained in a site can display a link to itself on the Quick Launch bar. Site templates, such as the Team Site template, set this flag automatically. For example, the Team Site template displays links to all lists and libraries created in the site except the Announcements list.

You can easily add or remove a list or library from the Quick Launch bar using the list's settings:

1. **Browse to the list or library you wish to remove from the Quick Launch bar on a site.**

   For example, in a site using the Team Site template, click the link in the Quick Launch bar or click the View All Site Content link to browse to a list not included on the Quick Launch bar, such as the Announcements list.

2. **Choose Settings⇨List Settings or Settings⇨Library Settings.**

   The Customize page appears.

3. **In the General Settings section, click the Title, Description and Navigation link.**

   The General Settings page appears.

4. **In the Navigation section, indicate whether to include the list or library in the Quick Launch bar.**

5. **Click the Save button.**

   The links in the Quick Launch bar update to reflect your changes.

SharePoint also provides a Quick Launch page that behaves very similarly to the Top Link Bar page. You access the Quick Launch page by clicking the Quick Launch link in the Look and Feel section of the site's Site Settings page.

You also can disable the Quick Launch bar entirely for a site. You can add a site hierarchy called a *Tree View* to the left navigation panel instead of the Quick Launch bar. If you leave the Quick Launch bar enabled, the Tree View appears below the Quick Launch bar. To perform either of these tasks, follow these steps:

1. **Browse to the Site Settings page for the site you wish to manage.**

2. **In the Look and Feel section, click the Tree View link.**

   The Tree View page appears. Figure 11-8 shows the Tree View below the label Site Hierarchy.

3. **In the Enable Quick Launch section, indicate whether to enable or disable the Quick Launch bar.**

4. **In the Enable Tree View section, indicate whether to enable or disable a Tree View in the Quick Launch bar.**

5. **Click OK.**

Figure 11-8:
Tree View
navigation.

Exploring Administrative Options

You'll be glad to discover that many of the administrative tasks associated with sites and site collections are available from the browser. You can use two different menus to access all the major administrative features for site collections and sites in SharePoint:

- ✔ **Site Actions:** The Site Actions menu is in the upper-right corner of a SharePoint page. You must at least be a member of the *Site* Members group in SharePoint Server 2010 or the *Site* Owners group in SharePoint Foundation 2010 to see the Site Actions menu. Here you find links to administrative pages and page-editing features. The list of shortcuts available on the Site Actions menu depends on the features enabled in the site's template. Sites based on site templates that use the Publishing feature list commands related to editing publishing pages. Sites with fewer features, such as team sites, offer basic commands for editing Web Parts pages.

- ✔ **Site Settings:** You can access virtually all SharePoint's administrative pages for a site via the site's Site Settings page. The Site Settings page for a top-level site in a site collection includes a set of links related to administering the site collection. You can access a site's Site Settings page via the Site Actions menu.

You can access additional administrative features related to Web applications, site collections, and the server itself at SharePoint's Central Administration site.

Generally, site collection administrators don't access Central Administration. However, in SharePoint 2010, companies can configure SharePoint for multi-tenancy, similar to a hosting provider. With this option enabled, your SharePoint administrator can delegate certain administrative features to you in Central Administration.

Site Actions

The Site Actions menu is available to users who are members of the *Site* Members group in SharePoint Server 2010. Members of the *Site* Visitors group and other groups that are restricted to Read Only permissions can't see the Site Actions menu. No individual permission is related to accessing the Site Actions menu. Rather, the ability to see the Site Actions menu is determined by whether the user belongs to a group with the permissions to access commands found on the Site Actions menu. For example, a group with the Add and Customize Pages permission can see the Edit Pages command on the Site Actions menu, which enables members of that group to see the Site Actions menu. See Chapter 13 for more about setting permissions.

The Site Actions menu provides shortcuts to commands commonly used by administrators, contributors, designers, and hierarchy managers when working with SharePoint sites. Which menu commands are available depends on your permissions and on the kind of site. Figure 11-9 shows you how the Site Actions menu looks for a member of the *Site* Owners group in a SharePoint team site.

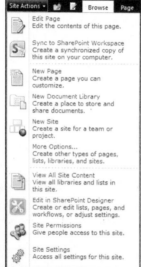

Figure 11-9: The Site Actions menu.

You can always change which group has permission to access the commands on the Site Actions menu. See Chapter 13 for more information on setting permissions.

Site Settings

You access a site's administrative features through the Site Settings page. To access the Site Settings page, choose Site Actions➪Site Settings in a non-publishing site (such as a team site) or choose Site Actions➪Site Settings➪Modify All Site Settings in a publishing site (such as a collaboration portal site). Figure 11-10 shows the Site Settings page.

You can also access a list of all the sites created in a site collection by choosing Site Settings➪Site Hierarchy. The Site Hierarchy link is in the Site Collection Administration column. Click the Manage link in the Site Hierarchy page to access the Site Settings page of any site listed in the site collection's site hierarchy.

The URL for the Site Settings page is

```
http://sitepath/_layouts/settings.aspx
```

You can append the path `_layouts/settings.aspx` to any SharePoint site's path to view the site's Site Settings page.

The header of the Site Settings page displays the Site Information section, which shows the following information about the site:

- ✔ **URL:** The URL to access the site's home page.
- ✔ **Mobile Site URL:** The URL to access a mobile version of the site for use on handheld devices.

The Site Settings page displays links to administrative pages in the following categories:

- ✔ **Users and Permissions:** Find links for managing people, groups, administrators, and permissions.
- ✔ **Galleries:** Access libraries of reusable content available to a specific site or all sites in the site collection.
- ✔ **Site Administration:** Access links for administering the site and its structure and features.
- ✔ **Look and Feel:** Set the site's title and configure navigation. SharePoint 2010 sites also let you set the site's master page, title, theme, welcome page, and other features that impact the way the site appears.
- ✔ **Site Actions**: Provides additional administrative options, such as managing site features.
- ✔ **Site Collection Administration:** Access links relevant to administering the entire site collection. You must use the Site Settings page of the top-level site in a site collection to access administrative links in the Site Collection Administration column. When you view the Site Settings page of a subsite, you see the Go to Top Level Site Settings link in the Site Collection Administration column. Clicking that link takes you to the top-level site.

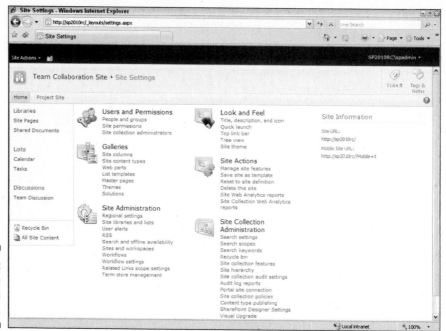

Figure 11-10:
The Site
Settings
page.

Chapter 12

Securing Your Team Site

In This Chapter

▶ Managing groups in SharePoint

▶ Handling security for lists, libraries, and documents

▶ Giving access to administrators

SharePoint is a great tool for storing documents and managing calendars and contacts. But how do you know that your information is secure? Although your IT department makes sure that your network and servers are secure, managing the security for your SharePoint content falls on you as the site steward.

When securing your site, you need to perform three basic tasks. I list them here in the order of the frequency you perform these tasks, from most often to not very often:

  ✔ **Managing SharePoint group membership:** When it comes to that dreaded time to manage SharePoint security, what you really need to be thinking is, "To which SharePoint group do I need to add this person?" If you don't have an existing group and you instead find yourself descending into a morass of permission levels, inheritance, and other such incomprehensible stuff, somebody needs to take away your browser. The reality is that assigning permissions — breaking inheritance and assigning groups — should be a rare event, if done right.

  ✔ **Assigning permissions to sites, lists, libraries, or folders:** Deciding which groups get access to what is an important task, and one you only want to think about infrequently — most usually at the time (or ideally before) you create your team site. In other words, granting Read Only, Edit, and Delete permissions to the content in your site should be a set-it-and-forget-it task if you make those assignments to SharePoint groups. When these permission assignments are granted to your SharePoint groups, you only have to manage who is in each group.

  ✔ **Managing administrative access:** Even less frequently do you need grant or revoke administrative access to your site.

In this chapter, I explain these three tasks.

Using SharePoint Groups

SharePoint uses groups to manage the process of granting someone access to the content in a team site. Each SharePoint group maps to a set of permissions that define the tasks that a user can perform. Most of your users fall into one of SharePoint's three default groups:

- ✔ *Site* **Members:** Confers the Contribute permission level for users, which allows them to add, edit, and modify list items and browse sites. Most end users fall into this category for a team site.

- ✔ *Site* **Owners:** Grants full control. A site owner may or may not use the site on a regular basis, but the site owner can delegate administrative and design tasks to others. Also, a site owner may or may not be a technical person.

- ✔ *Site* **Visitors:** Have read-only access to the site and can create alerts. Users who need Read access to a site but don't need to contribute content are visitors.

Access to your site and its content is managed through *group membership*. Adding and removing users from SharePoint groups is the most efficient way of granting and revoking permissions.

A top-level site has a single set of *Site* Members, *Site* Owners, and *Site* Visitors. The actual names of the groups are determined by the name of the site. For example, if your site is named *Projects,* SharePoint calls your groups Projects Members, Projects Owners, and Projects Visitors.

These three groups are created and named when the top-level site is created. All the lists, libraries, and subsites that are created below the top-level site use these groups and have the same set of people inside the groups. By default, all the content and subsites in your top-level site have the same permissions, dubbed *permissions inheritance.*

For people to access your team site, you must add them to one of these default groups. For example, to add someone to the *Site* Members group:

1. **Log into the site as a site owner and then choose Site Actions⇨Site Permissions.**

   A list of SharePoint groups appears.

2. **Click the Members group for your site.**

   A list of the users who are already group members appears.

3. **Choose New⇨Add Users.**

   The Add Users page appears, as shown in Figure 12-1.

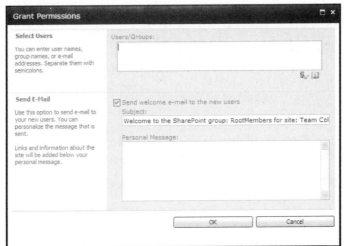

Figure 12-1:
Add users.

4. **In the Select Users section, type the names of individual user accounts or domain groups in the Users/Groups text box.**

   Type the names in the form of domain\account. For example, if your domain name is SP and the domain group name is Employees, type **SP\Employees**.

   If you don't know the names of user accounts, you can type the e-mail address. SharePoint tries to map the e-mail address for the account. For example, the e-mail address employees@sp.com resolves to SP\Employees in my domain. Chances are you can use the e-mail addresses from your address book in Outlook.

5. **To search for user accounts, click the Book icon. Use the Select People and Groups dialog box to select user accounts.**

   If you can't find the accounts you need, check with IT for assistance.

6. **Click the Check Names icon to resolve the account names with the identity management system.**

   The Check Names icon is the check mark icon below the Users/Groups text box. When you click this icon, SharePoint tries to find the user account in the identity management system, such as Active Directory (AD). If SharePoint can't find the user, you can't add the account. If the names won't resolve, see IT for assistance.

7. **Click OK.**

I recommend using domain groups instead of individual user accounts to assign users to SharePoint groups. Check with IT to determine whether domain groups are available to meet your needs. However, if you just have a few people to add to your SharePoint group, it's silly to ask IT set up a domain group. Just go ahead and manually add your users.

Members in the *Site* Owners SharePoint group create the permission structure for a site. The site owner should have a pretty good understanding of who needs to access the site and what that access should be. This means that members of IT usually shouldn't be site owners. Instead, you want members of the business departments to take responsibility for site ownership.

Permissions are contained within a site collection. Therefore, all the people, groups, and permission levels defined for a site collection are available to every site, list, and library within the collection. Permissions inheritance is in place by default, so all the content and subsites in SharePoint inherit permissions from their parents.

Web sites, lists, libraries, folders, and list items are all securable in SharePoint.

When a site collection is created, all the content structures within the site collection inherit permissions from it. For example, when you create a new site collection using the Team Site template (see Chapter 13), all the sites, lists, and libraries in the portal inherit permissions from the top-level site. The default permissions configuration for a site collection is as follows:

- ✔ The *Site* Owners, *Site* Visitors, and *Site* Members groups are created.

- ✔ The primary and secondary site collection administrators are added to the *Site* Owners group. These administrators are specified when the site collection is created.

- ✔ Default SharePoint groups in publishing sites, such as Approvers and Hierarchy Managers, are created and given appropriate permissions.

The site collection's site owner takes responsibility for planning the permissions. If desired, the site owner can delegate the responsibility of implementing the permissions to the Hierarchy Managers group in publishing sites. In team sites, the owner has to create a new permission level that confers the Manage Permissions permission to those individuals and groups assigned to it.

SharePoint also provides the following set of specialized administrative groups for publishing sites that enable the site's owner to delegate responsibility:

- ✔ **Approvers:** Enables Approve permissions, which allow users to approve items and override document check-outs.

- ✔ **Designers:** Grants permission to change the look and feel of sites with style sheets and themes.

- ✔ **Hierarchy Managers:** Enables Manage Hierarchy permissions, which makes it possible to manipulate the site's hierarchy and customize lists and libraries.

In addition to providing several kinds of administrative roles, SharePoint 2010 provides the following groups for restricting access:

✔ **Quick Deploy Users:** Is used for moving content from one server to another, such as from a staging server to a production server.

✔ **Restricted Readers:** Can view only items and pages but can't see any item history.

Figure 12-2 shows common SharePoint groups, their permission levels, and their permissions. The permissions are cumulative as you move clockwise starting at the top.

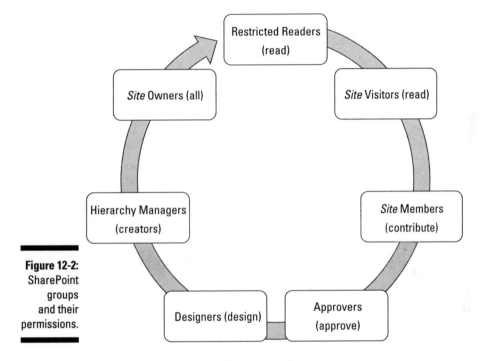

Figure 12-2:
SharePoint
groups
and their
permissions.

After you know how to add new users and domain groups to a SharePoint group, finish setting up security for a site collection by doing the following:

1. **Add user accounts or domain groups to the *Site* Visitors group.**

   The *Site* Visitors group has Read permissions, which enables this group to view the site collection's content.

   I suggest you add the Authenticated Users domain group to the *Site* Visitors group. This enables all your network users to access your site collection.

2. **Add user accounts or domain groups to the *Site* Members group.**

   Members of the *Site* Members group have Contribute permissions, which allow them to add content to the site collection.

3. **Add users to the Hierarchy Manager and Designers groups in publishing sites.**

   You may want to create a separate permission level for consultants. SharePoint team sites don't have these groups by default, but you can create similar groups if you need that kind of role.

4. **Configure unique permissions for content structures in and below the top-level site.**

   You have to stop inheriting permissions from the top-level site before you can create unique permissions for sites, lists, and libraries. See the section, "Breaking inheritance," later in this chapter, for details.

5. **Add sites to the site collection.**

   You can inherit permissions or use unique permissions when you create the site.

Remember that everything *in* the site collection inherits *from* the site collection by default. Make sure your site collection permissions don't grant too many people access.

To make contacting site owners and designers easy, consider adding the Contact Details and Site Users Web Parts to your sites, as shown in Figure 12-3.

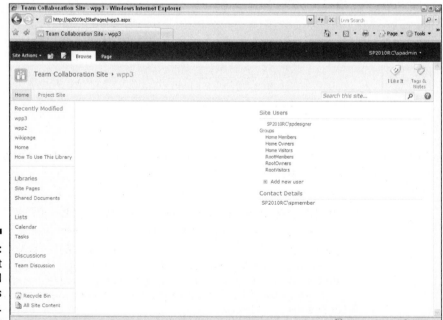

Figure 12-3:
Contact
Details and
Site Users
Web Parts.

Securing Lists, Libraries, and Documents

In theory, you could set up security once for a site collection and allow everything to inherit. In reality, you may not want everyone to have the same access. In order to create unique permissions for a site, library, list, or folder, you have to stop inheriting permissions from the parent.

Breaking inheritance

You must be in a subsite to break permissions; the following steps don't make sense otherwise.

To stop inheriting permissions in a subsite from a parent site, follow these steps:

1. **Browse to the Site Permissions page for a site (choose Site Actions⇨ Site Settings⇨Site Permissions).**

   The Site Permissions page is displayed with a message reading `This Web site inherits permissions from its parent.`

2. **Click the Stop Inheriting Permissions button in the Permission Tools tab Edit group.**

   A message window appears reading, in part, `You are about to create unique permissions for this Web site.`

3. **Click OK.**

   The Site Permissions page is displayed with a message reading, `This Web Site has unique permissions.`

   The site's permissions levels and SharePoint groups are no longer Read Only.

4. **Click the Grant Permissions button on the Ribbon to grant permissions to users and groups.**

   The Grant Permissions dialog box appears.

5. **In the Select Users section, enter the SharePoint Group you want to grant permissions to access the site, list, or library.**

   This is where you want to use your SharePoint Groups — *Site* Members, *Site* Visitors, or *Site* Owners. What if users are in your group that you don't want to have permissions to the subsite, list, or library? You need to create a new SharePoint group and grant that group permission to the subsite, list, or library.

6. **In the Grant Permissions section, select the Grant Users Permissions Directly radio button.**

7. **Select the permission level that matches the permissions you want to grant.**

   The default permission levels for team sites are Full Control, Design, Contribute, and Read. You can create your own permissions levels by clicking the Permission Levels button on the Ribbon if you need additional groups of permissions.

8. **Click OK.**

   The users who are members of the SharePoint group you entered in Step 5 are granted permissions.

Be careful about adding users to groups at the site, list, or library level. You're actually adding users to the entire site collection group. Individual subsites, lists, and libraries don't have their own SharePoint groups.

To re-inherit permissions from the parent site, choose Inherit Permissions in Step 2. Any changes you've made are discarded, and the site inherits the parent's permissions.

After you stop inheriting permissions, the parent's permissions are copied to the site. I suggest you delete the parent's permissions and start fresh with your custom permissions. Otherwise, you can easily get confused about which permissions you want to use.

Follow these steps to remove existing permission assignments:

1. **Browse to the Site Permissions page for a site (choose Site Actions⇨ Site Settings⇨Site Permissions).**

2. **Place check marks next to the permission assignments you wish to remove.**

   Remember to leave yourself with permissions; otherwise, you won't be able to access the site.

3. **Click the Remove User Permissions Button and then click OK to confirm the deletions.**

   All the permissions are deleted for the selected permissions assignments.

Allowing a site's content structures to inherit permissions from the site is usually sufficient. Don't try to secure everything individually. But at times, you need to secure a folder in a library or limit access to a list. You may want to delegate ownership to a list or to library administrators.

To manage permissions, the user must have the Manage Permissions permission. You must be a member of the Hierarchy Managers group to edit permissions.

To create unique permissions for a list or library, follow these steps:

1. **Browse to the list or library. To do so:**

   a. *Access the Library or List tab.*

   b. *Click the Library Permissions or List Permissions button in the Settings group.*

   The Permissions page appears.

2. **Manage the permissions as you would for a subsite.**

   Managing permissions on lists and libraries is the same as managing permissions for subsites.

Follow these steps to create unique permissions for a list item, document, or folder:

1. **Browse to the list or library where the item is stored and click the down arrow at the right of the item name.**

   The item contextual menu appears.

2. **Choose Manage Permissions.**

   The Permissions page appears.

3. **Follow Step 4 in the preceding list.**

Managing permissions is tricky, and the steps I outline here are my recommendations. These aren't the only ways to manage permissions. Try a scenario to help you better understand permissions. Assume you have a site with the SharePoint groups I outline here.

SharePoint groups	*Members*
Site Members	John, Bill, and Steve
Site Visitors	Mary, Sue, and Sally

Everything in the site inherits from the top-level site. In this scenario, those in the *Site* Members group have Contribute permissions whereas those in the *Site* Visitors group have Read permissions.

Assume you create a new subsite and you only want your *Site* Members to access it. You don't want *Site* Visitors to even know the subsite exists. You'd break inheritance on the subsite and remove the *Site* Visitors group.

Assume you have a document library for policy documents, and you want John and Sally to have Contribute permissions. I recommend creating a new Policy and Reviewers SharePoint group at your top-level site and then adding John and Sally as members to the group. You aren't done here, however. You haven't actually granted the group permission to anything yet. You have to browse to the document library, break inheritance from its parent, and then grant the Policy Reviewers SharePoint group the Contribute permission level.

Why not just add John and Sally to the document library and grant them the Contribute permission level? That approach will certainly work, but it's hard to manage. That approach obscures that John and Sally have some permissions granted outside the context of a SharePoint group. I like to be able to look at my SharePoint groups and have a good idea of what the role of that group is based on their names on the site. If you start adding users individually to subsites, lists, and libraries, it becomes difficult to get a big-picture view of how your permissions for the site are configured.

Viewing a group's permissions

You can easily check the permissions for a given group to see everything that group has been granted access to in your entire site collection. To do so:

1. **Browse to the top-level site in your site collection.**

2. **Choose Site Actions➪Site Permissions.**

   The list of SharePoint groups in your site appears.

3. **Click the name of the group you want to manage permissions for.**

4. **Choose Settings➪View Group Permissions.**

   The View Site Collection Permissions window appears, as shown in Figure 12-4. All the sites, lists, and libraries that the group has permission to access appear in the list.

Everyone who is a member of the group has those permissions.

View Site Collection Permissions -- Webpage Dialog

Team Collaboration Site
View Site Collection Permissions: Team Collaboration Site Visitors

Use this page to view the permission assignments that this SharePoint group has in this site collection. In addition to the listed URLs, this group has access to any sites, lists, or items that inherit permissions from these URLs.

URL	Permission Level
http://allsp10/sites/tca	Read

OK

Checking a user's permissions

Sometimes, you just want to know who has permission to do what in a given site. SharePoint 2010 provides just such an animal:

1. **Browse to the site where you want to check a user's permissions.**

   This command only checks permissions within a single site. You have to check each site manually.

2. **Choose Site Actions⇨Site Permissions.**

3. **Click the Check Permissions button on the Ribbon.**

4. **Enter the name of the user or group whose permissions you want to check for the current site in the User/Group field, and click the Check Now button.**

   The permissions appear in the bottom of the window, as shown in Figure 12-5.

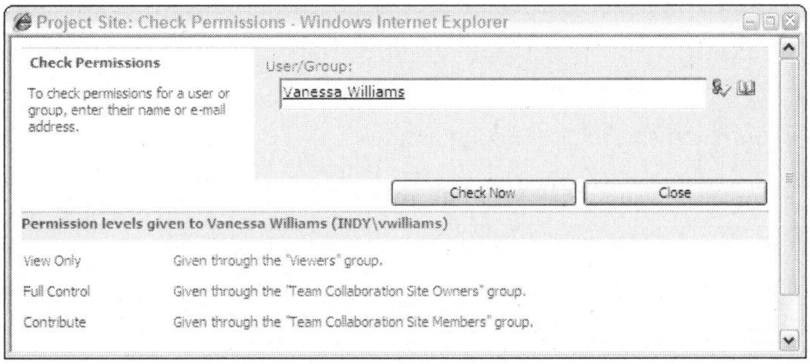

Figure 12-5: View a user's permissions to the current site.

Putting it all together

I often encourage site owners to create their own SharePoint groups instead of using the built-in Visitors and Members. There's something about naming your own groups that makes managing them more intuitive. Maybe because you probably don't refer to your coworkers as *members.*

By creating your own groups, you can very easily tell someone, "Oh, you need to add the new guy to the Accounting Clerks group in the team site." Because you've already assigned proper permissions to the Accounting Clerks group throughout your site, the new guy is guaranteed to have all the access he needs. When the not-so-new guy gets promoted a year later, you can change his membership to the Accounting Supervisors group and then get back to important stuff like eating cake.

Granting Administrative Access

You'll find a number of different administrator levels in a SharePoint deployment. Administrators usually have full access over the domain they've been charged with administering. The levels of administrators in SharePoint are

- ✔ **Server administrators:** By virtue of having local administrator access to the physical server, a server administrator can do anything from the server console. Server administrators are usually members of the technical staff.

- ✔ **Site collection administrators:** These administrators can access everything within a site collection. SharePoint allows you to appoint a primary and secondary administrator for each site collection.

- ✔ **Site administrators:** Members of the *Site* Owners SharePoint group are the site administrators. If subsites inherit permissions, a site administrator has full access to each site.

To set the site collection administrators for a site:

1. **Click the Site Permissions header in the People and Groups page (choose Site Actions⇨Site Permissions).**

   The Permissions page appears.

2. **Choose Settings⇨Site Collection Administrators.**

   The Site Collection Administrators page appears.

3. **Enter the user accounts for the people who are site collection administrators and then click OK.**

Assigning accounts to be site collection administrators is one time when it's acceptable to use individual user accounts instead of domain groups.

Viewing permission assignments

A site can have all the elements of an *authorization model* — people, groups, and permissions, in other words — but still not be secure. The deciding factor in securing SharePoint's content lies with the permission assignments made on securable objects such as sites, lists, and libraries. A permission assignment consists of permissions, *principals* (users and groups), and securable objects.

Permissions are the smallest unit for managing security in SharePoint. Permissions confer rights, such as View Pages rights or Add Items rights, that a user may have. In SharePoint, you deal with following three permission types:

✔ **List:** Permissions related to accessing lists and list items.

✔ **Site:** Permissions related to accessing sites, pages, and permissions.

✔ **Personal:** Permissions related to creating personal views of Web pages.

When managed properly, you never have to work with permissions on a case-by-case basis because permissions are never assigned directly to principals. Rather, they're assigned to *permission levels,* which are assigned to default SharePoint groups. You can also assign permission levels directly to user accounts or custom SharePoint groups you create.

Follow these steps to view a list of permission levels for a site:

1. **Choose Site Actions⇨Site Permissions to access the site's People and Groups page.**

   A list of groups and their corresponding permission levels appear, as shown in Figure 12-6.

   If you've assigned permission levels to user accounts or domain group accounts outside SharePoint groups, you see them listed here.

   Each site inherits its site permission assignments from its parent site or has its own unique permission assignments.

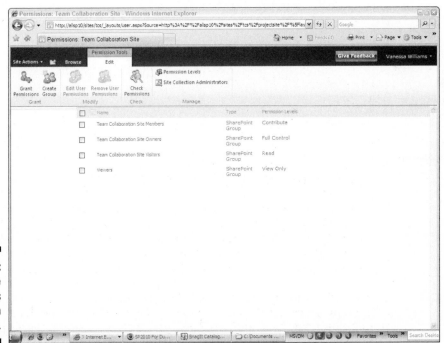

Figure 12-6:
View the site's permission assignments.

2. **Click the Permission Levels button on the Ribbon.**

   The Permission Levels page appears. You can use this page to create new permission levels or modify existing ones.

3. **Click a permission level, such as Contribute, to view or modify the permissions in the permission level, as shown in Figure 12-7.**

   Note: The permissions you see might not be the entire set of permissions available in SharePoint. The server administrator can limit the list of permissions available to a Web application using Web Policies.

Keep in mind that the Permissions Levels page doesn't really show individual permissions. Instead, the page shows permission levels.

Table 12-1 lists the permission levels, the rights they grant, and the SharePoint group they're assigned to by default.

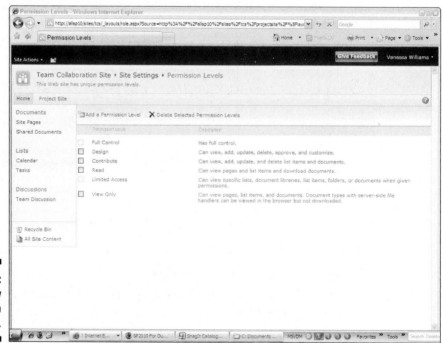

Figure 12-7:
View permission levels.

Table 12-1	Permission Levels	
Permission Level	*Rights Granted*	*SharePoint Group Assigned to by Default*
Full Control	Wield administrative access	*Site* Owners
Design	Change the site's look and feel	Designers
Manage Hierarchy	Manage the site's structure and permissions	Hierarchy Managers
Approve	Approve content	Approvers
Contribute	Add and modify content	*Site* Members
Read	View all content, including history	*Site* Visitors
Restricted Read	View and open	Restricted Readers
Limited Access	Open (same as guest access)	Quick Deploy Users
View Only	View items and pages	Viewers

Managing SharePoint Designer access

SharePoint 2010 allows you to configure which users can use SharePoint Designer 2010 to access your team site. Before you jump to the conclusion that you don't want anyone doing that, bear in mind that the role of Designer has changed with SharePoint 2010. Designer can be used to perform a lot of list and library management tasks. I suspect that more team sites will be granting access to Designer than in previous product versions.

To grant a user the right to use SharePoint Designer 2010 with your team site:

1. **Browse to the top-level site of your team site.**

2. **Choose Site Actions⇨Site Settings.**

3. **In the Site Collection Administration section, click the SharePoint Designer Settings link.**

4. **Choose the options that you want to enable.**

   Your choices are

   - *Enable SharePoint Designer:* Users who are *Site* Owners or who have Design permissions can use SharePoint Designer to access your site.

- *Enable Detaching Pages from the Site Definition:* I advise against allowing this unless you have a good reason to do so. Detaching pages can cause problems when upgrading later. I do this all the time when I'm developing, but then I implement my changes later in such a way that doesn't require detaching from the site definition.

- *Enable Customizing Master Pages and Layout Pages:* This is fine for publishing sites, although not usually required for team sites.

- *Enable Managing of the Web Site URL Structure:* This allows users to see the folder hierarchy. I usually allow this unless I think it will overwhelm the user.

5. **Click OK to save your changes.**

Chapter 13

Creating New Sites

....

In This Chapter

▶ Making sense of SharePoint templates

▶ Getting familiar with site hierarchy

▶ Whipping up a new site

▶ Immortalizing your site as a site template

....

SharePoint 2010 is basically a way to create Web sites without the need of IT or computer programmers. SharePoint provides you with a number of different kinds of sites you can create using site templates. A *site template* is essentially a blueprint that tells SharePoint what to create in the new site. Every site created from a site template looks the same. That's where you (and the rest of this book) enter the picture. In most cases, you quickly discover that you need the site to do something beyond what's provided in the site template. You need to change the name of your document library or create a new list. But you have to start somewhere — with a new site. And that's what this chapter is all about.

Getting Acquainted with Templates

SharePoint provides loads of templates you can use for creating sites. By far the two most popular that I see are the team site and publishing sites. But SharePoint offers a lot more choices beyond those two. What's more, your company can even create site templates that are specific to your company. Heck, when you get your site the way you like it, you can even create your own site template that you can use to stamp out new sites.

The term *site template* is overloaded. Technically, the site templates provided by Microsoft are *site definitions,* which is just an XML file that describes how to create a site. Site definitions reside on the file system. The site templates that you create from your sites are just Microsoft cabinet files that contain the objects required to stamp out a new site. Site templates are stored in the site collection and can be shared easily with other people. A site template is tied to one of the underlying Microsoft site definitions. I like to think of a site template as a macro. A site template creates a new site using the Microsoft site definition and then builds out the site using the objects contained in the cabinet file.

There is great debate among SharePoint professionals over creating custom site definitions. I am firmly in the camp that's opposed to custom site definitions. I've delivered dozens of sites without ever creating a custom site definition. Instead, I use features to package my customizations. If you need to do something that goes beyond a site template, look at SharePoint's feature framework. I discuss features in Chapter 21.

SharePoint provides dozens of site templates that fall into a handful of categories. Within each category, the templates are basically the same only with slight variations. Each category is optimized to serve a different audience or function.

By far, the two most popular site templates that I see used are the team site and the publishing site. Team sites are almost always the de facto standard for collaboration sites used for project teams. Publishing sites are usually used for public-facing Web sites.

Table 13-1 outlines the site template categories, lists the templates you can except to see, and when you should use them.

Table 13-1	SharePoint Site Template Categories	
Category	*Templates You See*	*When to Use Them*
Blank & Custom	Blank Site	When you want an empty container
Collaboration	Team Site and Meeting Workspaces	When more people will contribute content than read it; also when you want basic layouts
Content & Data	Blog, Contacts Web Database, Personalization Site, Document Center, Publishing Site, Enterprise Wiki, Visio Process Repository	When you need a site that specializes in content or data management
Search	Basic Search Center, Enterprise Search Center	When you need a site to display search results
Tracking and Web Databases	Assets Web Database, Charitable Contributes Web, Projects Web Database	When you want to use a Web-based database to create track of information

It's all about features

As you go about creating sites using different site templates, you quickly realize that a team site is vastly different from a publishing site, whereas a Contacts Web Database is different from both. These differences aren't really about the site templates. The differences are really about the features that are activated by these site templates.

SharePoint uses a framework for bundling functionality into packages called *features*. Each feature contains the Web pages, code, style sheets, images, and other resources to create the experience you have in the browser.

Features can reference other features. A site template (or site definition to be technically accurate) references features along with some other configuration information to create a new site.

The significance to you is that features are site template–agnostic. That is, they don't care in what site template they're used. So just because you create a site using a team site template, nothing stops you from activating the features related to publishing. I discuss feature activation in more detail in Chapter 21.

If you're creating new site collections, you see a slightly different set of categories along with a few additional templates. Also, the templates you have available to you are dependent on how your company has licensed SharePoint and what features they have turned on.

In a publishing site, you can control which templates can be used to create site templates. On the Site Settings page, click the Page Layouts and Site Templates link.

In this book, I specifically cover these following site templates:

- ✓ I cover team sites in Parts I and II. Team sites are the foundation for most of the sites in terms of functionality, so most of what you know about team sites applies to other kinds of sites as well. Or, as I like to say, a document library is a document library.

- ✓ I cover publishing sites in Parts III and IV. These sites are used for Web content management scenarios, where you have many readers and a few publishers.

- ✓ I cover Search Center site templates in Chapter 23.

I like to think of site templates more as examples from Microsoft on how you might do something, as opposed to a fully baked solution. I know many people perceive SharePoint as a product, and as such, expect it to work to their liking out of the box. (And, yes, this is how Microsoft markets it.) Although SharePoint is a product, it's also a *platform*, meaning a set of services that you can use to create your own solution. As a product, SharePoint probably meets 80 percent of your needs. The remaining 20 percent usually requires some creative thinking. SharePoint is an extremely powerful platform. A minimal amount of customization can go a long way. I have also found the inverse to be true: A large amount of customizations often adds very little value. My experience has shown that people who extensively customize SharePoint often have little knowledge of SharePoint's platform.

Understanding Site Hierarchy

Before I can explain how to create a new site, I need to give you some background on where sites live. (You may never need to know this.) Someone in your company may tell you to always use a certain process to create your sites because that person knows best and will decide where to put your site. However, you may need to know this information if *you* have to decide where to put your site.

SharePoint sites are organized into a hierarchy of containers. Some containers are sites that contain content, whereas other containers simply act as entry points into a group of sites. These containers map to Web addresses, which is how you access them.

The highest level container in SharePoint is a *Web application*, which is usually used to logically group together content and users who have similar needs. For example, say your organization consists of two different companies — Big Bagel Makers, Inc. and Big Donut Makers, Inc. The bagel makers and the donut makers have their own employees, business process, and content. What's more is that never the two shall meet (Melvyn Einstein shouldn't be sniffing around to learn how to make Homer Simpson's favorite donut).

To meet these business requirements, your IT department can set up two separate Web applications. Each Web application can have its own Web address. If you work for Big Bagel, use `portal.bigbagel.com`. Your cousin who works for Big Donut uses `portal.bigdonut.com` to access her content.

In this example, you know the Web address of your portal based on where you work in this organization. If your organization consists of one company, you may only have a Web application — `mycompanyportal.com`.

A Web application provides an entry point into a site hierarchy and allows IT to configure policies that apply to every site within that Web application. A Web application contains a group of *site collections,* which contain content such as Web pages, document libraries, and lists. A site collection can also contain a hierarchy of sites, or *subsites.* A site collection may also consist of only one site — the *root* or *top-level site.*

Creating Web addresses

The decisions for when to use Web applications or site collections have a lot to do with security and Web addresses. Companies usually have some URL navigation scheme in mind — `flashycompanyportal.companyname.com/departmentname goeshere`. SharePoint provides many ways to accomplish these URL navigation schemes. You can associate URLs with a Web application. You can also associate them with individual site collections so that `accounting.flashy companyportal.companyname.com` points to a site collection instead of a Web address. SharePoint also offers a *sitemap path,* which is a way to specify a path within a Web address. For example, if you want all team sites to follow the convention, `portal.company.com/teamsites/teamsite namegoeshere`, you could use a sitemap path of `teamsites` in the Web application that points to `portal.company.com`.

All this configuration happens at the farm level in Central Administration, which probably isn't something you can access. I share this with you because I want you to know you have an alternative for using site collections and subsites to create Web addresses. I've encountered many enterprising power users who realize that they can create their own Web addresses using nested subsites. Although that works, it can create a real navigational nightmare when users have to navigate through three or more levels of site home pages to get to their site. Creating a good Web address hierarchy is a combination of farm level configuration and site collection configuration. If you find yourself creating subsites for no other reason than to provide navigation, you may need to talk to IT about helping you figure out a better approach.

Publishing sites have a Site Content and Structure tool (accessible from the Site Actions menu by selecting the Manage Content and Structure option) that you can use to view the site hierarchy within a site collection. This is a really cool tool because you can use it to move documents between libraries within the same site collection. Figure 13-1 shows the Site Content and Structure tool.

Many organizations use the site collection as their container of choice for creating new sites, which is clearly how Microsoft intended for site collections to be used. To state that another way, it's usually better to create a new site collection than it is to create a new site within a site collection.

One of the big reasons this is true relates to how permissions are managed in SharePoint. Permission groups are managed at the root or top-level site, as I discuss in Chapter 12. If you already have a site collection set up with the permissions you want and you expect your new site to use these same permissions, creating a new site in your existing site collection is acceptable.

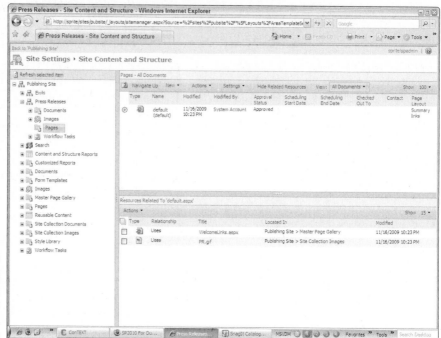

Figure 13-1:
Displaying
a site's
hierarchy.

However, if your new site needs a completely new permissions model, you probably want to create a new site collection. The following list summarizes my recommendations for creating site collections:

✔ **If you want a new site to have the same permissions of an existing site collection,** create your new site in the site collection where permissions are configured. Your site automatically inherits permission settings from the root or top-level site.

✔ **If you want a new site that has a unique permissions requirement,** create a new site collection and configure permissions to meet your requirements. By default, any new sites or content you add automatically inherit these permissions.

As is always the case with SharePoint, the recommendations listed in the preceding list aren't hard and fast rules. There are legitimate reasons for breaking them. For example, your IT organization or hosting company may allow you only one site collection. In that case, you don't have much choice — you have to create your new site in the existing site collection, stop inheriting permissions from the parent Web site, and configure new permissions.

Displaying content from other site collections

Many of the Web Parts in SharePoint tend to favor displaying content within the same site collection. The Content Query Web Part, for example, queries lists and libraries within a site collection and displays the results on a page. There are at least two ways to display content from the lists and libraries in your site collection in another site collection.

Using the Data Form Web Part in SharePoint Designer 2010, you can create a SharePoint data source that queries content from a SharePoint site at the Web address you specify. You must have permissions to view the content in order to query it.

Using SharePoint's search functionality, you can display content with a Search Web Part. If the content is indexed by SharePoint (and it is by default) and you have permission to view the content, you can configure a Search Web Part to return the content.

SharePoint is intended to be a collaboration tool. That implies a more simplistic permissions model than most companies allow. Although SharePoint can accommodate any permissions model you throw at it, you probably can't maintain it in a single site collection. That's all I'm sayin'.

SharePoint content is stored in a database, not on the file system. Multiple site collections are usually stored in a single content database, although you can store a single site collection in one content database. Although you don't have an upper limit on content database size, you do have a practical limit. When databases grow too large, they can take too long to back up and restore. You'll find that it's also easier to move content databases than just the content inside them. For these reasons, IT will sometimes use separate site collections.

Creating a New Site

The process of creating a new site is actually quite easy. As I describe in the "Creating Web addresses" sidebar, earlier in this chapter, the harrowing task of deciding where to create the site requires some forethought.

As I mention at the beginning of this chapter, SharePoint provides a number of templates for creating new sites. Most organizations will decide for you which templates you're going to use; it's usually either a Team Site template or a Publishing Site template. The other templates are specialized.

You can create a new site collection in SharePoint in two ways — by using Central Administration or through Self-Service Site Creation. Using Central Administration requires elevated permissions, which are usually restricted to IT personnel.

Self-Service Site Creation is a feature of SharePoint that allows IT to delegate the authority of creating new site collection to end users like you. IT needs to provide you with the Web address for accessing Self-Service Site Creation, but it usually looks like this:

```
http://webapplication/_layouts/scsignup.aspx
```

As you may have surmised, Self-Service Site Creation is configured for each Web application. To enable it, use the Application Management page in Central Administration; it's either off or on.

The process for creating a new site or site collection is fairly similar; follow these steps:

1a. **To create a new site collection, browse to the Web address provided by IT for Self-Service Site Creation.**

1b. **To create a new site within an existing site collection, browse to the site collection where you want to create the new site and then choose Site Actions⇨New Site.**

All things new (new lists, new libraries, new sites) can be also created by clicking the Create button on the All Site Content page.

2. **Click the template you want to use to create your new site.**

Figure 13-2 shows the animated Create screen. (***Note:*** The animation requires the browser to have the Silverlight plug-in installed.)

The templates are presented in categories, such as Collaboration, Enterprise, and Content & Data. Clicking a category on the left displays a list of templates on the right.

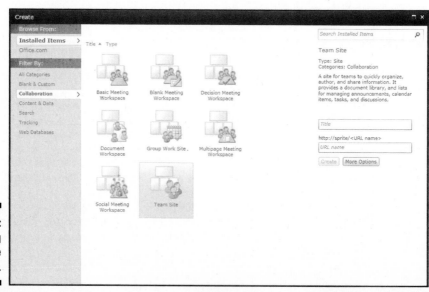

Figure 13-2:
Browsing site templates.

Figure 13-3 shows the typical browser experience if you aren't using the Silverlight browser plug-in. This is also how the screen appears for creating new site collections. This screen presents templates with the categories displayed as tabs. Click a tab to see the site templates in that category.

Of special interest is that in the Custom tab, you can create a site where the user selects the template later. This is nice if you're creating a new site collection for someone else and you don't know which template they want to use.

3. **Enter the title in the Title field and the Web address in the URL field for your site.**

4. **Click the More Options button to display additional settings for creating your new site.**

Creating a new site within an existing site collection requires some thought about the site's navigation. Because a new site collection is the top-most site in the site hierarchy, all subsites can inherit its navigation settings. The More Options button displays these navigation inheritance options along with the ability to inherit permissions from the parent site.

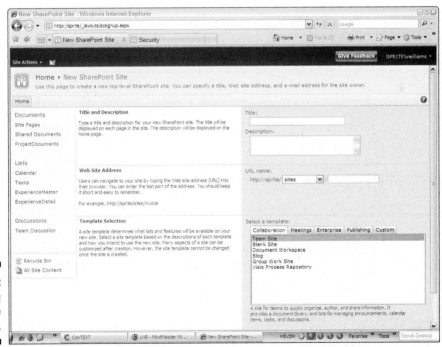

Figure 13-3:
Creating
a new site
collection.

I always suggest inheriting navigation and permissions from the parent site, unless you have an explicit reason not to. For example, if you know you want your subsite to use its own navigation across the top, you could opt not to inherit the Top Link bar of the parent.

You can always change your navigation and permissions settings for any site by choosing Site Actions➪Site Settings.

5. **Click the Create button.**

SharePoint creates your new site using the template you selected.

Creating Your Own Site Templates

If you have a site configured to your liking and you want to reuse it to create another site, you can create your own site template. When you make a site template of your site, it stands alongside Microsoft's templates, and you can use it to create new sites.

A user-created site template isn't the same as the site templates provided by Microsoft, but it functions similarly.

Creating a template from an existing team site

The process for creating your own site template is ridiculously easy. Make sure you have your site configured the way you want it, and when you're ready to create your site template, follow these steps:

1. **Browse to the site that you want to use to make your site template and then choose Site Actions➪Site Settings.**

2. **In the Site Actions section, click the Save Site as Template link.**

   You can also perform this task in SharePoint Designer 2010.

   The Save Site as Template option is available only for sites that don't use publishing. When you enable publishing features, this option is no longer available. I address how to handle publishing sites later in this section.

You can bypass this restriction and create a site template of publishing sites. I advise against doing so because the results are difficult to troubleshoot. In other words, everything may look fine on the surface and then you discover the site isn't working properly later. Publishing sites have their own process for templating for a reason.

3. **Enter the filename for your site template in the File Name field.**

   You can use any name you want. SharePoint appends the file extension .wsp to your filename.

4. **Enter the template name and description in the Template Name and Template Description fields, respectively.**

   The template name and description are visible in the Site Template gallery, so I suggest making them useful.

5. **(Optional) Include the site's content, such as list items and files in document libraries, by selecting the Include Content check box.**

6. **Click OK.**

SharePoint saves your site as a site template in the User Solution gallery. This gallery is where your site templates and any custom features you create are saved. You can browse to the User Solution gallery, download your site template file, and share it with other people. By uploading the file into the User Solution gallery of their sites, they can use your site template to create new sites.

You can follow the steps in the section, "Creating a New Site," earlier in this chapter, to create a new site from your site template. Figure 13-4 shows a custom site template in the Solution gallery.

Please note that site templates are used only to create a new site. No link exists between your site template and the new site. Updating your site template doesn't update any sites you've created already with the site template. If you need to update sites, the proper approach is to use features, which I discuss in Chapter 21.

You can also create templates of your lists and libraries. If you don't need your entire site but want a single list or library, create a template. Your templates appear alongside Microsoft's list and library templates and can be used to create new lists and libraries. Save a library as a template in the library's Settings page.

Site templates created by end users are saved as WSP files, which is a Microsoft cabinet file. The .wsp file extension is also used for custom solutions. Previous versions of SharePoint used the .stp file extension. Now all site templates and custom solutions share the same file extension.

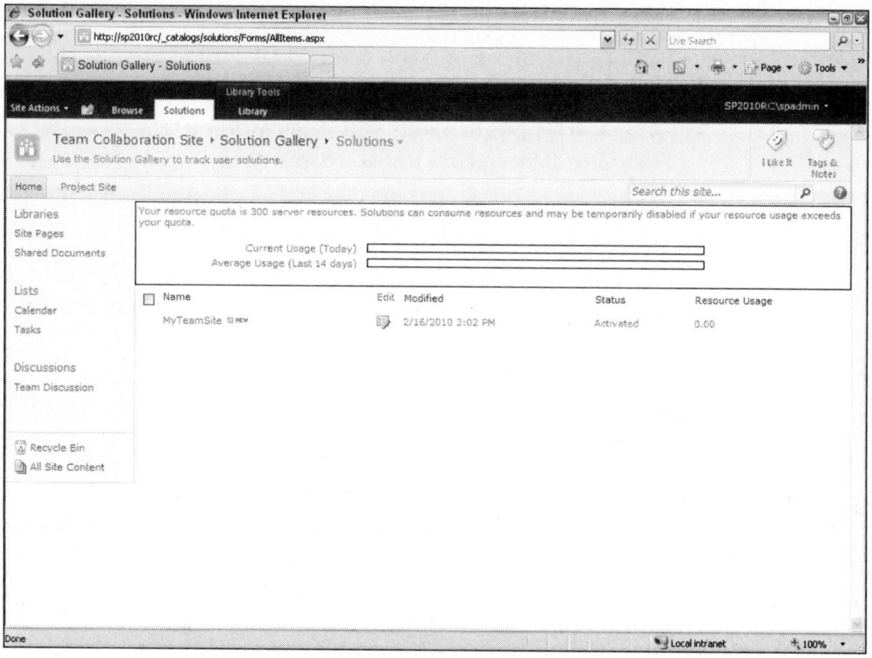

Figure 13-4:
A custom
site
template in
the Solution
gallery.

Creating a template from a publishing site

If you need to create new sites from an existing publishing site, the easiest way to do so is by creating a copy of the site. The following process only works to create a new site in an existing publishing site collection:

1. **Browse to the publishing site collection where you want to create a copy of an existing site.**

2. **Choose Site Actions⇨Manage Content and Structure.**

   The Site Content and Structure tool opens.

3. **In the right pane, click the site you wish to copy.**

4. **Hover over the site name, click the drop-down arrow to display a contextual menu, and choose Copy, as shown in Figure 13-5.**

   The Copy dialog box appears.

5. **In the Copy dialog box, click the place where you want to create the new site and then click OK.**

   A message appears informing you that SharePoint is performing the Copy operation. When the copy completes, the screen refreshes.

6. **Navigate to your new site and test it.**

Figure 13-5:
Choose
Copy to
make a copy
of a site.

SharePoint places all the pages in the new site in Draft mode. You need to publish your pages before they're visible to site visitors. (See Chapter 15 for details on publishing and approving pages.)

The Copy operation can be taxing on the server, so I suggest using this tool in non-peak hours. The Copy operation of the Site Content and Structure Tool works for lists and libraries also.

You may be wondering how the Copy operation works. Under the covers, this operation is the same as performing an export and import using the command line. The export process creates a *content migration package,* or *CMP,* file. The file can be transported to another site collection, or even another server farm, where the content and structure is imported. This is an extremely powerful command, and I use it any time I need to move content. Like WSP files, a CMP file is a Microsoft cabinet file and can be inspected by changing the file extension to .cab. Exports and imports can be scheduled in Central Administration using Content Deployment Jobs. This is a great way to copy content from an internal authoring farm to a public-facing Web site.

Part III
Putting On Your Webmaster Hat

The 5th Wave   By Rich Tennant

©RICHTENNANT

"Jeez — I thought the page template just defined the background on the screen."

In this part . . .

Here I cover some of the fun stuff, such as changing your plain vanilla site to something a little less . . . SharePointy? Enter the publishing site, stage left.

Unlike team sites, which are about characters and collaboration tools, publishing sites are about the audience and what they see and experience. SharePoint publishing features help you control how your site shows its face to the world. Want to customize your navigation, get rid of the left navigation completely, or hide those ugly application pages? No problem.

A SharePoint publishing site is well-equipped with tools that help you create portals and public-facing Web sites. A publishing site makes applying consistent layouts and navigation across your site possible. You can also use Web Parts to roll up content from one part of your site and present it with a different costume on your home page.

Chapter 14

Getting Started with Portals and Web Sites

In This Chapter

▶ Mastering the basics of publishing sites

▶ Creating and fixing your pages

▶ Choosing or changing a page layout

▶ Selecting the allowed page layouts for a site

▶ Changing the master page of a site

*N*owadays everyone expects their Web sites to have a content management system. SharePoint users are no different. People don't want to have to type their content in multiple places. They want to enter it once and reuse it throughout their site. That's the role of a content management system, and that's what SharePoint's publishing sites do.

SharePoint's publishing sites are very useful for creating portals and public-facing Web sites. For internal portals, the business community often stands up portals with very little or no IT intervention. Common uses for internal portals include sites that aggregate users and content based on geography, business units, or business service. Business service portals are very popular for things like a self-service human resources portal or internal communications portal. For smaller companies, their entire company portal may consist of a single publishing site.

I usually recommend using a publishing site for the company portal with separate site collections for team collaboration sites. Although internal communication usually owns the company portal, team sites should usually be less restrictive.

Public-facing Web sites may require some design assistance because these sites tend to have more stringent branding requirements. If the branding is implemented properly, business owners can maintain the site's content on an on-going basis. A company may choose to put their entire Web site in SharePoint, whereas others choose smaller micro-sites that they want the business to be able to maintain. For example, a marketing micro-site is a good use for SharePoint because the marketing group can maintain the branding and content.

SharePoint 2010 includes another site template, the *Enterprise Wiki,* that has similar content management capabilities of publishing sites. The Enterprise Wiki, however, is geared more for collaborative information publishing, similar to Wikipedia. (I discuss Enterprise Wikis in more detail in Chapter 23.)

This chapter introduces you to SharePoint's publishing sites and shows you how to start adding your own content.

Exploring SharePoint's Publishing Site

SharePoint provides a site template for creating Web content management sites — the *Publishing Portal template.* The Publishing Portal template includes a number of interesting elements that you can use to kick-start your portal or Web site project, including

- ✔ A branded master page that changes the site's look and feel.

- ✔ Several variations of layouts for your site's landing pages and subpages, referred to as Welcome pages and Article pages by SharePoint.

- ✔ An enhanced Site Actions menu that provides access to commonly used administrative tasks in publishing sites, such as modifying site navigation and viewing reports on site content.

- ✔ A preconfigured Pages library with versioning and approval workflows enabled by default. (See Chapter 15 for more details on the Pages library and approval workflows.)

- ✔ Search Center that provides basic and advanced search capabilities. (See Chapter 23 for more details on search.)

- ✔ Sample content including a home page and a subsite for managing press releases.

The Publishing Portal site template can be used to create new site collections. Usually when you're creating a new portal or public-facing Web site, it should reside in its own site collection. Using a separate site collection allows the portal or Web site to reside in its own database and makes it easier to manage permissions. The features used to customize a publishing site apply to all the content within the site collection. (I discuss creating new site collections in Chapter 13.)

You can add a publishing site to an existing site collection by using the Publishing Portal template. You have to enable publishing features for the site collection, which you can do on the Site Settings page of the top-level site.

Blank or publishing site?

Although using SharePoint's Publishing Portal template is a great way to kick start your portal or Web site, sometimes the template makes too many choices for you. For example, my clients rarely want to use approval workflows, so I find myself turning off workflows and deleting a lot of sample content. Sometimes it's better to start with a blank slate and add what you want. That's where the Blank Site template comes in.

Instead of creating a new site with the Publishing Portal template, you can use the Blank Site template and then enable publishing features in your template. With the features enabled, you can add pages, configure libraries, change layouts, and brand your site.

The functionality of publishing sites is delivered by Microsoft using several features. In the browser, you see two features — the SharePoint Server Publishing Infrastructure at the site collection level, and the SharePoint Server Publishing feature at the individual site level.

Figure 14-1 shows the home page of a site created using the Publishing Portal template.

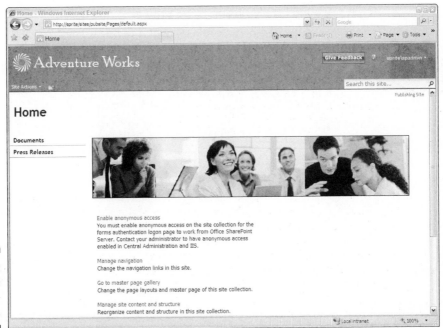

Figure 14-1: SharePoint's publishing site.

Creating and Editing Pages

One of the first tasks you want to perform in a new publishing site is to create new Web pages or edit the pages provided in the site template. Pages in a publishing site are created automatically in the Pages library. This library is preconfigured with approval workflows. See Chapter 15 for details on approval workflows.

You can create new publishing pages only in the Pages library. This means all your pages have the word *Pages* in their Web addresses. There's no way around this if you want to use publishing pages. You can create folders in the Pages library, which is useful if you have a set of pages you want to manage separately but don't want to create a new subsite.

To create a new page in a publishing site:

1. **Browse to the site where you want to create the new page and then choose Site Actions➪New Page.**

   The New Page dialog box appears, as shown in Figure 14-2.

2. **Enter a new filename for your page in the New Page Name field.**

   Any spaces are converted to a dash. I suggest that you do not use spaces in your filenames.

3. **Click the Create button.**

   SharePoint creates a new page and displays it in Edit mode.

It helps to have a plan for the pages you want to create. See the sidebar, "Blank or publishing site?" for planning suggestions.

You can edit pages by choosing Site Actions➪Edit Page. Alternatively, browse to the Pages library any time you want to manage multiple pages.

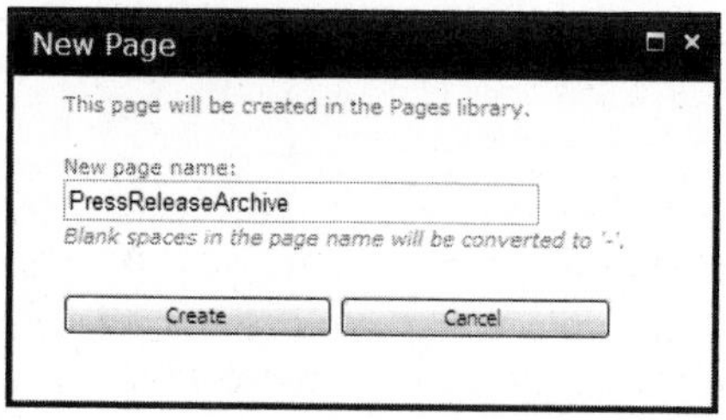

Figure 14-2:
Creating a new page in a publishing site.

New Page

This page will be created in the Pages library.

New page name:

PressReleaseArchive

Blank spaces in the page name will be converted to '-'.

[Create]   [Cancel]

Adding Content to Your Page

SharePoint's publishing site provides a rich editing experience that makes it easy for a non-technical person to create Web pages. Adding your content to the page is a snap. SharePoint provides many kinds of content containers that you can use when creating your page, including

- ✔ Single-line text boxes for entering a simple text line, such as the page's title
- ✔ Multiple-line text boxes for entering paragraphs, bulleted and numbered lists, and tables
- ✔ Tools for adding images, video, and Web Parts

The containers that you see on the page are determined by the *page layout* used to create the page. The page layout is the template or form that determines what type of content you can put on the page (text, image, and video) and where the content goes on the page.

SharePoint provides a number of page layouts, but you can also create your own (see Chapter 16). By default, a publishing site uses the Body Only page layout, which provides a single multiline container for adding all your content to the page.

SharePoint provides four types of page layouts. The type of layout you choose is determined by the information you need to display on the page. Within each kind of page layout provided, a number of layouts are available. Each layout provides a different way of displaying the same kind of information. Table 14-1 provides a summary of the layouts provided for each layout type.

Table 14-1	SharePoint Page Layouts	
Layout Type	*Type of Information Displayed*	*Example of Layouts Provided*
Article page	Supports news content with images, bylines, and article dates	Article with no image; article with image on the left or the right
Enterprise Wiki page	Supports community editing with rating and categorization	Rich text box with rating stars and a Category drop-down list
Redirect page	Captures the Web address of a page you want to automatically forward users to	Hyperlink field for entering the forwarding address
Welcome page	Acts as the starting or landing page for a site	Web site table of contents, "splash" page with an image and two areas for links

Create a new page layout any time you want to present a new type of information or present that information in a new format on the page. (See Chapter 16 for details.)

Adding content to your page

Most page layouts include a multiline text box you can use for entering lots of different kinds of content. This text box includes plenty of formatting options and commands for inserting images and videos.

Depending on the page layout you're using, your page may have several more containers for adding content. Some of these containers may be specialized; for example, just for adding an image or a hyperlink. (I discuss creating layouts using different kinds of containers in Chapter 16.)

To add content to your page, follow these steps:

1. **Place your cursor inside the page's text box.**

   This text box is often called Page Content, but it may be named differently depending on the page layout you're using.

2. **Enter your text into the page, applying formatting as desired.**

   The Ribbon displays several formatting options you can use for formatting your text. These options can be disabled, as I discuss in Chapter 16, so your Ribbon may look different from the one you see in Figure 14-3.

When your branding is properly implemented, you don't have to apply formatting to content. For example, you can enter a bulleted list, and it formats automatically in a consistent way with the site's branding. (See Chapter 20 for details about applying consistent styles across content.)

3. **To view the HTML mode for the content, click the Edit HTML Source button in the Markup group on the Format Text tab of the Ribbon.**

   The HTML Source appears in a separate window. You can use this option if you want to copy and paste HTML markup into the page.

4. **Use the buttons on the Insert tab to insert other kinds of content into your page, such as tables, images, videos, links, and Web Parts.**

You don't have to upload your images and videos before inserting them. The insert process prompts you to upload your image or video to the site, as shown in Figure 14-4. (I discuss working with images and videos in more detail in Chapter 21.)

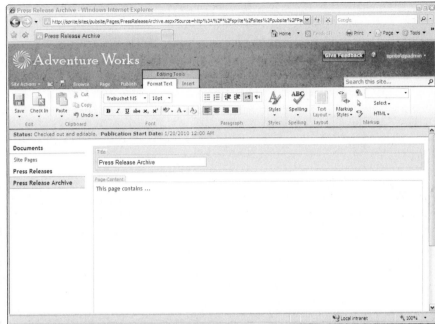

Figure 14-3:
Ribbon showing text-editing options.

Figure 14-4:
Insert videos, images, and links.

If you have content you want to give users to use on pages, consider adding it as reusable content. You just enter your content in the Reusable Content list in the root of your site. A user can insert the content into his page. Common uses for reusable content include privacy statements and copyright information.

Changing the page's layout

For good practice, choose your page layout type before entering any page content; although you can change page layout types later, that sometimes leads to unexpected consequences.

What about copy and paste?

Site contributors often want to use Microsoft Word to create their content. Although you can copy and paste your content from Word into a SharePoint page, it will usually contain a lot of extra styling and characters. Although you can use the formatting option to remove all inline styles, here are several ways to avoid this situation:

- **Avoid page layouts that use one big content container.** Instead, create page layouts that look like forms and make it easy for people to enter the content as smaller chunks of text.

- **Train users to clean text before pasting it into SharePoint.** A common approach is to ask people to paste their text into Notepad and then copy and paste it again into the SharePoint page.

- **Give users a Word document template.** Create a document template that removes all extraneous styling and allows users to access only hierarchical block-level formatting, such as bullets and headers. This formatting is styled easily in SharePoint and requires no conversion effort, manual or automated.

- **Use document conversion.** A SharePoint page and a Microsoft Word document are essentially the same kind of file — they're both XML files. Therefore, you can easily convert from one format to the other. SharePoint supports automated document conversion.

To create a new page, choose Site Actions⇨New Page, give your new page a title, and click the Create button. Your new page appears, with the site's default page layout applied. In publishing sites, as I mention earlier, this should be a Body Only Article page.

Follow these steps to choose and apply a new page layout to your new page:

1. **Make sure you're in Edit mode, for example by looking for the Editing Tools tab.**

   If you aren't in Edit mode, click the Edit icon above the Ribbon (it looks like a piece of paper and pencil).

   You can also click the Page tab and then click the Edit icon. The Editing Tools tab appears with the Format Text and Insert tabs in it.

2. **Locate the Page Actions section on the Ribbon.**

   The Page Actions section is on the Page tab. This section includes the Preview, Page Layout, Make Home Page, Incoming Links, and Draft Check options.

3. **Click the Page Layout drop-down list and choose a page layout.**

   The page layouts available for this site are shown, grouped by type, with a thumbnail representation of each layout; see Figure 14-5.

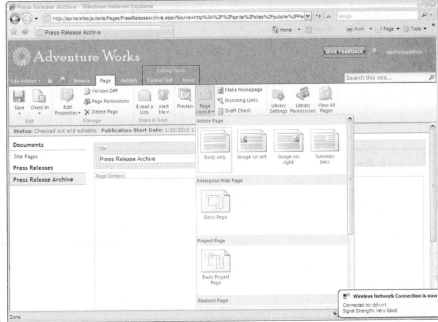

Figure 14-5:
The Page
Layout drop-
down list on
the Ribbon.

Think about the contents of your page to make sure the layout is what you need.

 4. **Edit the content as you normally would, and be sure to select Save and Close or Check In on the Page tab when you're done.**

Your changes are saved and the page is no longer in Edit mode.

The steps to change the page layout after you enter page content are no different than those to choose the initial page layout. But you should choose the new page layout carefully; does it have the same containers as your current page? Will you need to rearrange a lot of the content?

If your current page uses Web Parts and the new page layout doesn't have a corresponding Web Part zone, the Web Parts will either move to another zone or close. Content in controls (such as byline and date) will disappear if you apply a layout that doesn't contain those fields.

However, simple changes, such as going from an Article Left page to an Article Right page (where the only difference is the location of the image), go very smoothly.

Setting Page Layout Defaults

The *default page layout* differs according to the type of site you're in. And don't confuse this default page layout (what you get when you select Site Actions⇨New Page) with the home page or default.aspx page, which is determined by the site template definition. So for example, the home page may be a Welcome Summary Links page, but the default page layout for new pages on the site may be an Article page layout.

The default page layout is the assumed most common page layout needed for the site. (This choice can be changed in the Site Settings by accessing the Master Pages and Page Layouts link, however — see the "Changing the Master Page of a Site" section, later in this chapter.) The default page layout for publishing sites is an Article page, Body Only.

If you choose Site Actions⇨New Page, your new page will have the site's default page layout. (Likewise, if you use the New Page link in the Pages library.) If on the other hand, you select the New Document button on the Documents tab in the Pages library, you can choose a page layout type and then a specific layout, during the creation phase of the page.

In the interest of standardization and ease of use, define which page layouts users can use to create new pages. SharePoint 2010 gives you quite a few choices when it comes to controlling the default choices for site templates, page layouts, and inheritance of these settings in your site collection.

To define the page layouts available for use in a site:

1. **Select Site Actions⇨Site Settings.**

   The Site Settings page is displayed, oddly enough.

2. **Locate the Look and Feel section.**

3. **Click the Page Layouts and Site Templates link.**

   The Page Layout and Site Template Settings page appears. This page shows three sections: Subsite Templates, Page Layouts, and New Page Default Settings.

   In the first and second section, you can inherit what's been chosen at the parent level, choose any/all options, or select your own choices for this subsite on down.

   The third section, New Page Default Settings, allows you to determine whether you want to inherit the default page layout of the parent or choose your own.

4. (Optional) Use the radio buttons and list items to specify options for site templates (refer to Figure 14-6).

You can specify that subsites inherit the same settings applied to their parent site (select the Subsites Inherit Site Templates from Parent Site radio button), permit subsites to use selected site templates (select the Subsites Can Only Use the Following Site Templates radio button), or you can allow a subsite to use any site template (select the Subsites Can Use Any Site Template radio button).

The Add and Remove buttons activate, depending on what's allowed, and you can move site templates to the *left* (not allowed) or *right* (allowed) as desired. You can use the buttons or double-click a site template title to move the choice from box to box.

Select the Reset All Subsites to Inherit These Preferred Subsite Template Settings check box if you wish subsites under this level to use these choices as well.

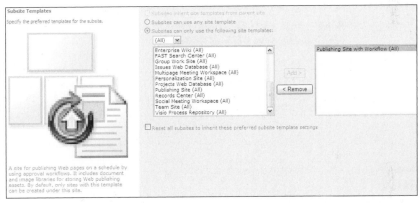

Figure 14-6:
Select templates that can be used to create new sites.

5. For Page Layouts, select the Pages in This Site Can Only Use the Following Layouts option.

The left (not allowed) and right (allowed) choice boxes become active. Use the Add and Remove buttons, or double-click, to place page layouts in the correct box (see Figure 14-7). Notice that the content type proceeds the page template title (in parentheses).

6. Select the Reset All Subsites to Inherit These Preferred Page Layout Settings check box if you wish subsites under this level to use these choices as well.

Remember that this choice can be overridden by a site owner at a subsequent level.

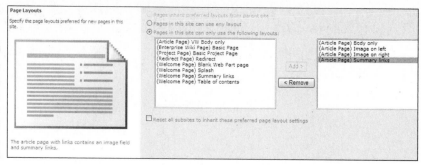

Figure 14-7:
Select page
layouts you
can use
with this
site.

7. **In the third section, choose the Select the Default Page Layout option, if applicable.**

If you choose the Select the Default Page Layout option, a list box appears with the page layouts listed. Choose the page layout you want as a default (see Figure 14-8). Usually this would be the most commonly used page layout for the site.

8. **Select your options concerning the New Page URL and/or inheritance settings for new page settings.**

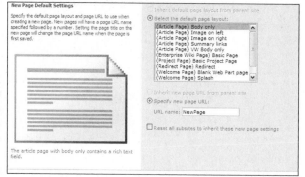

Figure 14-8:
Set the
default new
page layout.

9. **Click OK to apply your choices.**

Test your choices by creating and modifying several (or more!) new pages in your site before releasing to your editors.

Changing the Master Page of a Site

SharePoint 2010 includes two master pages: *v4* and *nightandday*. By default, the master page of a publishing site is v4.master.

To apply a different master page, follow these steps:

1. **Select Site Actions⇨Site Settings.**

   The Site Settings page is displayed.

2. **Locate the Look and Feel section.**

3. **Click the Master Page link.**

   The Site Master Page Settings page appears. This page has three sections — Site Master, System Master, and Alternate CSS.

4. **Choose to have the site inherit from the parent site master by selecting the Inherit Site Master Page from Parent of This Site radio button, or apply a specific master page by selecting the Specify a Master Page to Be Used by This Site and All Sites That Inherit from It radio button, and then selecting an option from the Site Master Page drop-down list (see Figure 14-9).**

5. **Select the Reset Subsites to Inherit This Master check box if you want subsites of the current site to use the same master page.**

6. **Set the site to inherit the system master page by selecting the Inherit System Master Page from Parent of This Site radio button, or specify a different System Master Page by selecting the Specify a System Master Page for This Site and All Sites That Inherit from It radio button and selecting an option from the System Master Page drop-down list.**

   The system master is applied to system-based pages, such as library pages. You don't have to have the same master for the site pages and the system pages.

   You can configure the site to inherit the alternate CSS of the parent, use the default SharePoint CSS, or use an alternate CSS. If you have a CSS attached to a custom master, you may not need an alternate CSS. On the other hand, if you're using the v4.master or the Night and Day master and you just want to apply different colors, spacing, or images, you can point to an alternate style sheet.

7. **Inherit the alternate CSS from the parent site by selecting the Inherit Alternate CSS URL from Parent of This Site radio button, or specify SharePoint Foundation default CSS by selecting the Use Microsoft SharePoint Foundation Default Styles radio button, or specify an alternative CSS option by selecting the Specify a CSS File to Be Used by This Publishing Site and All Sites That Inherit from It radio button and browsing to an existing CSS using the Browse button.**

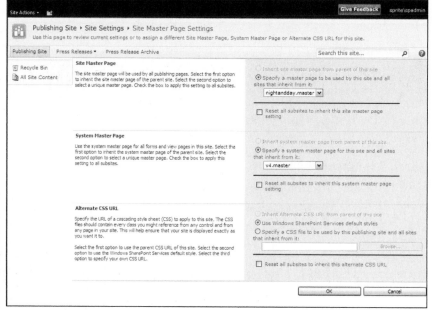

Figure 14-9:
The Site
Master
Page
Settings
page.

8. Click OK to apply your changes.

If you just chose a site master, you need to click a publishing page to see the results.

If you don't like the predefined SharePoint 2010 master pages, you can create your own custom master for your site. (See Chapter 20 for an overview of what this involves.)

Many resources are available on the Internet to give you branding guidance. You can also find many resources that you can contract to do the work if you decide not to do it yourself.

Chapter 15

Approving Content for Publication

In This Chapter

▶ Choosing between moderation options

▶ Enabling Content Approval

▶ Enabling Approval workflow

*T*rust, but verify: Sometimes you want to let folks create document library or list items but you don't want those items unleashed on an unsuspecting world before someone approves them. SharePoint has a few ways to help you enact and enforce content governance policies to define what gets published and under what conditions, how many revisions are retained, and how they're secured and tracked. Depending on the complexity of your approval process, you can use the standard Content Approval option, or you can create a more sophisticated — and custom — approval workflow.

In this chapter, I help you decide which process to use, and I walk you through using both processes.

Deciding Whether to Use Content Approval or Approval Workflows

Before you apply Content Approval or an approval workflow, make a few governance decisions:

- ✔ **Which lists and libraries contain (or will contain) content that will require approval?** This isn't the time to turn loose your inner control freak; your goal is to apply the minimum level of content governance necessary to achieve your approval goals.

- ✔ **What kind of approval process do you need?** Is the approval just a thumbs-up or thumbs-down process that Approvers can track and manage? If so, Content Approval will probably make you very happy. Or do you need a way for Reviewers to provide feedback and a way to track tasks associated with the reviews? In which case, you need an approval workflow.

✔ **Who needs to know about items that need approval?** Do you want Approvers to be notified when something needs their approval? If so, you need an approval workflow, with or without Content Approval.

✔ **Do you want the process to start automatically or do you want a manual trigger?** If you want a manual trigger, you need an approval workflow.

Choosing the Content Approval Option (Everything in Moderation)

Content Approval is approval-light; it's a publishing function that you turn on or off at the list or library level and it has just a handful of configuration settings. Content Approval — or *moderation* — doesn't include item routing or notifications, and it doesn't facilitate reviews and commenting. What Content Approval does do is help to ensure that drafts and new uploaded content don't get published to your list or library until someone with some authority says it's okay, and the Content Approval process controls who can see those things in the meantime.

Content Approval also can specify (in the case of documents) whether items must be checked out before they can be edited. And Content Approval can hide draft documents from everyone except the item author and those users with Approve permissions on the list or library (contrast this with draft item security on libraries without Content Approval enabled in which you can limit views only to users with library-level Read permissions or users with library-level Edit permissions). I sometimes use Content Approval on libraries in which my team stores documents that are intended for clients, if I want to review the documents before the client sees them.

This is a subtle distinction, but specifying that only the item author and users with Approve permissions can view items means that the author can check in an item without exposing it to the view of other readers or editors until it's formally published and approved. I find this useful in cases when I have multiple authorized contributors to a library and I want to keep them from seeing each others' work until someone (the Approver) says it's okay. This also gives me a way to let authors work on drafts without readers looking over their shoulders (few things are more frustrating than editorial feedback on something you're still working on!).

Is it drafty in here? Turning on Content Approval

By default, Content Approval is turned off and (usually) any user with Read access can see Draft items in most libraries. Sites created with the publishing site template, however, already have Content Approval turned on in the Pages library.

To turn on and configure Content Approval, follow these steps:

1. **Access Content Approval by going to your Library or List Settings page in your list or library and clicking the Versioning Settings link.**

   The Versioning Settings page appears.

   You see options to retain versions, specify who can see drafts, and — in document libraries — document check-out options.

2. **Enable Content Approval by selecting the Yes radio button below Require Content Approval for Submitted Items.**

   Notice that the options below Who Should See Draft Items in This Document Library? become available, as shown in Figure 15-1.

   You need to decide whether readers, editors, or only authors and Approvers can see drafts. I usually enable Content Approval partly because I don't want to expose items to just anyone before they meet some level of credibility or *done-ness* as indicated by the ~~Good Housekeeping~~ SharePoint Approval. So I select the Only Users Who Can Approve Items (And the Author of the Item) option.

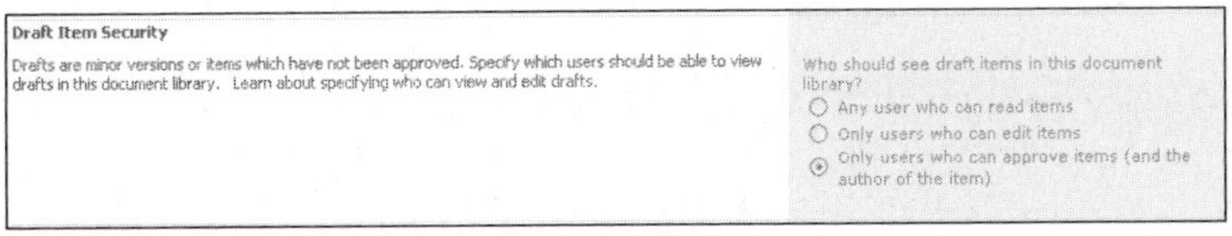

Figure 15-1:
The Draft Item Security settings are available.

Draft Item Security

Drafts are minor versions or items which have not been approved. Specify which users should be able to view drafts in this document library. Learn about specifying who can view and edit drafts.

Who should see draft items in this document library?
- ○ Any user who can read items
- ○ Only users who can edit items
- ◉ Only users who can approve items (and the author of the item)

3. **Verify the Document Version History settings in the Document Version History section.**

   You can specify versions *without* turning on Content Approval. I skip a detailed discussion of Document Version History settings here; it's pretty boring anyway.

4. Click a Draft Item Security option in the Draft Item Security section.

The security referred to by draft item security — Read, Edit, and Approve — maps to SharePoint's Visitors, Members, and Approvers groups. (See Chapter 12 for details on managing security groups.)

5. Click a check-out option in the Require Check Out section.

Flip to Chapter 2 if you aren't sure which option to choose.

6. Click OK to save your changes.

You return to the Library or List Settings page from whence you came. The items created in (or changed in) the list or library are subject to approval (unless of course you disable Content Approval later).

If Content Approval is active, when users add an item to the list or library, they see a note that items require Content Approval in the item properties window (see Figure 15-2). The item appears in Draft status in the list or library view until it's checked in for the first time, and then it changes to Pending until it's approved.

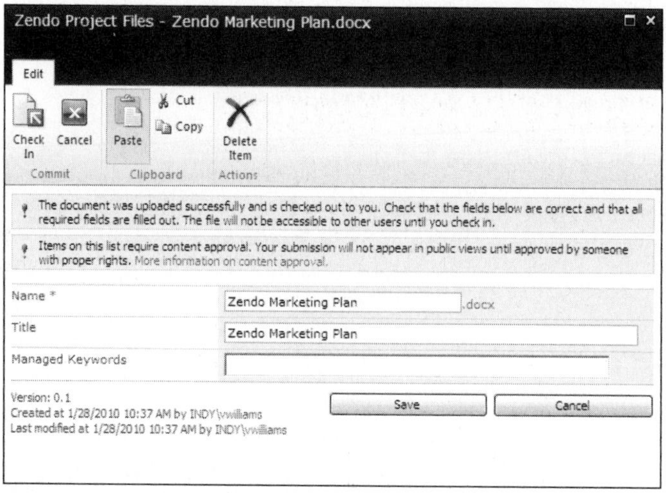

Figure 15-2:
A document's properties with an approval note.

Identifying Approvers

You need to specify who the Approvers include, generally by adding users to the created Approvers group. (See Chapter 12 for information about groups and permissions.)

Oh, and by the way, Content Approval isn't just about Big Brother — or, if it's me, nosy Big Sister — checking someone else's work. I may want to ensure that things can be checked in and versioned, but that they aren't displayed to Readers until they're formally approved. In these cases, I set the same person or people both to create and to approve items.

Casting an approving eye

In a library that has Approval turned on, when a new document is created and a major version is published, the Approval status is marked Pending and designated Approvers can approve, pend, or reject the item either from the list view by choosing Approve/Reject from the Edit menu, or by using the View Document Properties window. In either case, when you select Approve/Reject, you're presented with the aptly named Approve/Reject window, as shown in Figure 15-3, with the Pending option selected by default. At this point, you can leave a comment in the Comment text box but leave the item as Pending, or you can select the Approve or the Reject option to approve or reject the item with or without comment. (Rejecting without comment is pretty poor form, though.) The action, name of the person who took it, and timestamp are recorded in the item's Version History.

Figure 15-3:
The
Approve/
Reject
window.

You can get a quick view of all your items that are in a Pending status by choosing Site Actions➪Site Content Reports, and then choosing Pending Approval from the View drop-down list (see Figure 15-4).

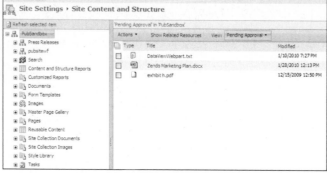

Figure 15-4:
View docu-
ments with
Pending
Approval
in the Site
Content
Report.

Unless alerts are enabled on the list/library or the item itself, the item originator won't know you've taken an action until the next time that person is in the list/library and checks the Approval status on the item. I recommend using alerts with Content Approval unless you have some alternative process whereby Approvers make it part of their daily routine to check for pending items.

Disapproval: Not just for stern parents

Everyone wants approval, but sometimes you don't get it. Sometimes an Approver rejects an item. When this happens, the item is changed to Rejected status and then it's visible only to the author and anyone with per-mission to manage the list.

When you first enable Content Approval on a library, all items are approved automatically.

Getting alerts on approval/rejection status

When an item is marked Pending with Content Approval turned on (and no associated approval workflow), that item just sits there, marinating in its own Pending status until someone notices and either approves or denies it. When the list/library I'm managing sees a lot of traffic, I rely on the Approvers to check for Pending items because they're working in the list/library all the time anyway. But another way to make sure Approvers get the heads-up is to set alerts (see Chapter 6).

If you turn off Content Approval, be aware that Pending and Rejected items, which were hidden from public view, are now viewable. I recommend resolv-ing all Draft, Pending, and Rejected items before disabling Content Approval; it's a dirty trick to reveal someone's draft to the world when she isn't expect-ing it!

Configuring Approval Workflows

Approval workflows can layer additional functions on top of Content Approval, or approval workflows can go it alone.

Approval workflow by itself doesn't affect who can see Draft items, and unlike Content Approval, doesn't control Item permissions. Approval workflow does create a task and an e-mail notification for each Approver when the workflow is initiated; for example, it can be useful for getting the attention of people who review documents but who otherwise don't spend a lot of time in the list/library.

In fact, because the notification and task include a link to the Pending item, an approval workflow is a good way to get the input of users who otherwise won't go to SharePoint. And approval workflow facilitates an exchange between the Approver and the author of the content by allowing the Approver to provide feedback on the document (better to have dubbed it Review workflow).

There are three components of using Approval workflow: Configuring the workflow for the list/library, initiating the workflow for a document or list item, and responding to the workflow.

Approval workflow options

Think of a workflow as a business process that you automate. Say you have a business process for reviewing and approving real estate contracts. This process may include someone drafting the contract, e-mailing a copy to someone who reviews it and then e-mails it to someone else for approval. The approval workflows in SharePoint provide all these options so you can automate the routing of the document from the person drafting it to the document's reviews and approvers.

You can select options for how you want the Approval workflow to work when you associate the workflow with your library, which I describe how to do in the next section.

The following list describes the options available for a approval workflows:

✔ **Approvers (Assign To):** Individuals and groups to whom the Approval tasks will be assigned. If you have multiple Approvers, you can also specify the order in which they're assigned the item. The Approval status doesn't change from Pending to Approved until all Approvers have approved the item.

Unless you have the Cancel on Rejection option enabled, if an Approver rejects an item, the approval continues to the next Approver and isn't cancelled as you might expect.

✓ **Approvers (Order):** Specifies whether the Approvers will be assigned the Approval tasks all at once or whether when one person approves, the next person is assigned the task, and so on.

Go with the standard — arrange Approvers in ascending order of importance so you don't bother the director until the managers have approved.

✓ **Add a New Stage:** Allows you to add a stage to the approval process. Don't get carried away here because you have to manage all those stages.

✓ **Expand Groups:** If selected, assigns an Approval task to each individual in each Approver group, rather than assigning a single task to the entire group. If you've also specified an order, all Approvers in the expanded group are treated as one Approver, and they're assigned the approval when the group is.

✓ **Notification Message:** The message that's sent to each member of each Approval group. All Approvers get the same notification message, and I recommend saying, "Please."

✓ **Due Date for All Tasks:** A date by which all tasks not completed are considered overdue; this overrides the Duration for Serial Tasks/Duration Units values.

✓ **Duration for Serial Tasks:** A number which, with the Duration Units field, determines how long each serial task can be active before being marked Overdue.

✓ **Duration Units:** With the Duration for Serial Tasks option, determines how long a serial task can be active before being marked Overdue.

✓ **CC:** Notifies specified people when the workflow is started but doesn't assign tasks to them (unless they're also in the Approvers group).

✓ **Cancel on Rejection:** Cancels the entire workflow if one Approver marks the item rejected. The item moves to Rejected status, and the item author is notified.

In any case, if Cancel on Rejection is selected, when one Approver rejects the item, this halts the Approval workflow for this round, until the item is resubmitted. I recommend listing the tougher critics as earlier Approvers to reduce the number of times you have to request approval from someone who's already given it.

✓ **Cancel on Change:** Cancels the workflow if the item is changed while the workflow is running.

> If you work in a regulated industry and are requesting approval of regulated items, I highly recommend enabling this option.

> ✔ **Enable Content Approval:** For the most reliable results, configure your Approval workflow before turning on Content Approval.

Need more options? You can create your own workflows or customize the approval workflows provided by SharePoint using SharePoint Designer 2010 or Visual Studio 2010.

Setting up an Approval workflow

Approval workflow is one of several workflow templates in SharePoint 2010. To set an approval workflow, follow these steps:

1. **Access the Library Settings page using the Ribbon in your library.**

2. **In the Permissions and Management settings options, click the Workflow Settings link.**

   The Add a Workflow page is displayed, as shown in Figure 15-5.

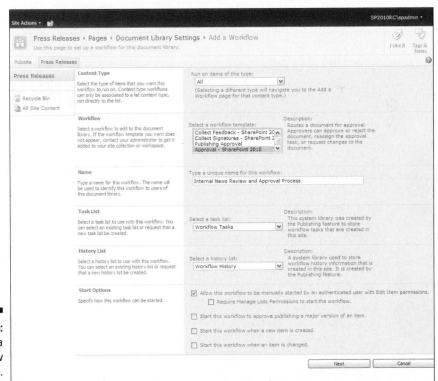

Figure 15-5: The Add a Workflow page.

3. **Click the Approval - SharePoint 2010 template option in the Select a Workflow Template list.**

4. **Enter a name in the Type a Unique Name for This Workflow text box.**

   I recommend choosing a name that describes the step in your business process this workflow fulfills. In my experiences, most business processes can have several approval steps, so calling it The Approval Workflow isn't meaningful.

   For example, if your approval workflow is actually a review workflow, call it the Author Review Workflow. If you need to add a second approval workflow, you could call it the Regulatory Editorial Review Workflow.

5. **Use the Select a Task List drop-down list to choose a task list.**

   I recommend going with the default — Workflow Tasks — unless you have a special reason for wanting to track this workflow in a list by itself.

6. **Use the Select a History List drop-down list to choose a history list.**

   Again, I suggest accepting the default, which is Workflow History.

7. **Select a Start option by selecting the appropriate check box.**

   Decide how you want the workflow to be triggered. If you want the workflow to start manually, select the check box Allow This Workflow to Be Manually Started by an Authenticated User with Edit Item Permissions.

   Note: You can have only one workflow that's triggered by publishing in a library.

8. **Click the Next button.**

   The Page Approval page appears, as shown in Figure 15-6. See the options I discuss in the "Approval workflow options" section, earlier in this chapter, and then specify the appropriate options.

9. **Click the Save button.**

By default, Content Approval is enabled on publishing portals. This can be confusing because when Content Approval is enabled, a document doesn't become visible to others until it's published. I've seen a few "It's right there," "No, it isn't," "Yes, it is!" exchanges that were a result of someone not realizing this and failing to check in and publish their document. To determine whether Publishing workflow is enabled on your library, open the document library and click the Properties icon for any document. If Workflows is an option, you're all set.

If you have an alert enabled on a library/list, and approval is also turned on for that library/list, you may not receive a notification until a new or changed item is approved and published.

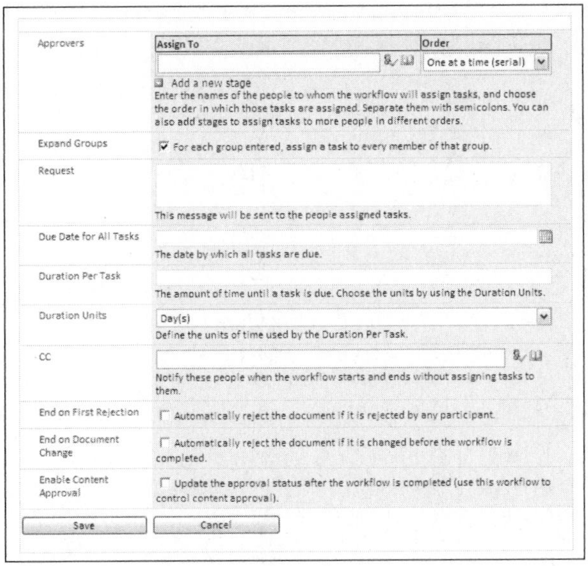

Figure 15-6:
The Page
Approval
page.

If you just need approvals, the Approval workflow may be overkill. Consider turning off workflow and just keeping approvals, with or without versioning. Items that require approval will quietly sit there (like my dog Rosie by the kitchen at dinnertime) waiting for someone to take notice.

Initiating a workflow

Configuring your library to use a workflow only solves part of the problem. If you don't have your library configured to kick-off automatically, then someone must manually start the workflow.

Manually initiate a workflow by following these steps:

1. **Browse to the item you want approved, click the drop-down list (see Figure 15-7), and choose Workflows.**

   You see the Workflows page for that library or list.

2. **Under Start a New Workflow, select the Approval workflow you want to initiate.**

   The form to initiate the workflow displays, populated with the default values specified during the workflow configuration; you can accept the defaults or change them (see Figure 15-8).

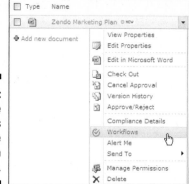

Figure 15-7:
Choose
Workflows
from the
drop-down
list.

The forms you see in Figures 15-6 and 15-8 are part of the workflow. You can customize these forms or create entirely new forms to meet your business process needs using InfoPath 2010, SharePoint Designer 2010, and Visual Studio 2010. The combination of tools you need depends on how sophisticated you need your workflow to be.

Figure 15-8:
Accept or
change the
workflow
options.

3. **Click the Start button.**

A Workflow task is created in the specified task list and is assigned to the first Approver. If e-mail alerts are enabled, an e-mail is sent to that person with a link to the item, instructions, and a link to the associated task. The Requestor also receives an e-mail indicating that the task has been started as well as a link to the item and the workflow status page.

Approving an item

If you're an Approver on an item, follow these steps to respond to an approval request:

1. **Review the item using the link in the e-mail request or by accessing the item directly in the library.**

2. **Enter comments in the Your Comments text box.**

3. **Click a button to indicate what you want to do with this item (see Figure 15-9):**

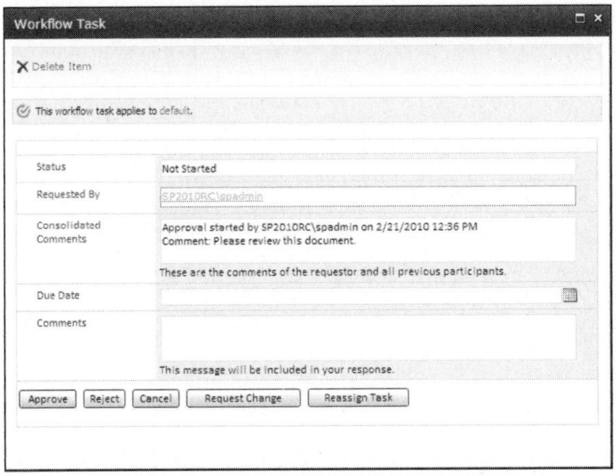

Figure 15-9: Task details for an Approver.

- *Click the Approve button to approve the item.* If you approve the item and there are no other Approvers, the task is marked Completed and the outcome is Approved. If there are other Approvers, the task is assigned to the next Approver on the list, if any, and the Requestor is notified. The task version history is updated.

- *Click the Reject button to reject it.* If you reject the item, the task is marked Completed and the outcome is Rejected.

- *Click the Cancel button to back out of this task.*

- *Click the Request Change button to indicate that further edits are needed.* The Workflow Task window displays, as shown in Figure 15-10. Enter the name of the person whom you want to make the change in the Request Change From text box, a description of your request in the Your Request text box, the task duration (if any) in the Duration for Serial Tasks, and select a time unit from the Duration Units drop-down list, and then click the Send button. A new task is created for the person you specified, and your task status is marked Completed.

- *Click the Reassign Task button to ask someone else to approve the item.* If you reassign the task, you're prompted to enter the name of the person to whom it should be reassigned. A new task is created and your task is marked Complete but the status is Delegated.

The Requestor is notified each time the task is updated.

Workflow Task	

✗ Delete Item

⊘ This workflow task applies to default.

Request Change From

Enter the name of the person to request a change from. If this field is left blank, the change request will be sent to the person who started the workflow.

New Request

This message will be included with your request.

New Duration

The amount of time until the task is due. To keep the existing due date, leave this field blank. To remove the due date, type the number '0'. Choose the units by using the New Duration Units.

New Duration Units   Day(s)

Define the units of time used by the New Duration.

Send   Cancel

Figure 15-10: Request the author to make changes.

Don't confuse status with outcome. *Status* merely indicates whether the workflow task is Active or Complete. *Outcome* is what tells you whether the item really passed muster and was approved. Whether the item was approved or rejected, the task status is marked as Complete when the last Approver has approved or rejected it. However, the task outcome indicates whether the item was approved or rejected.

You can also respond to an approval request by accessing the items using Site Actions⇨Site Content and Structure, locating the item in the site hierarchy, and then using the item's context menu to select an Approval option. Alternatively, you can also edit the task from Outlook or from the SharePoint task list.

Checking the status of an Approval workflow

Requestors and Reviewers can check the status of an Approval workflow as follows:

1. **Navigate to the site for which you want to check the status of one or more Approval workflows.**

2. **Choose Site Actions⇨View Site Content Reports.**

   The Site Content and Structure page appears, as shown in Figure 15-11.

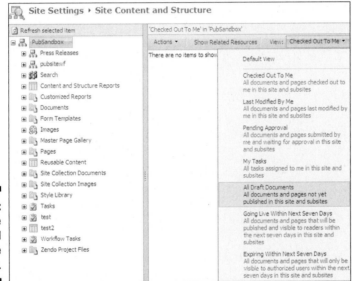

Figure 15-11:
The Site
Content and
Structure
page.

3. **To view the status of items specific to you, select an item from the View drop-down list:**

   • *For Requestors,* choosing Pending Approval displays all items that you've submitted for approval and aren't completed yet.

   • *For Approvers,* choosing My Tasks displays all tasks, including Approval workflow tasks, assigned to you.

4. **To view all tasks (your own as well as those assigned to other people), click Workflow Tasks in the navigation pane on the left and then choose All Tasks from the View drop-down list.**

   The Workflow Tasks – All Tasks page appears.

5. **Click any task to view its details.**

A light touch with Content Approval and Approval workflow can help facilitate reviews, support governance policies, and help you track and retain information about whether content has passed the right checkpoints before being formalized. Experiment with them alone or in combination until you hit on the process that works.

Chapter 16

Creating Page Layouts with SharePoint Designer

In This Chapter

▶ Working with placeholders, page layouts, and master pages

▶ Deciding on your content controls and content types

▶ Creating a new page layout in various ways

▶ Adding containers and controls to your layout

*I*n Chapter 14, I show you how to choose and apply different page layout templates in SharePoint 2010. Like many other applications, when I started with these templates, I was perfectly happy until I realized that I couldn't do this, or that, or that other thing (you get the picture). Sometimes you just need to create your own layouts.

Many SharePoint techies and branding resources may confuse what functionality they get from the master page (or the *outer template*) and what functionality they get from the page layout until they populate page content. Then they realize it'd help to have the title display (or not display) in a certain location, to have a certain Web Part embedded on the page, or to keep the content on the right to a certain width. Here's when shortcomings of a predefined page layout start to appear.

SharePoint 2010 comes with multiple default page layouts for a publishing site, as shown in Figure 16-1. Several of these are extremely flexible in terms of what types of content you can add and where on the page you can add them to. However, when you're using SharePoint for the Internet or across corporate intranet pages, you start to value the ease and control of specific page layouts you can provide your content editors.

I use some HTML terms in this chapter. After all, SharePoint page layouts are Web pages. Before you do any major modifications of a page layout or create a new page layout, you should be familiar with SharePoint and ASP.NET controls, HTML, and CSS. Minor modifications, such as changing the orientation of a Web Part zone or adding additional predefined controls, can be done with the SharePoint Designer 2010 interface without detailed Web design training.

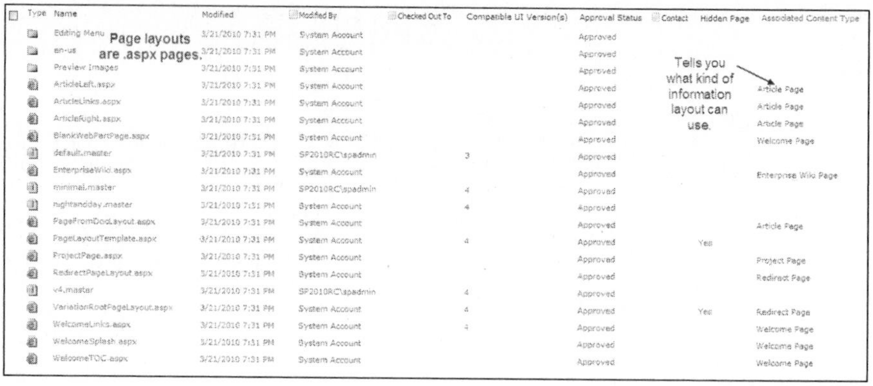

Figure 16-1:
The default
Page
Layouts.

Getting Inside a SharePoint Page Layout

Have you ever wondered what's going on behind the scenes in SharePoint? Cracking open a page layout is one of the easiest ways to do that. Start by opening one of the standard SharePoint page layouts in SharePoint Designer 2010:

1. **Open SharePoint Designer 2010 and then click the Open Site button and type (or paste) in the Web address to your publishing site.**

   You must access a site created using the Publishing site template to work with page layouts. (See Chapter 13 for details on creating new sites.)

2. **In the navigation pane, click the Page Layouts button.**

   A list of the page layouts in your site appears.

3. **Click the Blank Web Part Page layout file.**

   A summary of the file appears, which shows the file's versioning status and permissions as well as provides links to customize the file.

4. **In the Customization section, click the Edit File link, as shown in Figure 16-2.**

5. **When prompted to check out the file, click No.**

   Because you're just browsing, don't check out the file.

   The file opens in Design view for your viewing pleasure, as shown in Figure 16-3.

While Design view is interesting, the Code view is where all the real action takes place. To access the Code view of the page layout, click the Code button at the button of the screen, which you can see in Figure 16-4, along with the Code view.

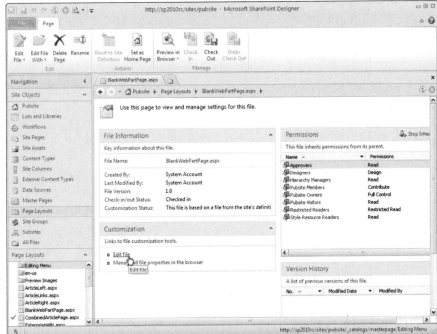

Figure 16-2:
Open a page layout for editing.

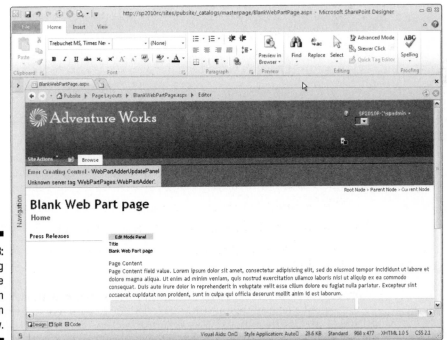

Figure 16-3:
Looking over the layout in Design view.

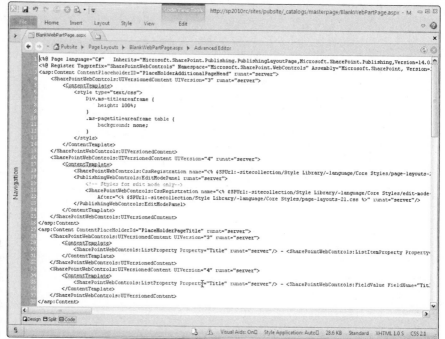

Figure 16-4:
Looking
over the lay-
out in Code
view.

If you're like me, the first thing you notice in the text editor is that all the text is highlighted in a sickly orange. That's because the page opens by default in basic Edit mode, which protects you from changing anything you aren't supposed to change. To make the highlight disappear, click the Advanced Mode button on the Home tab of the Ribbon.

Here I walk you through this page layout at a very high level and give you an overview of what you see (refer to Figure 16-4). Starting from the top, you see these elements:

- **Standard registrations and page directives:** The top of the ASPX page contains standard registrations needed for the page layout to work with SharePoint. *Warning:* Leave this code alone unless you know what you're doing.

  The page directives are everything that you see included in the symbols:

  ```
  <%@ some page directive here %>
  ```

  The directives at the top of the page are responsible for registering groups of controls with your page layout. Each directive designates a tag prefix attribute that defines the prefix that you must use to access the controls associated with the directive. If you try to use a control that isn't registered or you use an incorrect prefix, you get an error when you view your page in the browser. This is all ASP.NET stuff; it's not specific to SharePoint.

✔ **Content placeholders:** As you scroll down the page, notice that all the markup in the page is contained with special content tags that look like this:

```
<asp:Content ContentPlaceholderID=
"PlaceHolderNameGoesHere" runat="server">
. . . Markup goes here . . .
</asp:Content>
```

These content placeholders are predefined in the site's master page. Any content placeholder that you see in the page layout replaces the content that's normally found in the master page. For example, most master pages have a PlaceHolderLeftNavBar content placeholder where the Quick Launch menu and other navigation controls are placed. By placing this placeholder in your page layout, you can override what's in the master page and display your own content in that placeholder.

In most cases, you won't make any changes to the layout's page directives, but you'll most definitely be working with the content placeholders. That's the whole point of creating a page layout — to define something that you want to happen that's different than the master page.

All your changes must reside inside a content placeholder in your page layout.

Working with content placeholders

SharePoint Designer makes it easy to override placeholders from the master page. To put your content into a placeholder instead of using the master page's content:

1. **Open a page layout in Edit mode, which I describe in the preceding section, and check it out by clicking Yes when prompted to check out the file.**

   I recommend doing this in a non-production site. If you have to use a production site, be sure to discard your changes without publishing a major version.

2. **Place the page in Design mode by clicking the Design button in the lower-left corner of the screen.**

   You see a *WYSIWYG (what you see is what you get)* display of the page layout. Most of what you see actually comes from the master page.

3. **Hover your mouse over different areas of the page.**

   As you do, notice that names of placeholders appear. Those with *Master* in them display content from the master page. Those with *Custom* are in your page layout.

4. Find the PlaceHolderMain content placeholder and click it.

The PlaceHolderMain content placeholder is used to contain the body of the page, so it's usually the largest placeholder on the page.

One way to make sure you've selected the proper element is to use the Visual Aids tags at the bottom of the screen.

5. In the Visual Aids toolbar, click the `<asp:Content>` tag and choose Select Tag, as shown in Figure 16-5.

The entire tag is highlighted.

6. Click the Split button on the View tab of the Ribbon to display half the page in Code view and the other half in Design view.

The PlaceHolderMain content placeholder and its contents are highlighted. As you select different elements in Design view, notice that the code is highlighted in the Code view. This is a great way to browse through a layout and see how it works.

7. Select the PlaceHolderPageDescription content placeholder in Design view and click the arrow on the far right of the placeholder.

A smart tag appears. Any place you see these arrows, click them and then you see common tasks that are associated with that placeholder or control.

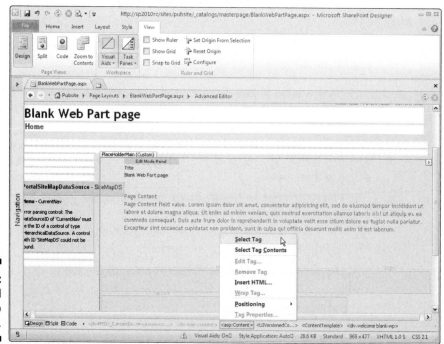

Figure 16-5:
Use visual aids to select tags.

8. **In the Common Content Tasks tag, click Create Custom Content.**

   The placeholder appears in Code view.

9. **In Code view or Design view, type** Hello world **in the PlaceHolderPageDescription content placeholder.**

10. **Preview your changes in the browser by clicking the Preview in Browser button on the Home tab of the Ribbon.**

As you may have surmised, the PlaceHolderContentMain placeholder is the one you use most often. The other placeholders are used for more specialized content, such as navigation bars and editing consoles. Another useful placeholder is PlaceHolderAdditionalPageHead. If you know anything about the markup used to create Web pages, you know that all Web pages have a head section where you place the title and references to style sheets and JavaScript files. Anything you put in the PlaceHolderAdditionalPageHead placeholder is merged into the master page's head section.

Page layouts and styles

Page layouts get styles from a myriad of places, including the core style sheet, page layout CSS, Edit mode styles, the style sheet attached to any master used, item styles for controls and Web Parts, such as Summary Link and Content Query, and the list goes on.

Chapter 20 talks about where to put your own styles if you create them. Figuring out what and where SharePoint styles are and how to override them are time-consuming processes. If you're creating custom page layouts, especially if you're following Web and accessibility standards and are using a CSS-based layout, at a minimum, you're probably going to write a few styles to position the content on the page, unless you started from a predefined layout.

The relationship between the page layout and a master page

In Chapter 14, I touch on the relationship between a master page and the page layout as well as how the master (the *outer template*) works with the page layout (the *inner template*). This relationship, and its dependencies, becomes more pronounced with custom-designed master pages and page layouts.

Although this chapter is about custom page layouts, not master pages, they often go hand in hand in a branded SharePoint Internet or intranet site.

Sometimes my clients are surprised when a custom master page doesn't look good with every out-of-the-box page layout or vice versa. This might have to do with fixed sizes versus fluid layouts or elements shown in the page layout that aren't styled in the master CSS. One example of this disconnect is when an out-of-the-box page layout contains an element, such as page bread-crumbs or navigation flyouts, that you may not have styled in a style sheet attached to the master.

If having your page layout work well with any master page in the site collection is important to you, test, test, and test and then make adjustments.

Having your page layout work well with a master page comes into play a lot with intranets. Examples of this are when different sites can be created under the site you planned, you don't foresee what combination of page layouts and master pages the owners and editors select, you don't know how many levels of navigation they'll choose, and so forth.

If you're creating an Internet or custom intranet site and have no intention of using anything but your custom master with custom page layouts, you can restrict the page layouts used.

Making Decisions before You Start

Depending on site complexity, you may need to consider making a new content type and/or additional site columns for your page layouts.

If your site needs are basic and you simply want a variation of an out-of-the-box page layout, skip ahead to the section, "Creating a New Page Layout," later in this chapter. However, if you want your pages to have additional fields beyond those provided in the Article Page and Welcome Page content types, consider the following:

✔ **Do you need a new content type for your pages?**

Do you want to be able to manage the pages by the content type, including rolling up content under just this type? Are the out-of-the-box page content types too detailed or too simple for your needs? If so, you need to create your new content type and add the necessary site columns. (Review Chapter 22 on content types to understand inheritance and how picking the parent content type can help or hinder your efforts.)

✔ **Do you need new field controls or site columns for your pages?**

Regardless of whether you create a new custom content type or use a predefined one, you may not have all the page fields or content fields you need.

For example, usually only one page content control is in a SharePoint out-of-the-box page layout. What if you need more than one content control? You can create additional site columns based on the Full HTML column type with formatting and constraints for the publishing type. Several other fields are created for publishing or content management as well, including images, hyperlinks, and summary links.

After creating and adding these to the appropriate content type, they're available to insert into your page layout.

✔ **Do you have what you need for branding, static content, and page layout?**

One of the compelling reasons for creating a new page layout is because you want to lay out your content in a different way on the page. Maybe you want to have four columns, to use tabs, or to have all your new pages display text to help the person using it to create a new page. Gather your thoughts around what you want to accomplish with this new layout.

Create a *prototype* (or a roadmap) before you actually create your page layout. In the process, think about stuff that you don't know how to do; if you can't do it outside SharePoint, you can't do it in SharePoint. If you aren't a whiz at HTML and CSS, don't fret. You can probably cobble together what you need by looking at other page layouts, and you can find lots of tutorials on the Web.

One way to discover interesting ways of using HTML and CSS is to use the browser to look at the source of any Web page, such as a SharePoint Web page. All browsers give you the ability to view the source of the Web page. Another good approach is to use the Firefox browser along with the Web Developer and Firebug extensions.

Creating New Page Content Fields

SharePoint's default publishing content types — Article Page and Welcome Page — usually provide most of the site columns you need for creating publishing pages. The site columns in a page layout's content types map to the fields that are available for entering content in the page layout. For example, both the Article Page and Welcome Page content types include the Page Content field. This is usually the main field on the page where users enter their content. What if you want your page layout to display the division of your company associated with each publishing page? You use a site column to add the division field to your page layout.

In this section, I describe how to create new site columns and associate them with content types, and how to add them to your page layouts.

Page layouts are supposed to be templates that your users use to create publishing pages. If those templates don't make it easy for your users to enter content, then they aren't very good templates. One way to make your page layouts better is to add the fields, or *site columns*, that allow users to enter their content.

Creating a site column for page content

In Chapter 4, I include detailed instructions on creating a new site column. However, if you need to make new page content fields to add to your page layout, here's an overview focusing on the publishing content column types:

1. **Navigate to the Site Columns Gallery by choosing Site Actions⇨Site Settings and then clicking the Site Columns link.**

   You're in the Site Column Gallery.

2. **Click the Create button at the top of the page to create a new site column.**

   The New Site Column page appears.

3. **In the Name and Type section, type a name for your site column in the Column Name field and then select your new column type.**

   The following types are part of the publishing framework (see Figure 16-6):

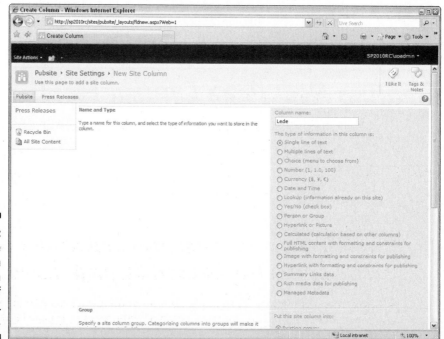

Figure 16-6:
A new site column showing a selection of full HTML content.

- *Full HTML Content with Formatting and Constraints for Publishing:* This is the same kind of column type as the out-of-the-box page content control; basically, a general HTML editor where you can add text, images, tables, hyperlinks, styles, and so forth.

- *Image with Formatting and Constraints for Publishing:* A publishing image control that allows for a hyperlink. Because this control is part of the publishing Web content structure, you can rely on the versioning and approval process of the page versus a Web Part.

- *Hyperlink with Formatting and Constraints for Publishing:* A publishing control that allows you to select a hyperlink to display in your Web page.

- *Summary Links Data:* Summary Links provide more benefits than a Links list or individual links you create because they come with the ability to create groupings and apply several predefined styles. Two Summary Link fields are provided out-of-the-box.

- *Rich Media Data for Publishing:* A container with all the publishing content management benefits for Silverlight content.

  Of course, all the other SharePoint column types you know and love, such as Choice fields and Managed Metadata, are fair game for page layouts.

4. **Select a group for your column using the drop-down list in the Group section.**

   Selecting a predefined group or adding your own makes it easier to locate in the Site Columns library and when you select it for inclusion in a content type.

   For the type of content I'm describing, you may want to add it to the Page Layout Columns group or a custom group.

5. **Select or add other properties as applicable.**

   These may include a description, whether the field is required or unique, and so on.

6. **Click OK to create your site column.**

   Your site column is created and can be added to content types.

You can use this same process for creating new page fields (information about the page, not content) for your custom layout.

Adding your publishing content site column to a content type used by page layouts

Before you can add your new site column to the page layout in the form of a content control, it must be included in a content type for page layouts. You can add your new site column to a new custom content type you made or add it to predefined page layout content types.

I discuss the predefined page layout content types, such as Article and Welcome, in Chapter 14. If you're using those content types to create new page layouts (for example, several new Article Page layouts), you can add your new site columns to that type for use, rather than create a new custom type.

If you're creating custom content types for your project, which could be desirable for long-term maintenance and content management in projects that have many variations from out-of-the-box SharePoint, add the site column in the same way to your custom content type.

I discuss creating new content types at length in Chapter 22; however, here are a couple items of note about content types for page layouts. You can *inherit* columns by picking predefined content types as parents for your new content type, automatically adding all the columns they contain. If you want more control over your custom type, you may choose a more skeletal parent with less base information.

Sometimes creating your first custom content type is easier than reviewing existing ones. To do so, follow these steps:

1. **Navigate to the Site Content Types Gallery by choosing Site Actions⇨Site Settings, and then click the Site Content Types link.**

2. **Scroll down to locate the Page Layout Content Types group and the Publishing Content Types group in the library.**

   Article Page and Welcome Page types are in the Page Layout Content Types group, and the Page type is in the Publishing Content Types group.

3. **Click the Welcome Page or Article Page link to open the content type.**

   You see the columns they contain, and near top of the page, you see their parent — the Page content type.

4. **Click the Add From Existing Site Columns link to add your site column to the content type.**

   The Add Columns to Content Type page appears.

5. **In the Select Columns section, select the column you created in the previous section.**

6. **Click OK.**

   The site column is added to the content type. Figure 16-7 shows the Welcome Page content with a new site column called Division. You still have to add the site column to your page layout in order for it to be visible to users when they create new publishing pages using your layout.

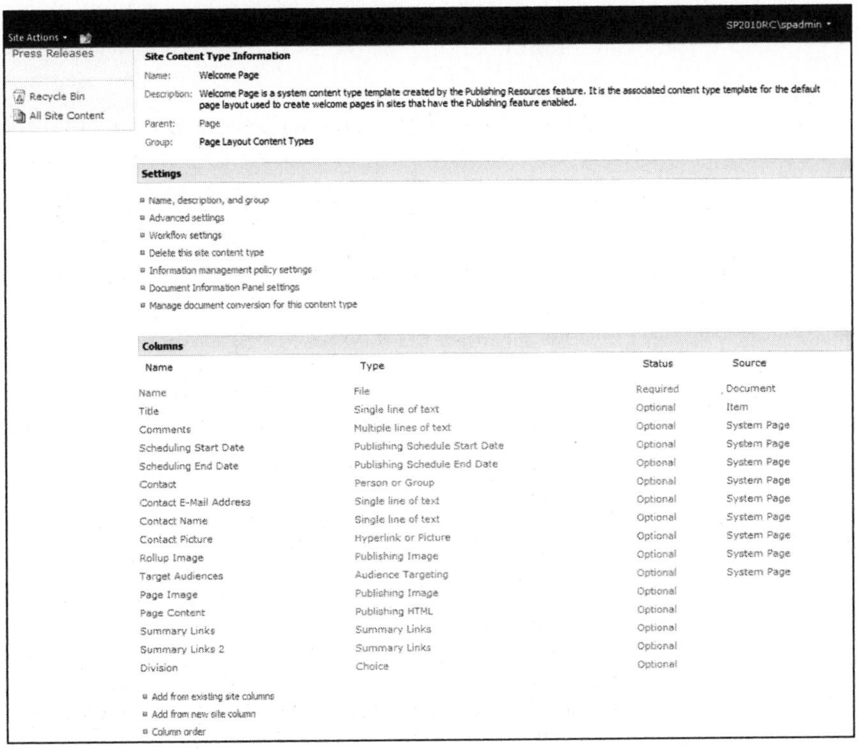

Figure 16-7:
Adding a site column to a content type.

Adding your site column to the page layout

With your site column added to the content type, now you have to add the site column to the page layout. Here's how:

1. **Open your page layout in Edit mode in SharePoint Designer 2010.**

   See the section "Getting Inside a SharePoint Page Layout," earlier in this chapter if you need a refresher for editing an existing page layout. If you want to create a new page layout, see the next section.

2. **Open the Toolbox by clicking the View tab on the Ribbon and then choosing Task Panes➪Toolbox.**

3. **In the Toolbox task pane, expand the SharePoint Controls pane.**

4. **Click the plus (+) sign to expand the Content Fields section.**

   You see a list of site columns, or content fields, listed, as shown in Figure 16-8. You can click the Refresh button to make sure you have the latest list of columns from the server.

The content fields you see listed here come from the list of site columns associated with the page layout's content type. If you don't see all the fields you expect, then double check your content type.

5. **To add your content field to the page layout, drag and drop the field from the Toolbox to your page layout.**

It doesn't matter whether you're in Design view or Code view. SharePoint Designer inserts the code that represents the field control.

You can't just drag a content control onto the page and rename the field-name property.

6. **Click the Save button on the File tab to save your page layout.**

Test that your change works as expected by creating a new publishing page that uses your page layout. I describe how to create new publishing pages in Chapter 14.

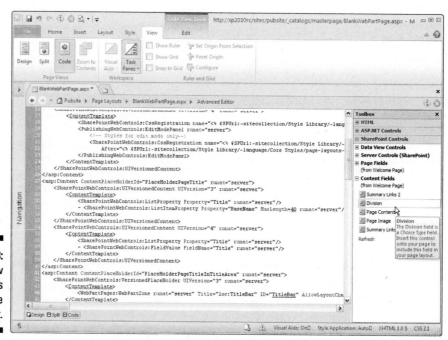

Figure 16-8:
Add new page fields to your page layout.

A word on custom

I hate to get hung up on *custom,* but you need to know the relevance of SharePoint customization in case IT starts to emit smoke and fire. *Customize,* in a SharePoint sense, means that you modified an out-of-the-box element and it's no longer part of the site definition. That can be a big deal, so don't take it lightly, and check with your IT SharePoint advisors if you're unsure.

I don't like to change out-of-the-box files from SharePoint, and in almost all cases, I don't have to. I generally create a new page from an existing layout and then change what I need. Technically, this becomes a different page layout, and even though it's custom to me, it doesn't "customize" the out-of-the-box page layout.

When I use *custom* in this chapter, I mean new page layouts, master, or content types. I wouldn't bring the wrath of IT down on you by suggesting you "customize" out-of-the-box elements.

Creating a New Page Layout

While it's possible to create a new page layout from an existing one, I don't recommend it. Instead, I suggest you create a new page layout from scratch. I believe it's too easy to make mistakes when you copy and modify an existing layout.

If there is an existing page layout that's close to what you want, then I suggest you study what you like about that layout and manually recreate it as a new page layout. Because a page layout is used in conjunction with a master page, you also have to be familiar with the structure of your master page. You can use SharePoint Designer 2010 to open your site's master page and review its structure and content placeholders.

Examples of modifications you may want to make to a page layout can include using DIV tags to create the structure of the page, inserting Web Part zones, adding new content controls, adding ASP.NET and HTML controls, adding additional styles in the head of the page, and/or attaching a style sheet for that page.

Make sure that you have SharePoint Designer 2010, that your organization supports you having it, and that you have the correct permissions before you start.

Page layouts and master pages, although they can be applied at a subsite level, reside in the top-level site in the site collection.

To create a new page layout:

1. **Open your publishing site in SharePoint Designer 2010.**

2. **Click the Page Layouts button in the Navigation pane.**

3. **Click the New Page Layout button on the Page Layout tab of the Ribbon.**

   The New dialog box appears, as shown in Figure 16-9.

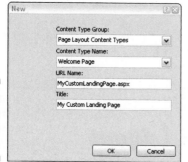

Figure 16-9:
Create a
new page
layout.

4. **In the Content Type Group dialog box, select the content type group for the content type you want to use.**

   If you're using SharePoint's publishing content types, then select Page Layout Content Types. Otherwise, select the content type group that you use in Step 4 in the section "Creating a site column for page content," earlier in this chapter.

5. **Select your content type from the Content Type Name drop-down list.**

6. **Type the filename for your page layout in the URL Name text box.**

7. **Type the title for your page layout in the Title text box.**

8. **Click OK.**

   SharePoint Designer 2010 creates your new page layout and opens it for you to begin editing.

A page layout is like any other kind of document in SharePoint. It's stored in a document library, has properties, and can be checked out, version controlled, and subject to content approval.

The document library where page layouts (and master pages) are stored is called the Master Page Gallery. You can access this library using either SharePoint Designer 2010 or the browser. To access this library from the browser:

1. **Browse to your site collection.**

2. **Choose Site Actions⇨Site Settings.**

    The Site Settings page appears.

3. **Click the Master Pages and Page Layouts link.**

    The Master Page Gallery opens.

Figure 16-10 shows the Master Page Gallery with a custom page layout.

Before you can start using your page layout to create new publishing pages, you need to check it in and approve the file. You can read about managing documents in document libraries in Chapter 8.

Your new page layout is available to you and your editors when you create a new publishing page or change the page settings for a publishing page of the same content type.

When you or your users initially select a page layout and then decide to change the page layout later, you can make changes only to other pages of the same content type. Therefore, if I have no specific need for a custom content type, I often choose the Welcome Page type so that my users can change the default home page of a site to my new page layout because the home page is usually some sort of welcome.

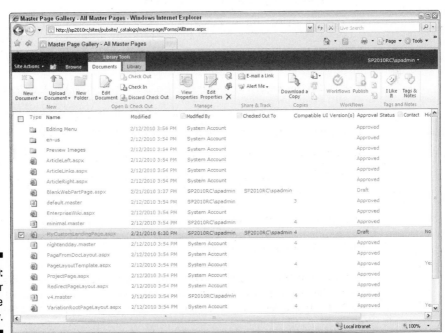

Figure 16-10:
The Master
Page
Gallery.

In the sections that follow, I tell you how to restrict the page layouts your editors can select and set the default page layout for new subsites in the site collection.

Putting Containers and Controls in Your Layout

You may be wondering what goes inside these content placeholders in your page layout. Although you can place text and HTML markup inside placeholders, most often you put fields, controls, containers, and Web Parts in your page layout.

A *page layout* is a kind of ASP.NET page. Most any controls that you might use in an ASP.NET page are fair game for SharePoint. A most notable exception is the regular ASP.NET data source controls. SharePoint has its own data source controls that you use instead.

If you really want to get hard-core with your page layout development, I suggest getting acquainted with creating Web sites with ASP.NET. Visual Studio Web Developer is a free download, and you can use it to get started in ASP. NET. Most of what you know in ASP.NET can be applied to SharePoint pages.

Here are multiple control types that you can put in a page layout to contain content:

✔ **Web Parts/Web Part zones:** Web Part zones are containers that contain other containers — Web Parts. Generally, you place zones in a way that defines the page layout using a combination of HTML/CSS positioning and inserted zones. By default, the zones are oriented *vertically;* the Web Parts inserted are stacked up and down, and you can move them above or below each other. Web Part zones, however, have properties that can be set in SharePoint Designer that allow Web Parts to sit horizontally next to each other.

In SharePoint 2010, you can insert Web Parts directly into a page layout without a zone; but remember, this should be done only when an element should be on every page using that page layout, and there are benefits to not using a zone or letting the page editors control the Web Part.

✔ **HTML controls:** HTML controls that can be inserted include HTML markups, such as IMG tags, DIV tags, paragraph tags, and HTML form controls, such as input boxes and submit buttons. You can manually type HTML in the page layout as well.

- ✔ **ASP.NET controls:** If you have .Net programming experience, you'll recognize many of the ASP.NET controls you can insert, such as standard controls like ad rotators, calendars, and ASP.NET form controls. These also include data controls, such as grid views and data sources, validation controls, such as RequiredFieldValidator, and navigation controls.

- ✔ **SharePoint controls:** Data View and server controls specific to SharePoint as well as page fields and content fields.

- ✔ **Page fields:** Site columns about the page itself; for example, Comments, Content Type, and Title Scheduling Start Date.

   To assist editors, you can place some of these fields in the Edit mode panel so that they can edit while they're editing the page instead of navigating to the page library to edit. Content shown in the Edit mode panel isn't visible to users viewing the approved page.

- ✔ **Content controls:** Controls on the page that store content, such as summary links, page image, and page content are different from Web Parts.

Page fields and content controls are site columns in the content type associated with your page layout. Any time you want to add a new field or content control to your page layout, you must add a site column to your content type.

Generally, SharePoint page layouts for publishing sites contain at least one content control (an HTML container) as well as Web Part zones. However, you can make additional field controls in the browser as site columns and add to page layout content types for insertion on the page.

I often find that I need a main page content control in the middle area of the page and a right-hand callout content control as an aside on the right.

Other field controls that are created already for your use in page layouts (depending on whether you're using the Article Page parent content type or the Welcome Page content type) include Page Image, Author, Byline, and so on.

What's so special about content controls? They're part of the publishing infrastructure and stored with the page information. That means they're part of the versioning of the page (meaning you can revert to a previous version of content) and the approval process (meaning visitors won't see the content until the page is approved). Web Part information is stored with the Web Part, so after you click OK on your Web Part changes, they're immediately visible.

I'd been entrenched in the SharePoint collaboration world for a while before publishing pages and control controls appeared in SharePoint 2007. So breaking the habit of using certain Web Parts for text and pictures (like the content editor) was hard for me at first. I missed being able to close the Web Part and modify the chrome as I wanted, which the page content control did not allow. However, finding that content in certain Web Parts didn't migrate across servers — you had to open the Web Part every time you needed to modify, plus no version control — showed me the content-control light!

Using the Edit Mode Panel

An Edit mode panel is visible only in, well, publishing page Edit mode. That makes this panel great for all kinds of information or properties that are helpful to your editors but that you don't want visible when the page is in Read mode.

If you insert an Edit mode panel into your layout, you can place page fields, such as Title or Schedule Dates, into this panel, allowing you and your editors to add or change this content while they're editing the page rather than going to the page library to add this information.

You can also add text about helpful training and tips into these Edit modes; for example, the optimal size for an image or hints on how to add or edit certain content. To insert an Edit mode panel on your page, follow these steps:

1. **Open your new or existing page layout in SharePoint Designer.**

   You can do this by navigating to the Master Page gallery and using the drop-down list on the page layout name, or by opening SharePoint Designer 2010 and locating the page layout in the _catalogs/masterpage folder. Make sure your page is checked out. You can insert an Edit mode panel in either Design or Code view, as shown in Figure 16-11. I tend to use Code view as much as possible to make sure my insertions are placed correctly and then use Design mode to cross-check.

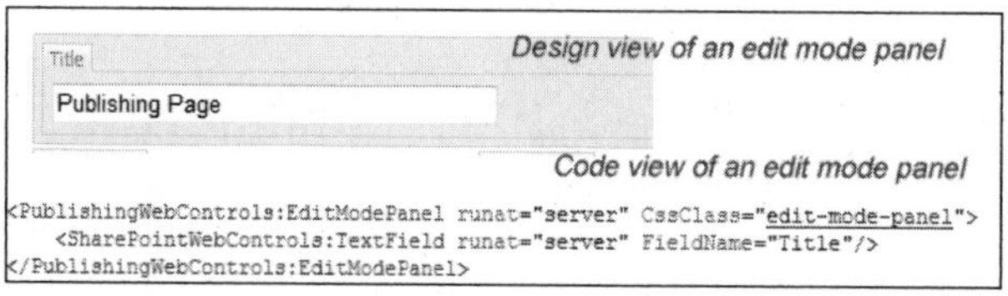

Figure 16-11:
Edit mode
panel of a
page layout.

```
Title                                    Design view of an edit mode panel
Publishing Page

                                         Code view of an edit mode panel
<PublishingWebControls:EditModePanel runat="server" CssClass="edit-mode-panel">
    <SharePointWebControls:TextField runat="server" FieldName="Title"/>
</PublishingWebControls:EditModePanel>
```

2. **Click the Insert tab on the Ribbon and then SharePoint drop-down list in the Controls section.**

   The SharePoint drop-down list includes data view controls and server controls. The EditModePanel control is in the Server Control section.

On the drop-down list, you can choose to open the toolbox to see all the insertable controls. If you have the toolbox open, locate the server controls (SharePoint) in the SharePoint Controls heading. You can drag the EditModePanel into your page code or right-click the control name and choose Insert.

3. **Insert the EditModePanel control using one of the methods that I describe in Step 2.**

   This code appears on your page:

   ```
   <PublishingWebControls:EditModePanel runat=server
   id="EditModePanel1">
   </PublishingWebControls:EditModePanel>
   ```

   Note: Both the opening and closing tags appear.

4. **Type or place content between the opening and closing tags.**

   Use the Controls section on the Ribbon or the toolbox to place content in the Edit mode panel. Page field controls, such as the page's title, are located in the Page Field Controls section of the SharePoint Controls categories. You can also type information directly between the opening and closing tags for your users.

   You may want to apply a style to your text input so that your text looks as polished as the rest of the page.

5. **When you're done with all your editing for this session and have published the page layout and approved (if applicable), test an instance of your new page and its Edit mode.**

   You don't see the Edit mode panel(s) while in the Read view of the page, only while in the Edit mode.

Multiple Edit mode panels may be placed on the page — be careful if you copy/paste — the IDs will need to be changed.

In this chapter, I don't go into creating other types of pages in a publishing site, such as including the system pages, like views or custom form pages. Many of these same techniques apply to those pages as well.

Chapter 17

Rolling Up Content to the Home Page

In This Chapter

▶ Publishing Web Parts to the home page

▶ Showing the site hierarchy

▶ Using a Data Form Web Part to create content from scratch

1 like to think of this as the How to Get Your Data Out of SharePoint chapter. Getting your stuff into SharePoint is pretty easy. You create a site, upload some files, enter a few tasks, and you're on your way. Things get tricky when you want to start displaying your content outside the current site.

In this chapter, I show you how to publish Web Parts, publish content to a page, display a site's hierarchy, create custom displays, and use the Data Form Web Part.

Publishing Web Parts

SharePoint's publishing sites provide three very important Web Parts that display content:

- **The Content Query Web Part** allows you to display content from anywhere in your site collection; it's useful for rolling up content to a home page or creating an archive view of content.

- **The Summary Link Web Part** allows you to manually select and order which items appear in the Web Part.

- **The Table of Contents Web Part** lists the site's hierarchy and is useful for creating sitemaps.

You don't need a publishing site to use these Web Parts. However, your site needs to have the SharePoint Server Publishing Infrastructure site collection feature activated.

Rolling up content

The Content Query Web Part is commonly used to display a list of news articles on a site's *landing page* (the first page visitors usually arrive at). Say you have three people creating new articles in your site. You can use the Content Query Web Part to automatically display a list of these articles on your department's landing page.

Follow these steps to use the Content Query Web Part:

1. **Insert the Content Query Web Part into your page and edit the Web Part's properties.**

   The Content Query Web Part is located in the Content Rollup section.

   See Chapter 9 for details on inserting Web Parts into a page.

2. **In the Query section of the Web Part, select the options that will return the items you wish to see in the Web Part.**

   The Query section provides many options, as shown in Figure 17-1, including:

   • *Source:* Select the location in your site hierarchy where you want to query items. If you want to display items regardless of where they appear in your site hierarchy, select the Show Items from All Sites in This Site Collection radio button and select the List Type, Content Type Group, and Content Type you want to display. For example, if you want to roll up all project tasks, use your Tasks List Type and List Content Type Group and Task Content Type.

   • *List Type:* Select the kind of list that stores your items from the drop-down list.

   • *Content Type:* Select the content type group and content type you want to use for query from the drop-down lists.

   • *Audience Targeting:* If you want the Web Part to honor any audience targeting settings on the items, select the Apply Audience Filtering check box.

   • *Additional Filters:* Include any additional fields on which you wish to filter by selecting from the drop-down lists. The list of available fields is determined by the list type and the content type.

For example, to display all tasks that aren't started, choose Task Status, Is Equal To, and Not Started from the drop-down lists (refer to Figure 17-1).

You can configure more query options for the Content Query Web Part with SharePoint Designer 2010.

Figure 17-1: Set the query options for your rollup.

Behind the scenes, this Web Part generates a query with SharePoint's query language, CAML (Collaborative Application Markup Language). You can write your own custom CAML query to use instead of selecting the options; you can find sites that tell you more about CAML by searching "CAML syntax" in your favorite search engine.

3. **In the Presentation section of the Web Part, select the options that will display your items.**

   Your options, as shown in Figure 17-2, include

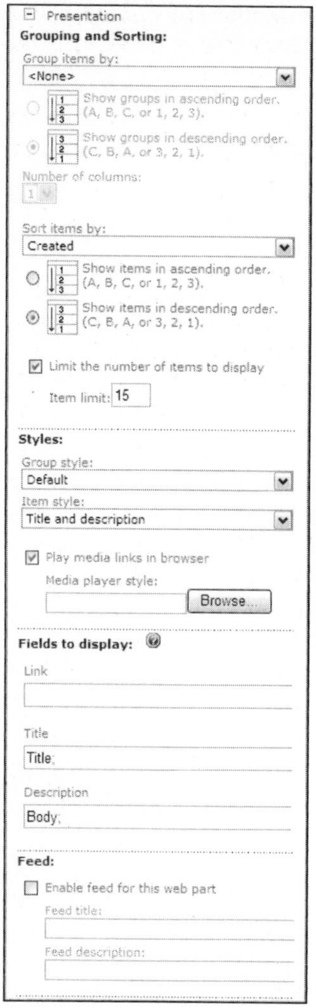

Figure 17-2:
Set the
Presentation options
for your
rollup.

- *Grouping and Sorting:* Select the columns by which you wish to group results in the Group Items By drop-down list. You can also choose to group results by site by selecting the Site option in the Group Items By drop-down list. You can select a column to sort by and limit the number of items displayed by choosing the Sort Items By drop-down list and selecting the Limit the Number of Items to Display check box, respectively, and then entering a number in the Item Limit field.

- *Styles:* Select the group style and item style you want to use to display your items from the Group Style and Item Style drop-down lists.

These styles determine what information appears. For example, Title and Description displays the item's title field, linked to the document or item, along with the description.

These styles are XSL templates, not CSS styles. You can create your own XSL templates using SharePoint Designer 2010.

- *Fields to Display:* Specify the fields that you want to map to the item style you select by typing them in the Fields to Display text boxes.

  In the case of most documents and articles, the Comments field is the default description field. For items, you have to decide which field you want to use. For example, the Tasks content type uses the Body field. I know this because I look at the Tasks Site content type. Enter the field name Body in the Description field and the value of that field appears in the Web Part.

- *Feed:* Indicate whether you want an RSS feed to be generated for the results of this query by selecting the Enable Feed for This Web Part check box.

4. Click OK.

Your query appears in the Web Part, as shown Figure 17-3.

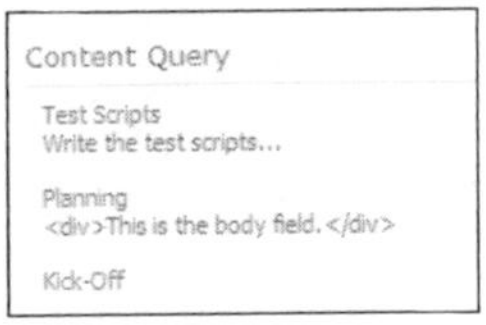

Figure 17-3: The query results for a Web Part.

Content Query

Test Scripts
Write the test scripts...

Planning
This is the body field.

Kick-Off

You can export a Content Query Web Part, rename it, and upload it to your site's Web Part gallery for reuse in other places.

Displaying a site's hierarchy

The Table of Contents Web Part is used frequently to display a sitemap or provide navigation for a subsite. No surprise: The Table of Contents Web Part is in the Navigation category when you insert it on a page.

The Table of Contents Web Part has three main sections in the configuration pane, as shown in Figure 17-4:

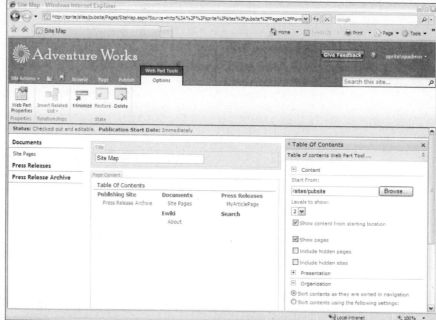

Figure 17-4:
Choose
options for
the Table
of Contents
Web Part.

✔ **Content:** Use this section to select where in the site hierarchy the Web Part displays. Enter the path to the page where you want to Table of Contents to begin in the Start From field. You can choose how many levels to display in the Table of Contents by using the Levels to Show drop-down list.

✔ **Presentation:** This section controls how the items display. You can choose to display everything in a single column or multiple columns and select how the header is styled by selecting an option from the Header Style drop-down list.

✔ **Organization:** Decide how you want the items sorted by selecting either the Sort Contents as They Are Sorted in Navigation or the Sort Contents Using the Following Settings radio button. If you choose the latter option, select applicable options from the Sort Sites By, Sort Pages By, and Sort Direction drop-down lists.

Creating custom displays with the Summary Link Web Part

Although the Content Query and Table of Contents Web Parts let you configure a query to display items, the Summary Link Web Part allows you to manually select the items that you want to display. These items can link to pages in the site or to external sites.

Like the Table of Contents Web Part, the Summary Link Web Part is in the Navigation category. Unlike the Table Of Contents and Content Query Web Parts, the Summary Link Web Part doesn't have special configuration items in the Web tool pane. Instead, you add items directly to the Web Part and then manually select how you want them presented and ordered.

Summary Link can also be added to a page layout as a field control. This approach stores your links with the page, instead of inside the Web Part. I usually use Summary Link as a control unless I need to create a reusable Web Part.

The Summary Link Web Part has a toolbar along the top, as shown in Figure 17-5, with these four options:

- ✔ **New Link:** Click this button to link to a new item in the Web Part. You can link to a page, item, or person. You can also link to content outside SharePoint.

- ✔ **New Group:** Create a new group that you can use to group the links you add to the Web Part.

- ✔ **Configure Styles and Layout:** Select the default style that's applied to new links or change the style on all links you already entered into the Web Part.

- ✔ **Reorder:** Move the items in the Web Part up or down to change the order.

Figure 17-5:
The
Summary
Links
toolbar.

The home page of publishing sites uses a Summary Link Web Part to display a list of tasks that one should perform. Somebody at Microsoft manually entered these Summary Links to provide you with a list of shortcuts to tasks commonly used in a publishing site. The steps here describe how to add a new Summary Link Web Part:

1. Insert the Summary Link Web Part on a page.

The Summary Links Web Part is located in the Content Rollup section. See Chapter 9 for details on inserting Web Parts into a page.

You can also edit the default home page of a publishing site.

2. **Click the New Link button on the Summary Links toolbar on the Web Part itself.**

   The New Link Dialog Box is displayed.

3. **In the New Link dialog box, as shown in Figure 17-6, enter the title and a description you want to display for the new Summary Link Web Part in the Title and Description fields, respectively.**

4. **Enter a hyperlink in the Link URL field or click the Browse button to browse to the item you want to select.**

   The Browse button launches an asset picker that you can use to visually select the item. I discuss the asset picker in Chapter 21.

5. **(Optional) Select an image to associate with the link by entering the path to the image in the Image URL field or by clicking the Browse button and browsing to the image.**

6. **Click OK.**

   The link appears in the list, as shown in Figure 17-7.

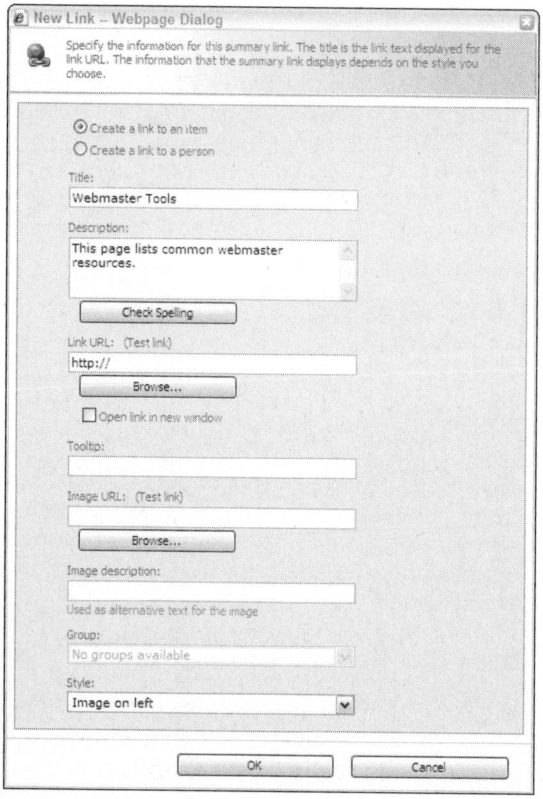

Figure 17-6:
Enter a new
Summary
Link Web
Part.

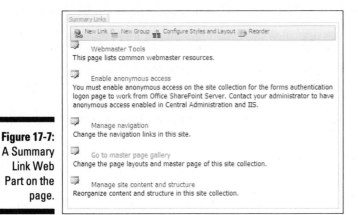

Figure 17-7:
A Summary
Link Web
Part on the
page.

Starting from Scratch

Sometimes, you may want to create a simple one-off Web Part that isn't tied to any of the styles provided by the Content Query Web Part. In those cases, you might want to use the Data Form Web Part. (You may not have worked with the Data Form Web Part before because it requires SharePoint Designer.)

This Web Part is often referred to as the *Swiss Army Knife of Web Parts* because it's extremely versatile; I use it all the time. In fact, most of the "custom" Web Parts that I create are actually Data Form Web Parts.

I always use a Web Part page when I'm working with the Data Form Web Part. When I have the Web Part configured the way I want, I export it into the page where I intend to use the Web Part.

Even if your company doesn't allow you to connect to their production SharePoint farm with SharePoint Designer, you can still use the Data Form Web Part. You can configure the Web Part with another instance of SharePoint, say, on your laptop or in a lab, and then import the Web Part into your production site.

To insert a Data Form Web Part, follow these steps:

1. **Open a new Web Part page in SharePoint Designer 2010.**

   You can either create your Web Part page in the browser and open it in SharePoint Designer, or you can use SharePoint Designer to create the new Web Part page for you. I usually choose the former because I like to have control over what and where I'm creating it.

2. **Click the Design tab to view your Web Part page in Design mode.**

3. **On the Insert tab, click the Data View button and choose Empty Data View.**

   SharePoint Designer inserts a new Web Part on the page, and a new set of tabs appears in the Ribbon, as shown in Figure 17-8.

After you insert the Web Part, your next steps are to select the data source, add your columns, and apply sorting, filtering, and conditional formatting as desired.

To select your data source:

1. **Inside the Web Part, click the Click Here to Select a Data Source link.**

   The data sources picker appears.

2. **Select the list or library you want to display in your Web Part and click OK.**

   The Data Source Details pane appears.

3. **Ctrl-click the columns you want to appear in your Web Part.**

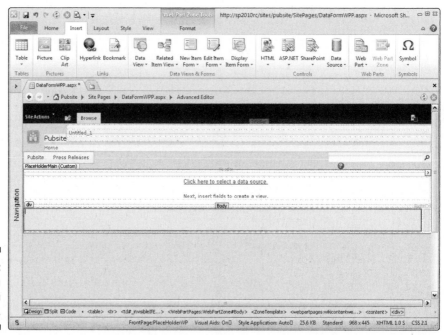

Figure 17-8:
Inserting a
Data Form
Web Part.

4. **Click the Insert Selected Fields As drop-down list and then choose an option to display the content.**

   You have several options, as shown in Figure 17-9:

   - *Single Item View or Multiple Item View:* Inserts the selected fields so that the Web Part displays one item at a time or several rows at once, respectively.

   - *Single Item Form or Multiple Item Form:* Displays a data entry form using the field(s) you select.

   - *New Item Form:* Displays a form for entering new items into your data source.

Figure 17-9:
Display
items in a
Data Form
Web Part.

You can create very complex data sources that query other sites and even join two lists. SharePoint uses its own query language, *CAML.* SharePoint Designer generates the CAML query for you, but you can also insert your own query.

Figure 17-10 shows a Data Form Web Part with Multiple Item View selected. When you have your data source inserted, the Ribbon activates the commands you can use, which you can also see in Figure 17-10.

Use the Design tab on the Ribbon to change the layout of the items in your Web Part. SharePoint Designer provides several built-in formats, as shown Figure 17-11.

Many of these formatting options also apply to the views you create for lists and libraries. For example, you can use conditional formatting with a list view.

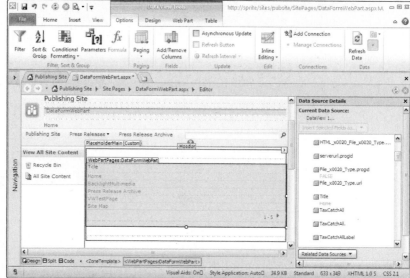

Figure 17-10:
Work with
data in a
Data Form
Web Part.

Figure 17-11:
Change the
display of
your data.

When the Data Form Web Part queries SharePoint, the data is returned as an XML document. XML documents have their own set of languages, XSL and XPath, that can be used to filter the data and display it exactly as you want. By viewing your Data Form Web Part in Code View using the View tab on the Ribbon in SharePoint Designer, you can view the XSL generated by SharePoint Designer. You can edit this XSL to display your data virtually any way you please.

Chapter 18

Configuring Site Navigation

- -

In This Chapter

▶ Configuring global and current navigation

▶ Adding static headers and links in navigation

▶ Creating your own custom navigation menus

- -

*P*ublishing sites have the same display options as team sites, which I discuss in Chapter 11. Both kinds of site use the Top Link bar for navigation across the top and the Quick Launch toolbar for navigating within the site. Both sites can optionally display a Tree View and use breadcrumbs.

One of the big differences between the two is that publishing sites are intended to use the site hierarchy as the site's navigation scheme. Using this approach, the site's navigation is displayed dynamically based on the sites and pages that exist in the site.

In reality, most people want more control over what displays in their site's navigation. They also aren't always interested in having the site's hierarchy match exactly to the navigation scheme.

In this chapter, I walk you through how to configure dynamic navigation based on your site hierarchy, show you how to configure static navigation, and discuss some additional navigation options.

The underlying controls used by team sites and publishing sites are the same. The data sources used by the navigation menus in publishing sites are optimized to work with portals and public Web sites.

Configuring Dynamic Navigation

The navigation options in a publishing site allow you to manage both the top navigation and the site's Quick Launch navigation in one page. SharePoint lets you manage the two major kinds of navigation found on most Web sites:

✔ **Primary navigation** is what your site visitors use to reach the main areas in your site, no matter where they are in your site. It's usually positioned somewhere in the top of the page and is consistent across every page in your site. SharePoint calls this your *global navigation.*

✔ **Contextual navigation** is usually found in the body of the page, usually on the left or right, and is used to access the pages within each major area of your site. This navigation is considered contextual because the navigation items change depending on where the visitor is in the site. SharePoint calls this your *current navigation.*

SharePoint provides two navigation menus that correspond with your global and current navigation. The Top Link bar is the global navigation menu that's usually present at the top of publishing pages. The Quick Launch menu provides the current navigation that appears along the left of most pages.

Both the Top Link bar and the Quick Launch menu are provided by the same navigation control — SharePoint's *AspMenu* control. This is a very powerful control that has a lot of settings.

SharePoint's publishing site assumes that you want your global and current navigation menus created dynamically based on your site hierarchy. Toward that end, configuring navigation in a publishing site requires two things:

✔ **A site hierarchy that matches your navigation requirements.** In other words, you have subsites for the major items in your global navigation and pages for the items below. Any time you want to create a new grouping of pages in the navigation menu, you have to create a new subsite.

This often leads to extensive nesting of sites, which I recommend you avoid. This is one reason that people start looking for alternative approaches to navigation.

✔ **The ability to think in terms of the current site you're setting navigation options for, its parent site, its sibling sites, and any children sites that may exist.** This can be extremely confusing to people, which is one reason why I see many people abandon dynamic navigation. It's too hard to keep track of what's happening where.

Configuring global navigation

In most publishing sites, you want all pages and sites to display the same navigation settings. SharePoint can dynamically display all subsites and pages within a subsite in your global navigation. Pages display in a drop-down list.

Each site in your publishing site can have its own global configuration settings. So you need to perform the following steps for each site. The settings you make in a subsite, such as whether to display pages, impacts navigation for the entire site, not just what the visitor sees when they're on that site. Follow these steps:

1. **Browse to the publishing site or subsite you want to configure global navigation for and then choose Site Actions⇨Modify Navigation.**

   The Site Navigation Settings page appears.

2. **In a parent site, such as the top-level site, use the Global Settings section to indicate whether you want to display navigation items that are below the parent site.**

   Select the Show Subsites options to display each subsite in the global navigation. To show the pages that have been created in the parent site, select Show Pages.

   Scroll down to the Navigation Editing and Sorting section of the page to get a sneak peek at your global navigation hierarchy.

3. **In a child site, use the Global Settings section to determine whether the subsite will display the same global navigation items as its parent site.**

   Select the Show Subsites and Show Pages options to display subsites and pages on the current site and any other site (parent or child) that opts to display navigation for the site you are configuring. Figure 18-1 shows the global navigation options for a child site.

   A child site can be a parent site to another site.

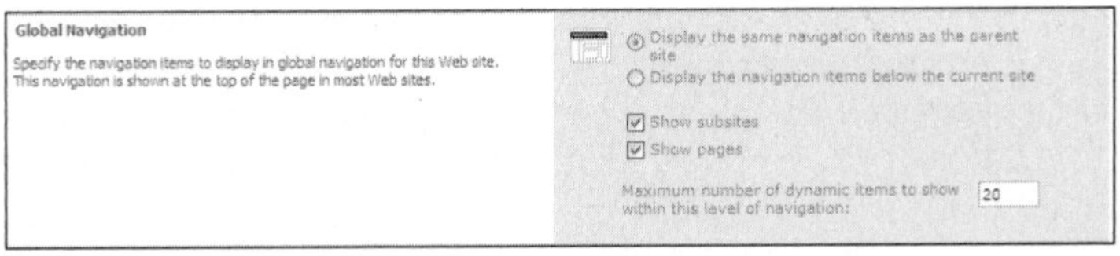

Figure 18-1: Global navigation settings.

> **Global Navigation**
>
> Specify the navigation items to display in global navigation for this Web site. This navigation is shown at the top of the page in most Web sites.
>
> ○ Display the same navigation items as the parent site
> ○ Display the navigation items below the current site
>
> ☑ Show subsites
> ☑ Show pages
>
> Maximum number of dynamic items to show within this level of navigation: [20]

For example, all publishing sites include a Press Releases subsite. If you enable Show Subsites and Show Pages, the top-level home site will also display any pages and subsites of the Press Releases navigation option. Figure 18-2 shows the Press Releases navigation menu from the parent site when the Show Pages option is selected.

4. **Click OK to save your global navigation settings.**

Figure 18-2: Press Releases displays its pages.

> Publishing Site ▸ All Site Content
> Displays all sites, lists, and libraries in this site.
>
> Publishing Site   Press Releases ▾   Press Release Archive
>   MyArticlePage
> Documents   Create
> Site Pages

I usually use two browser windows when configuring navigation. I use one browser window to configure the navigation and another to view the changes I made.

Figure 18-3 shows the global navigation menu for a typical publishing site. This site's parent site is configured to show subsites and pages. The subsite, Press Releases, is configured to show pages. Table 18-1 summarizes typical global navigation settings.

Figure 18-3:
Global
navigation
settings for
a parent
site.

Table 18-1	Typical Global Navigation Settings
Appears in Global Navigation	*When You Select This Option*
Subsites automatically appear in the global navigation as soon as they're created.	Select the Show Subsites check box in each site in your hierarchy. If this option isn't selected in the parent site, no subsites appear in your global navigation.
Pages automatically appear in the global navigation as soon as they're approved.	Select the Show Pages check box in each site in the hierarchy. If this option is selected in the parent site, the parent's sites pages appear as siblings to any subsites in the global navigation.
All sites have the same global navigation.	Make sure that in each site's global navigation settings, you select the Display the Same Navigation Items as the Parent option.

Configuring current navigation

Configuring current navigation settings for each site is similar to global navigation. You have the same options to automatically show pages and subsites. As shown in Figure 18-4, you have these options to determine what items appear in the site's current navigation:

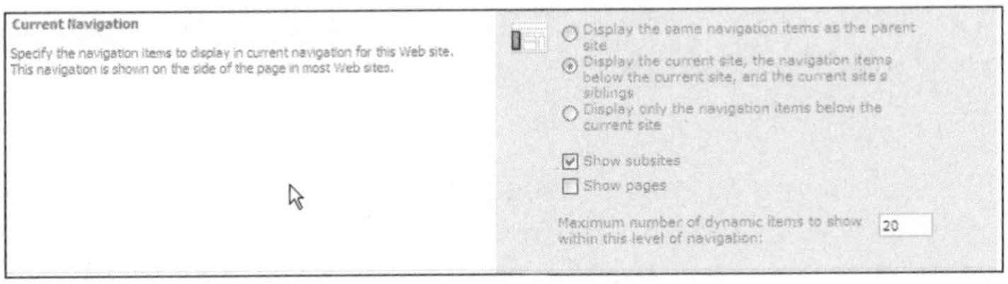

Figure 18-4:
Current
navigation
options.

> ✔ **Display the Same Navigation Items as the Parent Site:** This option displays the current navigation items using the settings of the parent site.

> ✔ **Display the Current Site, the Navigation Items below the Current Site, and the Current Site's Siblings:** This is the show-everything option. This option shows navigation items from the current site, parent site, sibling sites, and any children sites.

> ✔ **Display Only the Navigation Items below the Current Site:** This option doesn't show any sibling or parent navigation items or items from the current site; only items from child sites display.

Choosing the Show Pages and Show Subsites options makes navigation items show for pages and subsites in the current navigation of parent sites, sibling sites, and child sites any time those sites opt to show the navigation to the site you're configuring.

Configuring Static Navigation

Most clients I work with don't want pages and subsites showing automatically in their navigation. They usually want a static menu that doesn't change anytime someone decides to publish an article page.

You accomplish this by deselecting the Show Pages and Show Subsites options in the navigation settings for each site. You can then manually enter whatever navigation you want to appear in the global and current navigation for each site.

To manually configure your navigation items:

1. **Browse to the site you want to configure and then choose Site Settings⇨Modify Navigation.**

2. **Scroll down to the Navigation Editing and Sorting section.**

   This section shows a hierarchy of your global and current navigation items, as shown in Figure 18-5. The items you see here depend on the settings you make in the global navigation and current navigation settings of the page. For example, if you select the Show Subsites in Global Navigation option, you see subsites listed in this section of the page.

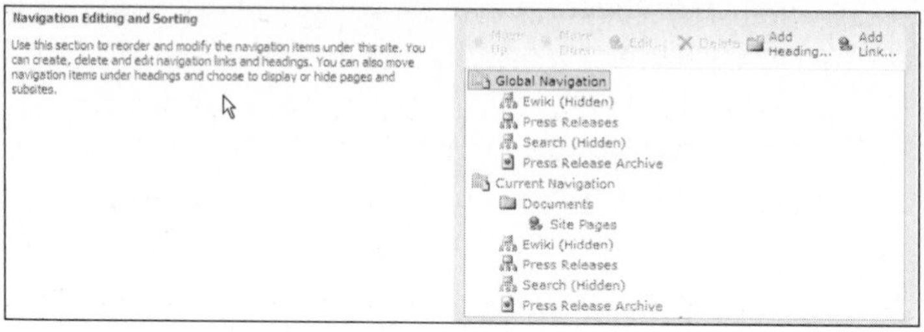

Figure 18-5:
View the
navigation
hierarchy.

3. **To add a new navigation to your global or current navigation, click the place in the hierarchy where you want to add the item.**

4. **Click the Add Heading button to add a new heading, or click the Add Link button to add a new link.**

   Figure 18-6 shows the Add Heading dialog box. The Add Link dialog box looks exactly the same. A heading doesn't require a Web address or URL. That is, you can use a heading to contain links without requiring that the heading point to anything in the browser.

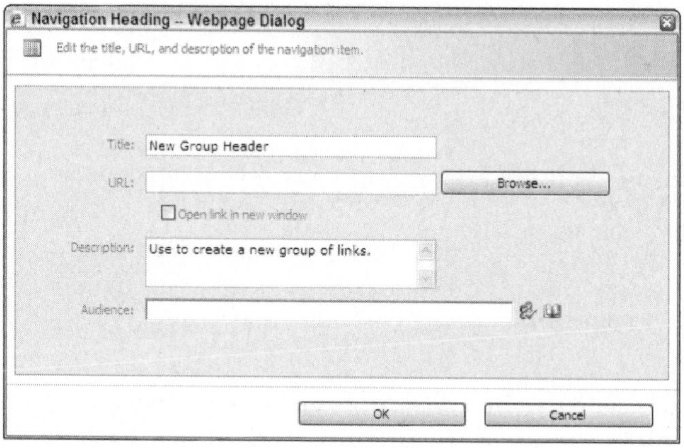

Figure 18-6:
Adding a
new head-
ing to your
current
navigation.

5. **Enter the details for the navigation item.**

   You have these options:

   • *Title:* The text you enter in this field appears in the navigation menu.

   • *URL:* Enter the page where the item links to. This is an optional field for headings.

- *Open Link in New Window:* Select this check box to open the link in a new window.

- *Description:* The text you enter in this field displays as a ToolTip when someone hovers over the navigation item.

- *Audience:* Use this text box to filter the navigation item so that only members of the selected audience can see the navigation item.

Get creative about adding navigation items. I often add static links to the current navigation for common tasks that people need to perform, such as managing a group's membership.

6. **Click OK to save your heading or link.**

The heading appears in the site's navigation hierarchy, as shown in Figure 18-7. Use the Move Up or Move Down buttons to reposition the item in the hierarchy.

Figure 18-7:
Your item
appears
in the
navigation
hierarchy.

7. **Repeat Steps 3–6 to add more links and headings to your navigation hierarchy.**

8. **Use the Hide and Edit buttons to make additional changes to the hierarchy.**

Click the Hide button to mark items in the hierarchy that shouldn't appear in the site's navigation. Click the Edit button to modify the title, description, link, or audience for a navigation item.

9. **Click OK to save your navigation settings.**

Looking at Alternative Ways to Generate a Navigation Menu

I'd be naïve to expect that you only need to use two kinds of site navigation. In reality, Webmasters and site visitors expect lots of ways to get to content. In Chapter 17, I discuss the *rollup* Web Parts. These Web Parts are often used to provide the additional navigation options that you want to see inside your Web pages, not just in the header and along the side.

One such Web Part, the Table of Contents Web Part, can be used to create a sitemap. A considered best practice is to provide a sitemap, and the Table of Contents Web Part dynamically generates it for you.

You can use a custom master page or page layout to control where the site's navigation menu appears on the page. For example, if you want the current navigation on the right instead of the left, you can move it in the master page. (See Chapter 16 for more about altering page layouts.)

In many cases, however, people want more control over the site navigation than SharePoint allows. Publishing sites provide great options for dynamically displaying the navigation based on the site's hierarchy. But what if you want to display two global navigation menus? What if you want to display navigation from a list?

Here are several options available:

- ✔ **Use a rollup Web Part, such as a Content Query Web Part or Data Form Web Part.** These Web Parts can be used to query lists and libraries and present the results any way you want. You can effectively create your own navigation menu using this option. These Web Parts work fine in a master page or page layouts.

- ✔ **Manually enter your navigation options in the master page or page layout.** I often see master pages with manually entered footer navigation. Why isn't there a place in SharePoint to enter your footer navigation items? I don't know the answer, but most people enter those items directly in the master page because they usually don't change very often.

- ✔ **Use an XML file to drive your navigation menu.** This approach can use SharePoint's standard navigation menu, AspMenu, to display navigation items using an XML file as a data source.

The last option starts to get a little techie, but is actually accessible to any power user who's been granted the rights to use SharePoint Designer. One of the nice things about using SharePoint's AspMenu navigation menu is that it already understands how to do flyouts and menu styling, so you aren't rolling your own navigation like you are with some of the other options. You're just providing an alternative data source instead of using SharePoint's publishing site hierarchy data source.

The following steps walk you through the process of using an XML file to drive your navigation menu:

1. **In SharePoint Designer 2010, create a new XML file by choosing File⇨All Files (see Figure 18-8).**

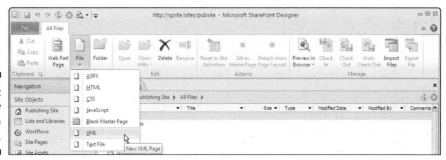

Figure 18-8: Add a new XML file to your site.

You can move this file to a document library where it can be version controlled.

2. **Enter your navigation items into the file.**

   Your file needs to follow the sitemap convention for navigation menus, which nests sitemap nodes inside one another (see Figure 18-9).

```
SampleNav.xml
Publishing Site ▶ All Files ▶ SampleNav.xml
1  <?xml version="1.0" encoding="utf-8" ?>
2  <siteMap>
3      <siteMapNode title="Root" url="">
4          <siteMapNode title="First Menu" url="http://www.live.com"></siteMapNode>
5          <siteMapNode title="Second Menu" url="http://www.live.com">
6              <siteMapNode title="Submenu" url="http://www.live.com"></siteMapNode>
7          </siteMapNode>
8      </siteMapNode>
9  </siteMap>
```

Figure 18-9: A sample sitemap file.

3. **Open the Web Part page, page layout, or master page in SharePoint Designer 2010 where you want to create your new navigation menu.**

   I suggest testing this in a Web Part page first, and then moving it into a page layout or master page after you test it.

4. **Drag and drop the data source for your XML file onto your page:**

   a. In Design view, click the location in your file where you want to insert the data source and then click the Insert tab on the Ribbon.

b. *Click the Data Source button in the Controls group and select the XML file, as shown in Figure 18-10.*

SharePoint Designer inserts the data source control into the page.

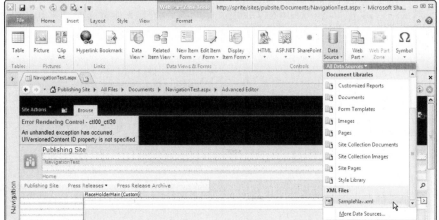

Figure 18-10:
Insert the
XML data
source in
your page.

5. **Right-click the data source and choose Properties from the contextual menu. Set the XPath property on your data source to the following value:**

```
/siteMap/siteMapNode/siteMapNode
```

This ensures that the root nodes in your file don't display in the navigation control.

6. **Drag and drop an AspMenu control onto your page from the toolbox.**

The AspMenu control is in the SharePoint Server Controls group of the Ribbon.

You may find it's easier to copy and paste the AspMenu control from the publishing master page than inserting the control from the toolbox. If you do that, make sure you give the menu a unique ID, such as `MyCustomMenu`.

7. **Configure the properties for the AspMenu control as follows:**

a. *Set the DataSourceID property on the AspMenu control to match the data source you created in Step 4.*

b. *Set the StaticDisplayLevels property to 1.*

c. *Insert a DataBindings elements to map the items in your XML file to the menu.*

Figure 18-11 shows the final markup for the control.

Figure 18-11:
Markup for
AspMenu
using an
XML data
source.

8. **Save your settings and refresh the page.**

   Figure 18-12 shows the menu on a Web Part page.

Figure 18-12:
A SharePoint
menu
displaying
custom
navigation
items.

> Publishing Site ▸ NavigationTest
> Home
>
> | Publishing Site | Press Releases ▾ | Press Release Archive |
> | --- | --- | --- |
> | Documents | First Menu | Second Menu ▾ |
> | Site Pages | | Submenu |
> | Press Releases | | |
> | Press Release Archive | | |

The example I just walked you through is but one way you can use an alternative data source to drive a navigation menu in SharePoint. I like to extend this approach by dynamically generating the sitemap file from items entered into a list. In Chapter 17, I touch on a way to generate the XML from a SharePoint list. When you have the XML, you can use an XSL template to transform it into the sitemap convention required by the AspMenu navigation menu.

SharePoint's navigation model is inherited directly from ASP.NET. Nothing is new or magical about how SharePoint handles site navigation. That means you have lots of options for customizing the navigation menus in SharePoint. In most cases, you either create a new navigation provider or a new data source while using one of the existing navigation menus to display the results.

Part IV
Putting a Bow on It

In this part . . .

Everyone wants to make SharePoint look less like
SharePoint. These chapters show you how to create
a new color scheme for your site or completely change
the site's look and feel by hiding and moving what you see
on the page. And I cover some of the hiding places
SharePoint uses for branding-related site assets.

Chapter 19

Changing the Look and Feel of Your Site

. . . .

In This Chapter

▶ Getting a handle on the Look and Feel section

▶ Changing the site icon

▶ Using SharePoint themes

▶ Creating a new theme with PowerPoint

. . . .

*N*ever underestimate the power of a site that's been made more attractive with color and graphics: It can be as simple as applying a color scheme that evokes the corporate colors, seasonal colors, or local sports teams. Photos of leaders, pertinent logos, even casual images can energize a team.

This chapter details how to change these elements with simple out-of-the-box options. No need for specialized technical skills!

However, you do need to take into account the type and level of your site. After designing the global pages of an intranet, you don't want to change the color scheme often, if at all, because familiarity is key for users to complete their tasks. Conversely, for a smaller department site, changes to the color and graphics can give a group a quick morale boost. I once stood in a middle of a small call center as the site owner changed the color theme to represent an upcoming holiday. The wave of oohs and aahs as each call rep viewed the updated site was humorous, but also drove home the point on how SharePoint Look and Feel options can mean a lot to users in little ways.

Color schemes in SharePoint are called *themes,* and in the 2010 version, they've been improved to let you choose color details and create new themes easily. You can also change the font or even import a color palette from a PowerPoint. How cool is that?!

If you do have (or are) a Web designer with HTML and *CSS (Cascading Style Sheets)* skills, make sure you read Chapter 20 to find out about branding your Web site. You can change much more with a custom style sheet than you can with themes. This book doesn't go into depth on either publishing sites or the instructions on creating custom master pages and page layouts. For exact style and layout control to make your SharePoint site look like a regular Web site, you may want to research SharePoint publishing sites and SharePoint Designer.

The Look and Feel Section of Site Settings

Most of the options I talk about in this chapter are in the Look and Feel section of the Site Settings page in your SharePoint 2010 site, which you can access from the Site Actions menu (see Figure 19-1). You must have designer or owner permission to change any of these items.

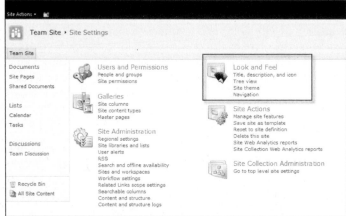

Figure 19-1: The Look and Feel section of Site Settings.

The Look and Feel section contains

- ✔ **Title, Description, and Icon:** This option allows you to change the title of the site, add or change the site description, add or change the site icon description, and change the URL of the site if necessary.

- ✔ **Tree View:** Allows you to enable Quick Launch menu (left navigation) or turn on the Tree View format of the Quick Launch menu. You can have one or the other, both, or neither. Consider whether you need left navigation if content is limited and you feel other navigation and content links suffice.

✔ **Site Theme:** This option allows you to choose whether you want to inherit a theme, select predefined themes, customize a theme, preview selections, and apply the theme to the current site and subsites if desired.

✔ **Navigation:** I detail Navigation options in Chapter 18. These include how top (global) and left (current) navigation is displayed, how navigation sorting is handled, and hiding, showing, and/or adding links to your navigation areas.

Team sites show the Quick Launch and Top Link Bar links instead of the Navigation link shown in Figure 19-1.

Although changing the title is helpful, especially if you're winging it when you first created the site, don't take changing the URL lightly. Remember users may have bookmarks or links to the URL that may be broken if you change.

Changing Your Site Icon

SharePoint team sites contain a site icon in the upper left. The default image in a collaboration team site looks like four colorful figures representing the team. SharePoint has a setting that allows you to change this image. I recommend a short (meaning *height*) square or rectangle. Microsoft has given helpful guidelines in the instructions and suggests a 60-x-60-pixel size.

Remember text is to the right of the image, so watch the length of your logo. If your icon is too tall, the header area becomes tall as well and distorts the look and feel.

To change the site icon:

1. **Upload your image to a document or picture library.**

   You may want to upload the image to the Site Assets library or create a new picture library to contain the image. The benefit of the picture library is that you can edit the image (including size) while in SharePoint because picture libraries have photo-editing capabilities that document libraries don't.

2. **Copy the URL of the image location before you navigate to Site Settings page.**

   Some image link options allow you to browse for your image, but the site icon option doesn't, so you need to copy that URL before you can update the site icon.

   One of the easiest ways to capture the URL is to right-click the link of the image in a library and choose Copy Shortcut from the contextual menu, as shown in Figure 19-2. If you won't use the URL immediately, you may want to paste it in a text file, such as Notepad, to use later.

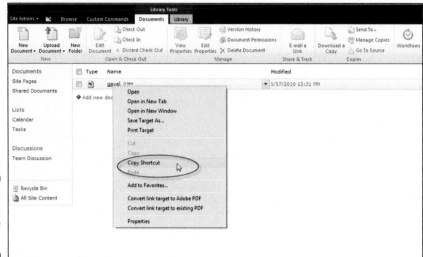

Figure 19-2:
Showing
how to copy
a shortcut.

3. **Choose Site Actions⊏>Site Settings.**

The Site Settings page appears. You see all the options in the Look and Feel section that I describe in the preceding section.

4. **Click the Title, Description, and Icon link in the Look and Feel section.**

The icon URL and description is the second options group.

Paste the URL you have copied into the URL field. You can use the Click Here to Test Link link to make sure that the URL correctly displays the image.

5. **Add a description for your icon in the Logo URL and Description section.**

The description you type under the icon URL becomes the alternate text for the image. Keep this description short, such as *Six Sigma Icon.*

6. **Click OK to commit your changes.**

You see your new icon in the header area, as shown in Figure 19-3.

You may want to copy the URL of the original icon if you ever consider changing back. If not, you can always navigate to a site with the original icon and copy the URL to replace it on your site.

A warning concerning using a relative URL for the site icon is geared toward your IT professionals. This warning reminds them that if the organization has multiple Web servers, the image needs to be copied to the same folder in each.

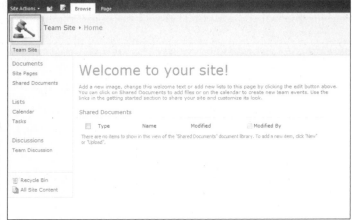

Figure 19-3:
A team site
with the
site icon
changed.

Changing the Theme of Your Site

A *theme* in SharePoint is a color scheme. In SharePoint 2010, the theme can include font choices as well. SharePoint comes with several predefined themes, and your organization may have added others as well to coordinate the look and feel of other sites.

As I mention earlier in this chapter, the site owner or designer can customize a theme through the browser, which in the past could be done only by hand-coding CSS or using a product like SharePoint Designer.

Themes don't change the sizing or placement of elements on the page, although this can be done with CSS. See Chapter 20 to discover the basics of what can be done with CSS versus themes.

To change the theme of your site, follow these steps:

1. **Navigate to the Site Settings page, Look and Feel section and then click the Site Theme link.**

   The Site Theme Settings page appears, as Figure 19-4 shows, with the following property sections:

   - *Inherit Theme:* If you're in a subsite, you can decide to inherit the same theme as the parent site, or define a theme for this site and any sites under it.

   - *Select a Theme:* View the default and see other predefined themes.

- *Customize a Theme:* Choose a predefined theme and then select individual color aspects, as well as choose a font for the headings and body text.

- *Preview Theme:* View what one of the predefined themes or your custom theme would look like on your site.

- *Apply theme:* Apply your new theme choices.

2. Try the different predefined themes by clicking one of the predefined themes to view the color and font assignments. Click the Preview Theme button to open a new window and see the theme applied to your site.

3. To customize a theme based on one of the predefined themes, select either the default or one of the predefined themes.

The colors of that theme display in the Customize Theme area. You have multiple selections for light and dark text backgrounds, accent colors, and choices for hyperlink and followed hyperlinks.

4. Change colors by clicking the Select a Color link next to each color.

A dialog box with a color chart appears. The current color is shown in the upper right, and as you choose a new color, it's shown in the lower right with its hexadecimal number.

In this Customize Theme section, you can also select a font for the heading and body text. The choices are contained in a drop-down list, and many should be familiar to you from other Microsoft Office applications. See the following section, "A note on fonts," before making your choices.

The palette suggested for Web sites contains colors that are considered *Web safe,* meaning that the color should remain true on most computer monitors. Unfortunately, this was only about 200 colors and didn't represent enough colors for most Web designers. Because monitors have improved in recent years, many more colors display uniformly online.

Often these colors are represented by their *hexadecimal number,* a six-character code that can contain both numbers and letters, preceded by a pound (#) sign. You don't have to pick a color from the palette shown in SharePoint. If you know the hexadecimal number of the color you want, you can type it.

I suggest testing your color choices by having users with different monitors view the site. Inside an organization, the different types of monitors may be limited. If you're creating a site viewed over the Internet, you may need to increase your test pool.

Some great Web sites can help you select colors and provide the hexadecimal code for that color. Some Web sites even provide you with a color palette based on a photo you upload!

5. Preview your theme by clicking the Preview button.

No matter how confident you are in your choices, previewing your selections, especially if you've changed multiple colors, is always a good idea.

6. **Choose where you want to apply the theme be selecting Apply to This Site Only or This Site and Reset Subsites to Inherit.**

   If you chose the Apply the Selected Theme to This Site and Reset All Subsites to Inherit This Setting option, all subsites under the current site inherit your new choices.

   These options are available only in publishing sites.

   Depending on the depth of your site collection, this could be an issue if you have multiple owners in subsites that took care in selecting their own theme that you just overwrote.

   When you create a custom theme, Custom Theme appears in the list box with the default and predefined options.

7. **Click the Apply button to commit your changes.**

   Your site (and subsites depending on your selections) reflects your new choices, as Figure 19-4 shows.

   If you want an easier, more intuitive way to create a custom theme, consider selecting a palette in PowerPoint to upload as a custom theme, which I describe later in this chapter.

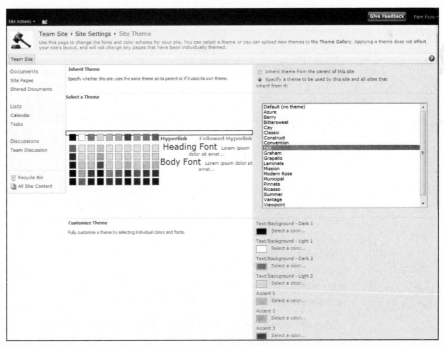

Figure 19-4:
A site theme.

A note on fonts

The most common fonts used in Web design used to be of two families — ones with *serifs* (the strokes that extend from letters), such as Times New Roman, and those without *(sans-serif),* such as Arial and Verdana. You couldn't guarantee what fonts users had on their computers, so those fonts were a safe default. They're also recognized as fonts with good readability. (For those reading this book that can't wait to pick Gigi, Jokerman, or Curlz MT, and you know who you are, you may want to hold up and read the "A word on usability" section, later in this chapter.)

Best practices when I first learned to design Web sites was that serif fonts were good for paragraph text and sans-serif fonts were good for very large and very small text (like headings and footer notes). The trend today for many sites is to use only sans-serif fonts.

Many companies have a large amount of font styles available on employee computers, especially as the options in MS Office have grown. However, if your users don't have the font you selected, the browser will convert to a default font.

As I describe earlier in this chapter in the "Changing the Theme of Your Site" section, while you're in the Customize a Theme section, you can choose different fonts for the heading and body text of a theme. These fonts don't have to be the same. Although you now have many options to select from, still consider best practices as well as any style guidelines that may be set by your organization.

A word on usability

I suppose the reason you have a SharePoint site is that you and your team are *using* it, and a big part of using a site is being able to read it. (See Figure 19-5 for an example of a usable Web site.) The following common checkpoints for Web sites might apply to your theme choices or perhaps your content on the team site pages as well:

✔ **Is there a strong contrast between the background colors and the text?**
Dark text on a white background is generally considered the easiest to read. The second best is very light text on a very dark background.

One area of SharePoint that this has been a problem with in the past is the Quick Launch menu or left navigation area where the contrast between the background and links isn't distinct enough. Be careful with your selections. Even if red and green are holiday colors, red text on a green background isn't very readable.

Figure 19-5:
A site theme applied.

✔ **Is the font simple and easy to read?** No matter that the Chiller font looks cool at Halloween, a whole page of Chiller will have your users running for the door, or at the very least not reading your site.

✔ **Are you using only a few colors?** Even though it seems like there are a lot of color options in the theme palette, many of them are similar in hue. Using the entire rainbow makes it hard for your users to focus on what's important.

✔ **Are link colors obvious?** If the text is black and links are navy blue or brown, it becomes difficult to identify them.

✔ **Is your *followed* (or visited) link color different enough from my unvisited link color?** A red hyperlink that changes to maroon when visited may not be enough of a visual cue to users that they've followed that link.

The benefits of themes

Although themes only allow you to change colors and fonts, they do have the benefits that take a lot of work to achieve using other methods. The colors also apply to the administrative pages, pop-up dialog boxes and windows, menus, and the Ribbon.

Whenever a discussion of branding occurs, one of the first thoughts should be can you achieve what you need with a custom theme or an alternative style sheet (which I discuss in Chapter 20), or do you need to totally customize the design of the page with custom master pages and CSS files?

Creating a Custom Theme for SharePoint 2010 Using PowerPoint

For many SharePoint site designers and owners, the thought of being able to customize their themes is very exciting. On the flip side, the task of choosing multiple colors may seem daunting to people who know what they like when they can see it but have trouble making the selections. If you're in either camp, you'll enjoy the capability to use PowerPoint to easily select a predefined theme or palette of colors or to make your custom choices and export that color file to SharePoint.

To create the Office Theme file using PowerPoint, follow these steps:

1. **Open PowerPoint and click the Design tab on the Ribbon.**

   When you open PowerPoint, a New Slide file is created. You don't need to worry about changing the slide type or adding slides.

2. **On the Design tab, select a theme.**

   The theme you select isn't particularly important, except that you may like the default color scheme. Remember the colors, not the graphics, are saved.

3. **To change the color scheme, click the Colors drop-down list on the Theme section of the Design tab, as shown in Figure 19-6.**

   The drop-down list shows the built-in color themes available. You can also choose Create New Theme Colors at the bottom of the list.

   If you choose Create New Theme Colors, the dialog box for selecting these colors opens with the colors of the current theme inserted as a starting point.

   Okay, you're going to get déjà vu one way or another. If you started with the SharePoint themes and have never seen the theme selections in PowerPoint, you realize that SharePoint and PowerPoint share the same options.

4. **Select new colors as desired and then type a name for your new theme in the Name field.**

   In PowerPoint, your custom named theme appears in the Custom area of theme choices.

Watch your fonts! Make sure that the PowerPoint fonts in the themes match your desired heading and body fonts for your SharePoint site. For example, when I picked unusual serif fonts in PowerPoint, such as Gigi, they were converted to Trebuchet MS in the Office Theme file. The default fonts of Calibri for titles and Constantia for subtitles in the default Office Theme file in PowerPoint carried over into another of my Office Theme files.

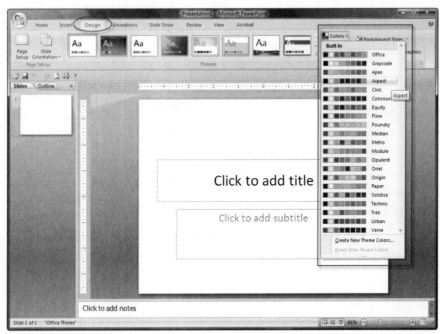

Figure 19-6:
Selecting
a theme in
PowerPoint.

5. **Save your PowerPoint file as an Office Theme by choosing File⇨Save As. Select Office Theme (.thmx) file as the Save as Type.**

   Consider saving the file to a location, such as your desktop or My Documents, so you can easily find it when you're ready to upload it to SharePoint.

To upload the Office Theme file to SharePoint 2010, follow these steps:

1. **Using the browser, open your SharePoint site and choose Site Actions⇨Site Settings.**

2. **Click the Site Theme link in the Look and Feel section and then click the Theme Gallery link in the description at the top of the page.**

   The Theme gallery, which is a SharePoint library, opens.

3. **Click the Add New Item link, as shown in Figure 19-7.**

   The Upload Document dialog box appears.

4. **Click the Browse button to upload a single file or click the link to upload multiple files if you've created more than one .thmx file in PowerPoint.**

5. **Upload your file(s) to the Theme gallery by clicking OK.**

   A dialog box appears with the selected filename. You can add a description before saving if desired.

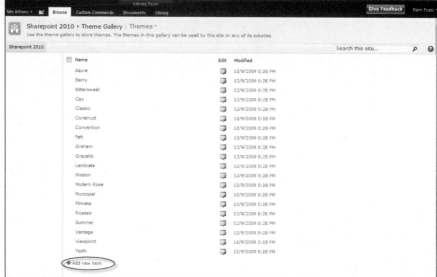

Figure 19-7:
The
SharePoint
Theme
gallery.

6. Click the Save button to save the file.

Your new theme is now saved in the SharePoint 2010 Theme gallery. You can see your new theme in alphabetical order by name in the theme choices. Choose your theme as you would choose any other theme.

Use the preceding steps to access the Theme gallery if you want to delete your custom themes.

Chapter 20

Branding Your SharePoint Site

In This Chapter

▶ Comparing publishing and collaboration site branding

▶ Branding your parts and pieces

▶ Using cascading style sheets

▶ Getting the layout of the Style library and the Master Page gallery

▶ Uploading your alternate style sheet

▶ Giving your site some animation

▶ Taking the next steps for branding

*P*art of my job entails making sure SharePoint sites don't look like SharePoint sites. My clients continually push to have attractive sites that aren't limited by the default, out-of-the-box options. In many cases, the decision to use SharePoint is done by IT for all kinds of good reasons, but the client's design and content needs may come from previous or related corporate sites, or a whole new concept being implemented by the Marketing department.

Neither the product nor my permissions in my first interactions with SharePoint allow me access to brand sites. After my initial frustration with not being able to design the page exactly the way I wanted, I got used to the default format of the page with its Quick Launch menu, full-screen sizing, and modest header. After all, they were often small collaboration sites, and in all cases, intranet sites, not exposed to the general public. In fact, many Internet sites seemed dated and busy after using SharePoint!

When I got involved on the technical and design side, I had to turn the wheel and think like a Web designer again. SharePoint 2007 introduced master pages, and via publishing sites you could make SharePoint sites with all the style, interactivity, and flair of regular Web sites. SharePoint 2010 offers all this functionality, while making it a little easier to incorporate popular animation effects found on today's Web. The efforts in creating these sites are *SharePoint branding*.

What is branding?

Branding, from marketing strategy, means to distinguish your product, service, or organization with a specific identity including logos, colors, fonts, and other imagery.

In this book, I use *branding* to refer to the files and actions required to modify and achieve a particular look and feel. Indeed, many of my clients have strongly branded their Internet or intranet SharePoint site. Others just wanted to create a more usable page for their content with elements shifted to different locations or apply a unique color scheme that can't be accomplished with a theme. I still refer to this as branding.

SharePoint 2010 enables you to use two popular technologies, Silverlight and AJAX, which are both very useful in creating dynamic user experiences.

Comparing Publishing and Collaboration Branding Options

I think it almost seems like there aren't hard-and-fast rules anymore. In collaboration sites, you used to start with the home page, and you got what you got in terms of layout based on the site template. Again, picking a theme and maybe changing the site icon was as far as you were going to get without coding. Now in collaboration sites, being able to use wiki pages for text and images, easily changing the wiki page layout, customizing a theme, and configuring navigation options go a long way to making team sites look more like Web sites, as shown in Figure 20-1.

Still, even with those options, you can't easily move the location of major elements such as navigation bars, insert JavaScript functions, use jQuery animations like carousels, and so on without diving into the technical options of what SharePoint provides to designers and developers for branding purposes. You don't find out how to get that detailed with your master page in this chapter, but you do find out where to start.

As soon as I say you can't do something with a collaboration site in terms of branding, techies start waving their hands saying that they have. And they probably did. To make your life easier though, if you really need to significantly change the appearance of a SharePoint site, start by using a publishing site template.

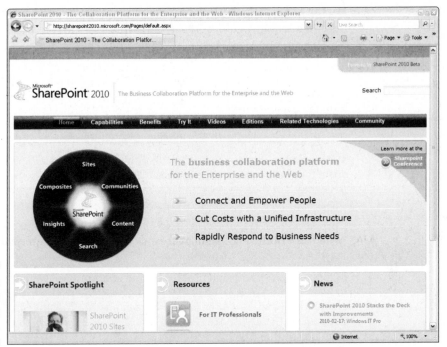

Figure 20-1:
A branded
SharePoint
site.

Publishing sites were created to be branded and include some predefined master pages and page layouts. They also allow you an option to link to an alternate style sheet. This option is helpful if the out-of-the-box files get you most of the way there, but you still want to change some design styles including minor positioning, sizes, and colors. You do need CSS (Cascading Style Sheets) skills to create this alternate style sheet, but you don't have to use third-party software to edit the pages of the site.

You aren't going to come out of this chapter as a SharePoint site designer. What you will know is the parts and pieces that comprise the branding files of SharePoint, where to find these files, and how to upload an alternate style sheet to your publishing site. I also share some helpful tips for SharePoint CSS and what you need to know in order to move forward with a complete branding effort.

Branding Parts and Pieces

The following list features the *parts and pieces* of a SharePoint branding effort. I always call them that because as I define a new branding effort, or help others with theirs, I always need to go down this list to make sure I cover all the bases:

✔ **Master pages:** The theme and general page template layout. One of the most common master layouts is the inverted L with the header and global navigation on top and secondary navigation on the left.

The master page contains HTML, linked or embedded CSS, and SharePoint placeholders for specific SharePoint items. Think of the master page as generally the header, top and left navigation, search, and footer. You don't need to use all these elements, but if you need any of them, the master page is the place to define their placement, and the CSS files associated with the master page is the place to style them.

Master pages can be applied to the public view pages and/or the system pages. System pages like the library views and the Site Settings page may not look as good in your master as the public view of pages. Designers can opt to create separate master pages for system pages or keep the `default.master` with a complementary theme.

✔ **Style sheets:** CSS styles in either separate files or embedded in the master and/or page layouts.

In the section "CSS Primer," later in this chapter, you get a run-through in what a *CSS rule* is — basically the visual properties for a specific element in your Web site. Style sheets can contain many, many rules. Sometimes the styles are separated into different sheets to make it easier to group large numbers of rules, for instance, all the rules for SharePoint controls. Often a master page has an associated style sheet for its look and feel that overrides the out-of-the-box styles SharePoint provides for those elements in a master page.

The *cascading* in CSS indicates that the same rule can be repeated at different levels. (I call it the *closest man standing wins.*) If several instances of the style are applied — such as a linked file to the master, but the same style with different properties embedded in the page layout — the embedded rule wins or applies. So, for example, Microsoft can describe the visual elements via its core SharePoint style sheets, but you might override them with your style sheet linked to the master and again override them on a specific page.

Besides styles used by the master and page layout for page items, positioning, and navigation, I also override SharePoint styles for controls that appear on list and Web Part pages, as well as define styles used by the content editors when entering text.

✔ **Images:** Graphics used for the logo, header, top navigation, left navigation, and so on.

These images are files used along with CSS to create the master template and aren't frequently, if at all, changed after the design is complete. They may include a background for the header, normal and other images for the top navigation, footer logos, and so forth. Unlike the images you may use in the content of the page, I suggest they be located in the Style library similar to the out-of-the-box master images so that only users with specific permissions can locate them.

✔ **Page layouts:** Defined layouts with specific content containers.

Master pages work with page layouts to provide the look and feel of the publishing page, as shown in Figure 20-2. The master contains the template branding elements, but the page layouts provide the arrangement and type of content containers in the content area of the page. Although a master page is generally applied site by site for all the pages, each publishing page has a layout that can be changed.

As I describe in Chapters 14 and 16, Microsoft has multiple page layouts available for publishing pages, and they can be used with a custom master page as well. The Blank Web Part page in particular can be very flexible. However, if your organization wants to limit the types of content that can be used, fix widths of zones, or create custom containers, it may find that creating custom page layouts can help users as they enter the content because the choices are more straightforward.

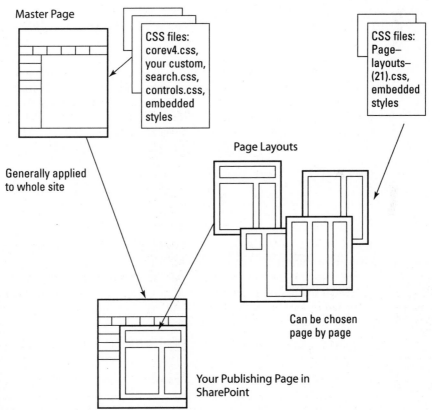

Figure 20-2:
Diagram of a master page, CSS, and page layouts.

Branding versus usability

I've implemented lots of highly branded SharePoint sites for internal use. The costs add up quickly, and I'm not convinced there's always a return on investment (ROI). If your SharePoint site is intended for internal use only, I advise against going gangbusters on flashy branding. Instead, put your money into improving the usability of your site, especially as it relates to adding and editing content.

To me, *usability* equates to little or no training. If your business users can create new pages and edit existing ones without training, you have a highly usable site. Not possible with

SharePoint? Think again. I've used a combination of Edit mode panels, JavaScript, and jQuery in page layouts to create editing experiences that make content entry a breeze for business users. Almost everything you see on the Web is fair game for SharePoint.

For internal sites, use your branding and training dollars to focus on usability instead. The usability of your site directly impacts your business users' productivity, which I guarantee has a much higher ROI than pretty sites and training classes.

   ✔ **Themes:** SharePoint site color schemes.

      Depending on what you brand in your site, you may still want to change or customize a theme in addition to the master page because the theme is far-reaching and the color scheme is applied to menus, system pages, the Ribbon, and so forth that visitors may not see, but your content editors will. Choosing a complementary color scheme completes the package.

Although I only list several branding elements or files, it still may seem daunting to teams with limited design resources. And no, you don't need to touch all these items in a branding effort. In fact, this chapter is more about describing the elements and giving you general guidelines.

If you *do* have a branding resource, he may opt to create a custom master page with an associated style sheet and images, but not custom page layouts. He may use an out-of-the-box master with an alternate style sheet and customize a page layout or two. Understanding what functionality or look and feel comes from each element goes a long way in deciding what to customize.

CSS Primer

This section provides a Cascading Style Sheets primer in very broad strokes. CSS can be very sophisticated and has entire books devoted to the subject.

In any history of HyperText Markup Language (HTML), you'll probably read how what initially was a markup language to describe the display of *content* (headings, tables for tabular data, bullet and numbered lists, and so on) got hijacked by the design and marketing folks in an effort to make the page look attractive.

Reading HTML documents with formatting tags wasn't only messy but inefficient. If you wanted to change all the blue words on the page to red in one fell swoop, it was awkward and error-prone. Enter CSS as a way to separate look and feel from the content. These style rules are often placed in the head area of an HTML document or in a separate file altogether that is linked to the HTML page (for SharePoint, it's often the master page). You can change the color of hyperlinks for an entire site in as long as it takes to type several characters!

Styles can be created for specific HTML elements, such as H1 (heading one). These styles apply automatically when those elements are used in the content. Custom styles, such as `.mystyleheader`, are specifically applied as desired. CSS is used for font, backgrounds, size and positioning, and many other visual instructions for the browser. The browser already has a default way of presenting text and headers, among other things.

Anatomy of a CSS rule

A CSS rule contains the element and one or more descriptors. The element can be an HTML element or a custom (class) style that can be applied as desired:

- ✔ **HTML element:** Properties descriptors in this HTML element example include the color of the text, font style, font size, and font family (pretty self-explanatory).

    ```
    h1 { color: red; font-style: bold ; font-size: 16px;
             font-family: arial; }
    ```

- ✔ **Custom class style:** The custom rule is the same, except that CSS has some shortcut formats, so I didn't have to individually type all the font elements.

    ```
    .mystyleheader { color: red; font: bold 16px arial; }
    ```

The HTML element and classes shown in the preceding CSS rules are called *selectors.* The rules defined for the selector are applied to everything in your Web page that matches the HTML element or custom class. The examples shown here are very simple. Selectors can get very complex when you need to apply rules to elements that are nested deeply in your Web page.

SharePoint has thousands of CSS rules, and it takes patience and experience to find, figure out, and create your own styles to override these predefined styles. On the other hand, if you want to change a couple font sizes, the background images of the top navigation, the logo, and/or the look of the left navigation, you may be able to copy the style sheet associated with a predefined master and modify those few items.

The `.mystyleheader` class is shown in the preceding list to easily define the difference between the HTML element and a custom class style. Class names used by SharePoint and created by you have more meaningful names.

When you're creating your own style names, as tempting as it might be to name a style `.redlink` or `.blueheading`, just as soon as you apply that style in multiple locations, I guarantee the team will want to change the color! So describe the element by its content intention, not its colors or properties.

Figure 20-3 shows several styles contained in the core `.css` file of SharePoint 2010.

```
A) corev4.css
← → ▢ Sharepoint 2010 ▸ corev4.css
270 text-decoration:underline;
271 }
272 table.ms-navitex td,span.ms-navitem{
273 background-image:url("/_layouts/images/navBullet.gif");
274 background-repeat:no-repeat;
275 background-position:left top;
276 padding:3px 6px 4px 16px;
277 font-family:tahoma;
278 }
279 .ms-navsubmenu1{
280 width:100%;
281 border-collapse:collapse;
282 /* [ReplaceColor(themeColor:"Light1-Lightest")] */ background-color:#f2f8ff;
283 }
284 .ms-navsubmenu2{
285 width:100%;
286 /* [ReplaceColor(themeColor:"Light1-Lightest")] */ background-color:#f2f8ff;
287 margin-bottom:6px;
288 }
289 table.ms-navselected{
290 padding:2px;
291 }
292 table.ms-navselected,span.ms-navselected{
293 /* [RecolorImage(themeColor:"Accent6",method:"Tinting")] */ background-image:url("/_layouts/images/SELECTEDNAV.GIF");
294 /* [ReplaceColor(themeColor:"Accent6-Lighter")] */ background-color:#ffe6a0;
295 background-repeat:repeat-x;
296 }
297 table.ms-navselected td{
298 background-image:url("/_layouts/images/navBullet.gif");
299 background-repeat:no-repeat;
300 background-position:top left;
301 padding:3px 6px 4px 17px;
302 }
303 table.ms-navheader td{
304 background-image:none;
305 }
```

Figure 20-3:
Part of
the core4.
css file in
SharePoint.

CSS resources

You can find many great online resources for discovering CSS, including the World Wide Web Consortium (W3C) for standards (www.w3c.org) and W3Sschools (www.w3schools.com) for CSS tutorials.

Also helpful in a CSS branding effort are browser tools, such as Firebug for Firefox and the IE Developer Toolbar for IE (Internet Explorer) 7, that allow you to find the CSS styles on a page with a click. I'm especially enchanted with the latest version of the Developer Toolbar baked into IE8. It has some great features for sleuthing CSS styles. These tools can be invaluable in tracking the actual style applied.

The Style Library and the Master Page Gallery

Most of the branding files are in one of two places — the Style library and the Master Page and Page Layout gallery from the Site Settings page (both only visible if you have the proper permissions).

Both these document libraries are contained in the top site of the site collection, so if you're the owner/designer of a subsite, you may need to work with the site collection owner/administrator to decide what changes you can make and how you can position and apply branding files.

Contents of the Style library

The Style library contains CSS files, Extensible Stylesheet Language (XSL) files, and images used by predefined master pages, page layouts, and controls in SharePoint 2010.

To locate CSS files in the Style library of a publishing site:

1. **Choose Site Actions➪View All Site Content.**

   The content of the site appears. The Style library is located in the Document Library section.

2. **Click the Style Library link.**

   Several folders appear in the Style library including en-us (for U.S. English) and Images.

3. **Click the en-us folder (or other language folder).**

   Other folders appear, including Core Styles and Themable, that contain predefined styles (see Figure 20-4). If you're making custom styles for a branding effort, create a folder under en-us to contain your custom styles for that site, so they're in a familiar location. However, you usually create that folder and its files in SharePoint Designer rather than in the browser.

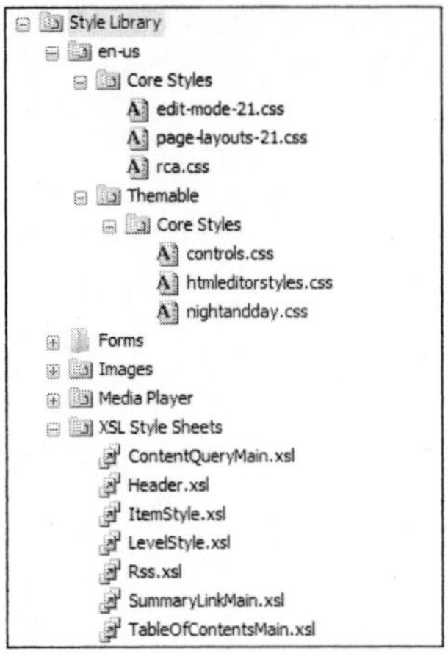

Figure 20-4:
The folder
structure
in the Style
library.

```
☐ Style Library
   ☐ en-us
      ☐ Core Styles
         A] edit-mode-21.css
         A] page-layouts-21.css
         A] rca.css
      ☐ Themable
         ☐ Core Styles
            A] controls.css
            A] htmleditorstyles.css
            A] nightandday.css
   ☐ Forms
   ☐ Images
   ☐ Media Player
   ☐ XSL Style Sheets
      ContentQueryMain.xsl
      Header.xsl
      ItemStyle.xsl
      LevelStyle.xsl
      Rss.xsl
      SummaryLinkMain.xsl
      TableOfContentsMain.xsl
```

4. **View the different CSS files in the folder.**

   Although these files can be opened with SharePoint Designer 2010 if you have it installed, I do *not* recommend this unless you are familiar with that product. See Step 5 for an alternative way to view the contents of a CSS file.

5. **To view the contents of a file, click the Library tab on the Ribbon under Library Tools and then click the Open with Explorer option.**

   The files appear in a folder window. You can right-click and choose Open with Notepad to view the content. I strongly suggest you *do not* edit these files, but you can copy and paste the content into your own Notepad file for review.

6. **Close the folder window when you're done.**

   Again, you'll find it's best not to modify the predefined SharePoint styles. Remember that you can override these styles in your alternate style sheet, in styles linked, or embedded in your custom files.

Viewing images used for predefined master pages

To find images used for predefined master pages, use the same steps as for CSS files in the preceding section, but click the Images link in Step 3 (after opening the Style library).

You may see folders to house specific graphics as well as images for SharePoint predefined master pages in the root of the folder. When you create custom branding, create a folder under Images and give it the site's name — this folder contains your images related to that master page. Don't place images for page content in this location and don't mix your images with the predefined images.

If you use the steps in the preceding section, while you're in the folder window containing the images, you can switch to one of the icons views in Windows Explorer to see what the images look like.

Master Pages and Page Layouts gallery

I describe options in a publishing site versus a collaboration site. If you're in a collaboration site collection, you may note the Master Page gallery in Galleries, but there isn't a link to apply a master page in the Look and Feel section.

In publishing sites, you have a Master Page and Page Layouts gallery as well as a Master Page option in the Look and Feel section. The Master Page link allows you to apply a different master page as well as upload an alternate style sheet.

To view the contents of the Master Pages and Page Layouts Gallery:

1. **Choose Site Actions⇨Site Settings.**

2. **Click the Master Pages and Page Layouts link in the Galleries section.**

   Several folders appear as well as library items that end in either .master (master pages) or .aspx (page layouts), as shown in Figure 20-5.

Figure 20-5: The Master Page gallery.

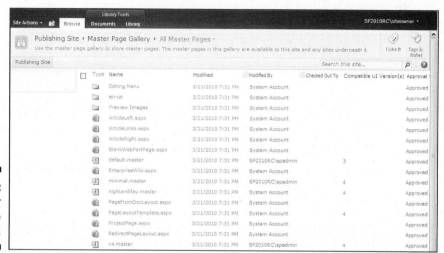

3. **Note the property fields shown for the files.**

   Showing in this library are the content type of the page (for page layouts, you may see Welcome Page and Article Page content types). You also see whether the file's approval status — Draft, Pending, or Approved. Remember, if someone is editing a page and it isn't published and approved, other users may not see recent changes.

4. **To view the contents of a file, click the Library tab on the Ribbon under Library Tools and then click the Open with Explorer option.**

   The files appear in a folder window. You can right-click and choose Open with Notepad to view the content. I strongly suggest you *do not* edit these files, but you can copy and paste the content into your own Notepad file for review.

5. **Close the folder window when you're done.**

Uploading an Alternate Style Sheet

Two of the questions you probably have are: When do you use the alternate style sheet, and what do you put in it? I don't know that a right or wrong answer exists, but I generally use an alternate style sheet if I want to keep the default.master or another predefined master that's applied, but override certain CSS styles linked to those masters, including the core.css.

Another reason I may upload an alternate style sheet is to override control styles or add styles for the HTML Editor Ribbon. If I create my own master page, I generally create a style sheet that links to the master page and don't use an alternate style sheet.

If you know how to make custom themes, you may not need to use an alternate style sheet to change colors and fonts for your site. See Chapter 19 for instructions on how to easily create a custom theme.

I suggest you use the tools I mention earlier in this chapter, Firebug and/or IE Developer Toolbar, to locate a style you want to change. Or you can copy the associated CSS file for the predefined master you want to use (for example, nightandday.css) or the core CSS file (corerev4.css), and modify a copy of those files to upload as your alternate CSS file. You need to include only the styles you want to override. In fact, you don't need to override every descriptor. If you only want to override the color, that's the only descriptor you need to include for the class or element. The site continues to use default styling for the other properties of the element.

You can edit a CSS file using any text editor or an HTML editor, such as Dreamweaver or SharePoint Designer. When you've completed your alternate style sheet, save it to the Style library where the other styles are located. As I mention earlier, I normally create a subfolder under /style library/ en-us.

To upload the alternate style file:

1. **Choose Site Actions⇨All Site Settings.**

   The Master Page link appears in the Look and Feel section.

2. **Open the Master Page settings by clicking the Master Page link.**

   The Site Master Page Settings page opens, as shown in Figure 20-6. This page has three sections, Site Master Page, System Master Page, and Alternate CSS URL.

Figure 20-6:
The Master Page Settings page.

3. **In the Alternate CSS URL section, select the Specify a CSS File to Be Used by This Publishing Site and All Sites That Inherit from It radio button.**

   The Browse button enables.

4. **Copy/paste the path to your file in the field or click the Browse button to locate where you uploaded your CSS file in the Style library.**

   If you click the Browse button, make sure you're in the correct folder by clicking the Style Library link on the left. In the examples I give, this style sheet would be in the `/style library/en-us/`*site name* subfolder.

5. **Select the file, if you clicked the Browse button, and then click OK.**

   You return to the Site Master Page Settings page. The path to your alternate style sheet appears next to the Browse button.

6. **(Optional) Select the Reset All Subsites to Inherit This Alternate CSS URL check box.**

   If you want all the subsites under the site you're on to use these same alternate styles, select this check box. If you don't want the child sites to inherit the styles, leave the check box blank.

7. **Click OK.**

   Your alternate styles appear.

Note your options in the Alternate CSS URL section in case you want to reset them in the future. You can select the Reset to Use the Alternate Style Sheet of the Parent Site check box (if there's an alternate style sheet) or select the Use Windows SharePoint Services Default Styles radio button.

Custom Branding

Although I talk about customizing page templates (layouts) with SharePoint Designer in Chapter 16, this book isn't meant to teach you how to use SharePoint Designer. That itself is a big topic that deserves its own book(s), blogs, and reference guides. Your organization may limit the use of SharePoint Designer and/or what you can do with the tool. Check that out before spending a lot of time studying the branding files!

Many bloggers specialize in SharePoint branding. They have reference tables, tutorials, and great examples to get you started. If you aren't a CSS expert, be prepared to spend a fair amount of time experimenting with your styles to get things just right. You might start checking now with your peers and friends to find those with CSS skills!

If you want to find out more on your own, one of the easiest ways to figure out SharePoint branding is to copy a predefined master page and its associated style sheet(s) and then study their content. If you're using SharePoint Designer, you can copy the content of these files directly into a new MASTER file or new CSS files in the site folder structure with the desired names.

Modify the CSS link in your new master page to point to your new style sheet. Now you can start to experiment with modifying the styles or changing the location of a couple elements in the master page.

The CSS file will probably have styles that link to images. As I mention earlier, I create a subfolder in /style library/images for my site and upload images I use for the master page to that folder. I then modify the links in the style sheet to point to my own images.

Please note that the markup in the master page includes placeholders for SharePoint content, HTML, and/or CSS positioning to give the page structure as well as new 2010 code related to the Ribbon, accessibility, and other new functionality. The placeholders are very important in that you must include required ones, or many page layouts don't work. As a general rule, spend 70–90 percent of your effort in the style sheets and the remainder editing the master page.

SharePoint 2010 includes a minimal master page you can copy that includes the required elements. I generally like to start with a predefined SharePoint master page or a master page that I've created already to speed up my development. However, that can be a double-edged sword. Sometimes, the process is faster and has less baggage than if I started with the minimal master.

Page layouts can override SharePoint elements placed in the master. For example, the master can contain instructions for a left navigation element, but a page layout, such as a Welcome Splash page, can override the master and not use that element.

Remember that a master page must be checked in, published with a major version, and approved before visitors can see changes. You need to do this at least one time to even have a new master page available to apply to your site. I recommend applying to a test site that others can't see. After a site goes live with your master page, you may want to keep your changes to a master page in a Pending (checked in and published, but not approved) mode until you're ready for others to see it.

The CSS files don't need approval — only a major version published for others to see needs this. Realize that when you're working in a CSS file that's connected to an active master page, users can see your changes as soon as you publish a major version.

Chapter 21

Managing Site Assets

In This Chapter

▶ Deciding where to store content

▶ Packaging assets in a solution

▶ Looking at a site's stats

*T*his chapter could be called Where to Find Stuff, Where to Put Stuff, and Stuff That's Good to Know about Stuff That Might Not Fit Elsewhere (unfortunately, that title was just too long). A lot of the stuff I talk about in this chapter I mention elsewhere in this book within the steps of a specific task. In this chapter, though, you get an overview of where you put the stuff created with those step-by-step tasks.

In fact, if you have a project going on or coming up, deciding on locations to store the content and establishing good naming conventions is a great mind-mapping exercise to break the tension of nailing down all the other details. Granted, you want your locations to be good choices, and your names clear and unambiguous, but this probably isn't going to be the hardest task you have (knock on wood).

In this chapter, I use the terms *pre-created* and *predefined.* Throughout this book, I use *predefined* to mean SharePoint 2010 has already set up the configuration template; for example, a document library. Using the Document Library template, you can create as many document libraries as you need with your own names. *Pre-created* means that SharePoint has gone one step further and made some libraries and lists for you when your site was created.

Figuring Out What to Put Where

When thinking about the problem of what to put where, it's important to differentiate between a user's content and site resources. A site's *resources* are the images, styles, scripts, and various other files that come together to create the user experience for your site. Of course, the site's users may also have all these files used as content.

So how can you tell the difference? The key differentiator between the site's branding resources and a user's content is who owns it. If the file — the video, image, or audio file — is intended to be used by the end users who maintain the site, it's user content. If those files aren't intended to be consumed in pages, I consider them off-limits to users. Figure 21-1 shows an example of how to differentiate files based on whether they're used for branding or used for content.

User content needs to always go in a library so that users can take advantage of all the great library features — check-out, versioning, and approval — that they may want for managing their content.

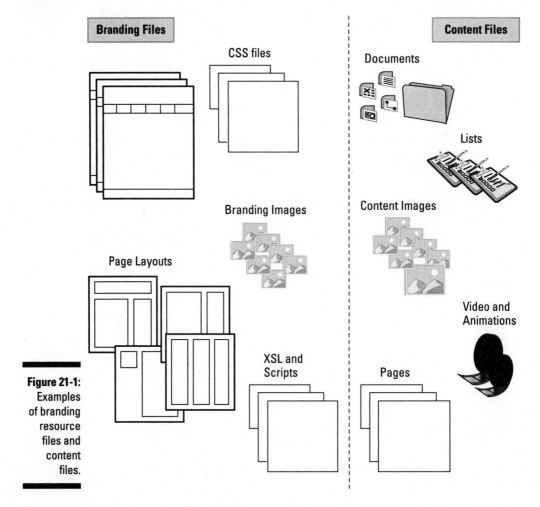

Figure 21-1:
Examples of branding resource files and content files.

Using standard naming conventions

Naming conventions are exactly what they sound like, conventions for naming things. Your organization, for example, may follow very specific standards and guidelines for documents and programming. If you aren't bound by any particulars, I suggest the names be short, clear, and without spaces (titles, however, can be longer and more informative).

I try to be consistent when naming documents, files, and images, especially with spacing and capitalization. If the naming conventions are different, it won't break anything, but it helps to plan ahead so that every time you name a file, you don't wonder, "How did I name that last time?"

Also, be careful about naming something that has a different meaning in SharePoint. The other day I had a coworker name a site *xyz*MASTER, and I was confused every time he talked about it. I live in the world of master pages, so it took an epiphany to understand he was talking about a site, not a master page.

Using libraries to store content

A document library can be used to store any kind of user content. However, SharePoint provides additional types of libraries that may be suited better for specialized kinds of content, which I summarize in Table 21-1.

Table 21-1	Kinds of Libraries for Storing Content
To Store This Kind of Content . . .	*. . . Use This Kind of Library*
Small videos, audio files, and images	Site Assets library or Picture library
Documents, such as PDF files	Document library
Individual PowerPoint slides for reuse	Slide library

So users can easily find resources, designate a library as a suggested asset location. Doing so causes the library to appear in the asset picker. Click the Suggested Content Browser Locations link on your site's Site Settings page to configure this setting.

Putting Web page content in default locations

SharePoint provides a number of default locations for storing content, such as Web pages. Team sites use the Site Pages library, whereas publishing sites use the Pages library. Table 21-2 lists some of the common locations SharePoint provides for storing resources.

Table 21-2	Default Locations for Content
To Store This . . .	*. . . Use This Default Location*
Documents	Documents library
Images on pages	Images library
Images in branding	Site Collection Images library
Master pages	Master Page gallery
Page layouts	Master Page gallery
Publishing pages	Pages library
Reusable Content	Reusable Content list
Style sheets	Style library
Themes	Themes gallery
XSL templates	Style library
Wiki pages and Web part pages	Site Pages library

In most cases, you aren't limited to using just the libraries provided by SharePoint. The exception is the Pages library. All publishing pages must be stored in the Pages library. And the galleries — Master Page gallery and Themes gallery — can't be changed.

You can use folders in the Pages library, unlike in previous versions of SharePoint.

You usually want to store site-wide resources off the root site. I generally recommend using a single Image library and using views and metadata rather than having a library at each site in your site hierarchy. But there are no hard-and-fast rules. Do what makes sense for your site and your organization.

Deploying content in folders or libraries

You have other options besides placing your resources in document libraries. With SharePoint Designer 2010, you can create a folder and place your items inside it. Or if you want to reuse items across several site collections (or even the entire farm), you can deploy items directly to the hard drives on the Web servers. Table 21-3 summarizes your options.

Table 21-3	Deployment Options
Put Stuff Here . . .	*. . . When You Want These Features*
In document libraries	To use the browser to upload files; to use check-out and version control
In folders off the site's root	To hide resources from the browser
In folders on the server	To make the same version of a given resource available across multiple site collections

Packaging Your Assets

At times, you want to package your site customizations for reuse. For example, if you create a snazzy branding scheme, you could package it and use it on another site. SharePoint's packages are *solutions,* which are a set of files that includes whatever files you want to package — scripts, master pages, style sheets, and so on — along with configuration files that tell SharePoint where to put these files. Use Visual Studio 2010 to package your files into a solution. Visual Studio 2010 has a set of tools that make it relatively easy to package your solution.

The files inside a solution are organized into groups dubbed *features,* which are logical sets of files that enable functionality in a SharePoint site. For example, you might package all your branding as a single feature in your solution or you could use multiple features. If you don't have good reason to use multiple features, don't.

If you plan to use your solution in a few site collections, you can upload your solution to each site collection's Solution gallery. The *Solution gallery* is a document library at the root of each site collection. A solution is a file with a .wsp file extension.

Your farm must have the user code solution feature enabled to create a solution. Otherwise, you have to deploy your solutions to the central solution store.

Alternatively, if your solution is going to be used throughout the entire SharePoint farm, you can have IT deploy your solution to the central solution store. Then every site collection in your SharePoint farm would have access to the files in your solution.

Creating a solution in Visual Studio

The following steps walk you through, at a very high level, the process to create a solution:

1. **With the browser and SharePoint Designer 2010, create the assets that you want to package.**

   For example, you might create lists, content types, page layouts, and style sheets.

2. **Create a site template of your site (see Chapter 13 for details).**

3. **In Visual Studio 2010, create a new project and use the SharePoint project template to import your template as a solution, as shown in Figure 21-2.**

   The Import wizard appears.

4. **With the Import wizard, select the items you want to include in your solution.**

   Visual Studio imports the items you select.

5. **Use the Solution Explorer to explore the imported items, as shown in Figure 21-3.**

   You can make changes to the configuration and asset files as necessary. Please see SharePoint's software development kit (SDK) for more details on working with features.

   You can use Visual Studio to check your files into a source control system, such as Team Foundation Server.

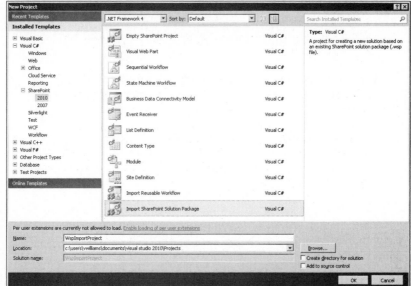

Figure 21-2:
Importing
a site
template
into Visual
Studio 2010.

Figure 21-3:
Explore
items using
Solution
Explorer.

6. **To build your new package, choose Build⇨Package in Visual Studio 2010.**

   Visual Studio packages your files into a new solution. This package file is located in the BIN directory of your project.

Uploading and activating a solution

You can give this file to your IT staff for deployment into a test environment, or you can upload it into the Solution gallery by following these steps:

1. **Browse to the site collection where you want to upload the solution.**

   I recommend using a test environment until your solution is thoroughly tested.

2. **Choose Site Actions⇨Site Settings.**

   The Site Settings page appears.

3. **On the Site Settings page, click the Solutions link in the Gallery section and then on the Solutions tab in the Ribbon, click the Upload Solution button.**

   The Upload Solution dialog box appears.

4. **Upload your solution file to the gallery using the Upload Solution dialog box.**

   The Activate Solution window appears.

5. **Click the Activate button on the Ribbon, as shown in Figure 21-4, to activate your solution in the site.**

   SharePoint activates the solution so that it can be used in the site.

Figure 21-4:
Activate
your
uploaded
solution.

After you upload your solution, you need to activate any features that are in your solution. Remember that your assets are organized into features. You activate features in the Site Settings page with the Manage Site Features link (for site-level features) or the Site Collection Features link (for site collection features), as shown in Figure 21-5.

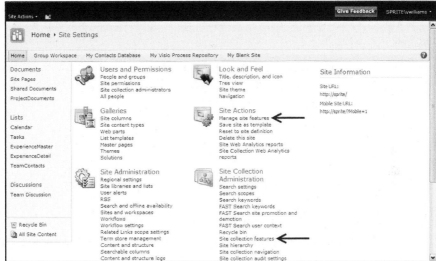

Figure 21-5: Managing features.

Collecting Statistics

At the top-level site collection is a pre-created document library for Customized Reports that has the templates to create Web Analytic custom reports for the site. Before reporting can be obtained, the feature for reporting needs to be turned on at the site collection level.

In the Site Actions section of the Site Settings page, you see the Site Web Analytics Reports and the Site Collection Web Analytics Reports links. Subsites also have a Site Web Analytics Reports link.

If you click these links (and reporting has been turned on and had time to create statistics), you see a multitude of information about your site and its visitors (see Figure 21-6). The report includes items, such as

- Total and average number of page views
- Total and average number of daily unique visitors
- Total and average number of referrers

✔ Top pages, visitors, referrers, destinations, and browsers

✔ Total number of sites, lists, libraries, and storage

Clicking the Analyze tab at the top of this library page allows you to change the date ranges and site scopes, as well as export reports and schedule alerts/reports workflows.

SharePoint 2010 also includes a Web Analytics Web Part that you can use to display the statistics for your site.

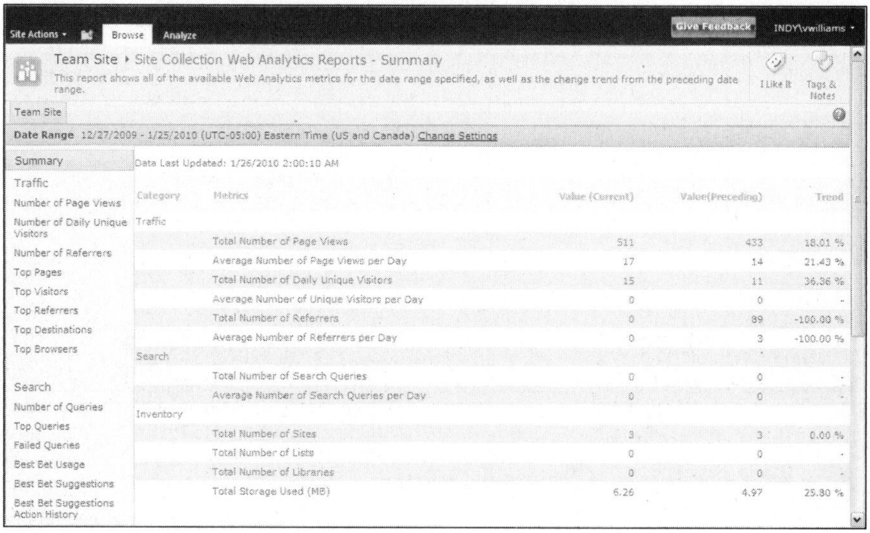

Figure 21-6:
A team
site Web
Analytics
Reports
Summary
page.

Category	Metrics	Value (Current)	Value(Preceding)	Trend
Traffic				
	Total Number of Page Views	511	433	18.01 %
	Average Number of Page Views per Day	17	14	21.43 %
	Total Number of Daily Unique Visitors	15	11	36.36 %
	Average Number of Unique Visitors per Day	0	0	-
	Total Number of Referrers	0	89	-100.00 %
	Average Number of Referrers per Day	0	3	-100.00 %
Search				
	Total Number of Search Queries	0	0	-
	Average Number of Search Queries per Day	0	0	-
Inventory				
	Total Number of Sites	3	3	0.00 %
	Total Number of Lists	0	0	-
	Total Number of Libraries	0	0	-
	Total Storage Used (MB)	6.26	4.97	25.80 %

Part V
Enterprise Services

The 5th Wave   By Rich Tennant

"It's web-based, on-demand, and customizable. Still, I think I'm going to miss our old sales incentive methods."

In this part . . .

*U*sing metadata instead of folders to organize content requires a shift in thinking, but pays off when you want to use search quickly. This part shows you how to use SharePoint's metadata and content types to manage content.

I also briefly touch on how you can turn key performance indicators, business intelligence, and dashboards into real-world SharePoint functionality that people can use. Hopefully, this part convinces you to explore the Business Intelligence Center, Excel Services, and PerformancePoint to take your SharePoint to the next level.

Chapter 22

Content Types and Metadata

In This Chapter

▶ Differentiating between intrinsic and extrinsic metadata

▶ Understanding metadata and term stores

▶ Adding your own personal touches

▶ Getting familiar with content types

▶ Using and reusing site columns

*M*etadata is typically defined as data about data. But that sounds much more technical than it really is because "data" can take the form of any information or content. For any information, or any set of information (or content object in SharePoint), there are things you can say about it, and the stuff you can say about it is metadata. Attributes, labels, characteristics, location, and types are all examples of metadata.

So if metadata is information about content and SharePoint is a content management system, why did it take me 'til Chapter 22 to talk about metadata? Well, the reality is that you can happily use SharePoint without giving much thought to metadata. But if you want to get the most of your content, using metadata to manage your content will make a big difference.

Understanding Intrinsic and Extrinsic Metadata

Metadata can be intrinsic or extrinsic. *Intrinsic* metadata is the static metadata that relates specific qualities of what it describes, such as file type or creation date. Intrinsic metadata is impersonal and can be applied to the content object without regard to the object's context or its relation to other content objects. Intrinsic metadata is pretty straightforward, and it can be useful for putting things in neat categories with other things that pretty much everyone can agree share intrinsic metadata traits (in fact, some intrinsic metadata, such as Save Date, can be determined by a computer without human input). Intrinsic metadata can provide a useful way to locate, filter, or group the data it describes. And intrinsic metadata often allows the consumer (person or system) to do something specific with or about the content object, like — in the case of file type — determine a software application that will open it. Simple search interfaces often make use of intrinsic metadata to facilitate the search process, and intrinsic metadata is sometimes very useful in finding information objects that display straightforward characteristics.

Extrinsic metadata is slipperier — it's subjective metadata that can be applied to content objects by association; users associate some trait, label, or characteristic with the information object in a way that's meaningful to them. Extrinsic metadata is more personal because it tends to rely heavily on context, and for a given content object, different people are likely to apply different extrinsic metadata to it. (Groups of people often will demonstrate trends in applying extrinsic metadata when presented with the same content object. More about folksonomies in the "Getting Personal with Folksonomies" section, later in this chapter.) If you've ever tagged a photo on Flickr, for example, that tag was extrinsic metadata.

SharePoint 2010 gives you lots of ways to apply and use both flavors (intrinsic and extrinsic) of metadata. And a combination of both improves findability and consistency of content objects. For best results, I recommend that you use a combination of metadata strategies — some controlled (content types, for example) and others that let users roll their own (such as social tagging).

1 Never Metadata 1 Didn't Like

When clients complain to me about their search results (such as they can't find anything or the search results aren't relevant), that's my cue to talk to them about metadata because how and where they handle metadata has a huge impact on the "findiness" of information.

If you have terms that you want to make sure everyone uses consistently, set those up as managed metadata terms. *Managed metadata* refers to a term or a set of terms that can be associated with multiple site collections. For example, if your company has four sales territories, you can set up a managed metadata term set to store that list of territories. Then, all sites can use these same terms each time they need to associate sales territories with content in your site.

Creating a term store

To create a new set of terms, your SharePoint site collection must be associated with a *term store* — a place to store and manage terms. The term store must be created by IT, but the management of the store and the terms within it can be delegated to you. In other words, it's not really the role of your IT department to manage your company's terms.

Managed metadata is configured through the managed metadata service application (MMSA). A SharePoint deployment can have many instances of this service, each configured with different sets of terms. *Web applications* (the containers that store site collections) can be associated with zero to many MMSAs. Terms are stored in a database separate from the site's content database.

Terms can be organized into a hierarchy. Additionally, terms can be grouped into term sets (which contain a hierarchy of terms), and each group assigned an owner. The owner can grant other people permission to manage the terms in that term set group. All this activity occurs in the Term Store Management tool, which is accessible from the Site Settings page of the top-level site in a site collection.

To open the Term Store Management tool:

1. **Browse to any site collection associated with the term store you want to manage and then choose Site Actions⇨Site Settings.**

   The Site Settings page is displayed. Odd, no?

2. **In the Site Administration group, click the Term Store Management link.**

   The Term Store Management tool appears, as shown in Figure 22-1.

   If the site isn't configured to use a term store, you see a message telling you so. Contact IT for assistance.

The Term Store Management tool is part of the SharePoint 2010 managed metadata service application. Like all service applications, MMSA is configured in Central Administration. To use the service, a Web application must be associated with at least one instance of an MMSA.

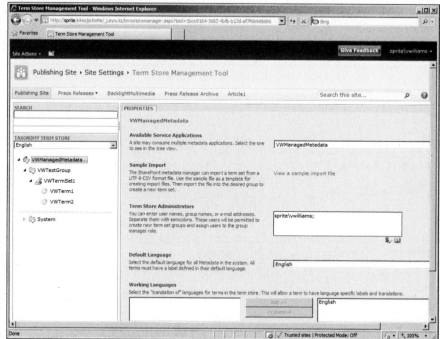

Figure 22-1:
Use the
Term Store
Management
tool.

The Term Store Management tool is divided into two panes. The left pane shows a Tree View of the term hierarchy, and the right pane shows the properties for the current item selected in the tree.

Tree View is a little persnickety to navigate. To expand items in Tree View, you have to click the arrow next to the item.

To add new terms to an item in Tree View, you have to hover over the item until you see an arrow. Clicking the arrow opens a drop-down list, as shown in Figure 22-2.

Importing a term set file

You can also import your term sets instead of manually entering terms. SharePoint 2010 provides a sample import file that you can use to see how to import terms. To get the `ImportTermSet.csv` file:

1. **Browse to the Term Store Management tool, as I describe in the preceding section.**

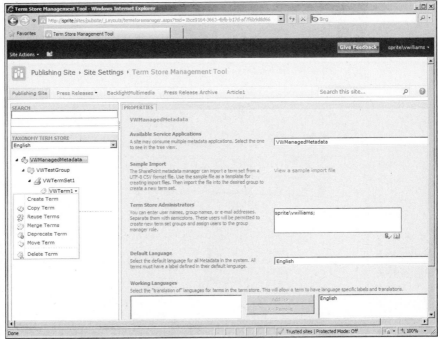

Figure 22-2:
Click an
item to view
a drop-
down list.

2. **Click the View a Sample Import File link and then save the resulting file to your desktop.**

   The `ImportTermSet.csv` file downloads to your desktop. You can edit this file to create your own import term file.

3. **Open the file in Excel or a text editor.**

To import a term set file:

1. **Click a term group in the hierarchy of your Term Store Management tool.**

   A *term group* is the highest level in your hierarchy. You can easily tell where you are in the hierarchy by clicking an item and viewing its properties in the right pane.

2. **Click the arrow on the group and choose Import Term Set from the drop-down list.**

3. **Browse to the file you created in the preceding set of steps and click OK.**

   The terms are imported into the term set. Figure 22-3 shows the term set included with the sample import file.

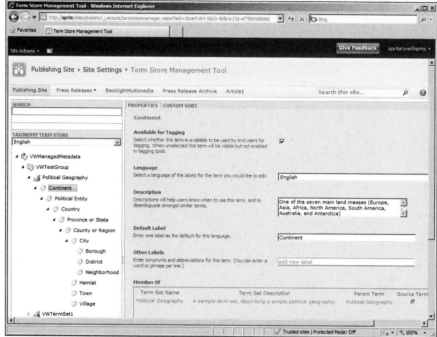

Figure 22-3:
Import
the sample
term set.

Adding a managed metadata column to a list or library

When you have these metadata terms, how do you actually get them in your lists and libraries? You add a managed metadata column type to your list or library. Recall that SharePoint 2010 provides several kinds of column types — Single Line of Text, Number, and Date and Time being a few. The Managed Metadata column type allows you to add a column to your list that points to some place in your term set hierarchy.

To add a managed metadata column to a list or library:

1. **Browse to the list or library where you want to add the managed metadata column.**

2. **On the Ribbon, click the List (or Library) tab and then in the Manage Views group, click the Create Column button.**

   The Create Column box displays.

   I discuss creating columns in more detail in Chapter 4.

3. **Enter a name for your column in the Column Name text box.**

4. **Select the Managed Metadata radio button.**

   Additional options for configuring a managed metadata column appear.

5. **In the Multiple Value field section, select the Allow Multiple Values check box.**

   Leave the check box deselected if you don't want users to be able to select multiple terms. *Note:* A column with multiple values can't be used for sorting.

6. **In the Display Format section, select either the Display Term Label in the Field or the Display the Entire Path to the Term in the Field radio button.**

   Displaying the entire path is helpful to provide context for the term.

7. **In the Use a Managed Term Set section, navigate to the section of the term set hierarchy you want to use in this column, as shown in Figure 22-4.**

   All term sets associated with your site appear in this section. Everything below the term you select appears for users to select as a value for the column.

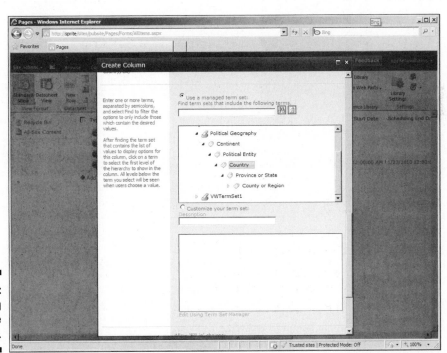

Figure 22-4:
Navigating
to the
term set.

8. **(Optional) If you want users to be able to enter their own value instead of selecting one, select the Allow Fill-In Choices radio button.**

   Only term sets that you designate as open allow this option.

9. **(Optional) Enter a default value for this column in the Default Value text field.**

10. **Click OK.**

    SharePoint adds the column to your list or library.

Figure 22-5 shows an example of the user experience when someone is selecting a term from a term set to use as a column value. The term set uses the hierarchy imported in Figure 22-3.

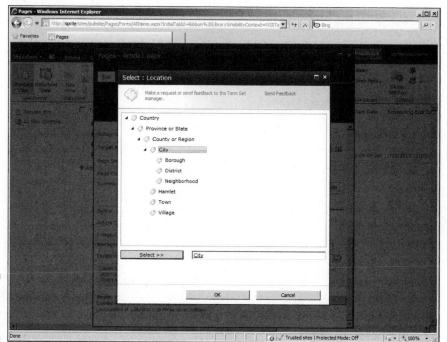

Figure 22-5:
Using a term in a column.

Getting Personal with Folksonomies

A *folksonomy* is a taxonomy (or set of terms) that arises as a result of people applying their own tags *(metadata)* to content objects. People use the tags that make sense to them, so over a period of time as more people tag, the folksonomy becomes more and more appropriate for the audience by associating content objects with the words and concepts people use to think about them.

SharePoint provides another kind of metadata, *keywords,* that you can use to apply free-form terms to content. Unlike metadata terms, keywords aren't organized into a hierarchy that users select from. Instead, users can enter any value into a keyword field. SharePoint 2010 provides an Enterprise Keywords column that's configured already for use as a free-form keywords field.

The Enterprise Keywords field is a site column. I discuss site columns in more detail later in this chapter, in the "Using Columns" section. The column uses a Managed Metadata column type that's configured to use the site's default keyword store. Each site needs to be configured with one default keyword store in an MMSA. The site can be associated with multiple instances of an MMSA, each with its own configuration settings, but only one can be designated as the default keyword store.

Enterprise Wikis use a Managed Metadata column configured to accept fill-in values, similar to how keywords work. Figure 22-6 shows entering a key-word into a wiki page. When someone enters a fill-in value with a Managed Metadata field, that value is available for everyone else to use.

Managed keywords provide a way to allow your users to enter their own free-form terms to a list item, document, or other library item. They're a useful way to allow users to create a free-form taxonomy, or folksonomy, of your items. *Social tags* are a kind of keyword, but they're used to vote or rate items.

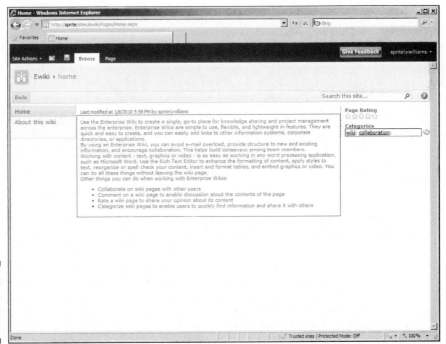

Figure 22-6:
Entering a keyword in a wiki page.

One of the benefits of going through all the trouble of using a hierarchy of terms to classify content is that you can use that same hierarchy to navigate to content. Figure 22-7 shows metadata navigation in a library.

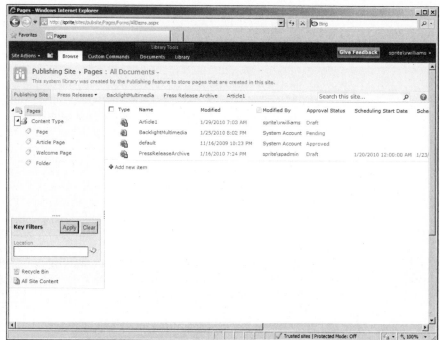

Figure 22-7: Using metadata to navigate in a site.

Understanding Content Types

What if you have a whole bunch of metadata that you want to reuse? For example, say you create a library for everyone to store documents related to a project. Over time, you develop a set of columns that allow you to track all the metadata for the documents. Then, you realize that you want to create a second library to store additional documents, but you want to use the same columns. Instead of manually recreating the library, you package your columns in a *content type* and then associate the content type with any library.

There's one catch, of course. You must use site columns in your content type. So you need to create all your columns as site columns, add them to a content type, and then associate the content type with each library where you wish to use it.

Creating a new site content type

Like site columns, content types have their own gallery where they're stored.
To create a new site content type:

1. **Go to the top-level site in your site collection and then choose Site Actions⇨Site Settings.**

   The Site Settings page appears.

2. **In the Galleries section, click the Site Content Types link.**

   A list of content types appears. Take a moment to scroll down the list.
   Notice that each content type has a parent. Your custom content type
   has to have a parent, too. The content type inherits the settings from
   its parent content type. Whatever columns are present in the parent
   content type automatically become part of your new content type, also.

   What's cool about this is that you can always be assured that you have
   the minimum columns required. In the case of a content type for a
   document, your content type knows that files must have a filename.

   What stinks is that you have another thing to think about when creating
   your content type. A good starting point is whether your content type
   relates to items or documents. The Item content types are for things like
   contacts, tasks, and announcements. Document content types are things
   like documents, wiki pages, forms, and so on. Anything inherited from
   Document content type automatically gets a Name field to store the
   filename.

3. **Click the Create link to create a new content type.**

   The New Site Content Type page appears, as shown in Figure 22-8.

4. **In the New Site Content Type page, type a name for your content type
   in the Name text box.**

   All the naming rules for lists, libraries, and columns apply here —
   namely, no spaces!

5. **Type a description that indicates how you intend to use the content
   type in the Description text box.**

6. **Select a parent content type from the Select Parent Content Type From
   drop-down list.**

   Each content type is assigned to one group. For a document, choose
   Document Content Types; select List Content Types for a list item. If
   you want to store files, such as podcasts, short video clips, and images,
   choose Digital Asset Content Types.

   Depending on the parent content type group you choose, a list of
   content types appears in the Parent Content Type drop-down list.

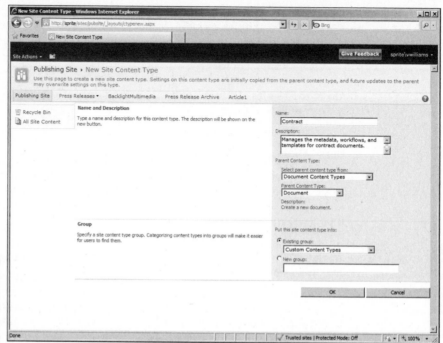

Figure 22-8:
Creating a
new content
type.

7. **Select the content type you want to use as the parent, or starting template, for your content type from the Parent Content Type drop-down list.**

8. **In the Put This Site Content Into section, indicate into which group to place your content by selecting either the Existing Group or New Group radio button.**

   If you select the Existing Group radio button, select a group from the drop-down list. If you choose New Group, enter a name for the group in the New Group text box.

9. **Click OK.**

   SharePoint creates the content type and presents you with the Manage Content Type page, but you aren't done yet. Use this page to add columns and configure your content type.

10. **(Optional) In the Columns section, click the Add from Existing Site Columns or Add From New Site Column link to add new or existing site columns.**

    You have two options here:

    • You can add existing site columns.

    • You can create new site columns and then they're added automatically to your site.

11. **(Optional) When you're done adding site columns, you can assign an order to the columns by clicking the Column Order link. The Column Order page is displayed; click the drop-down list beside each column to assign a numbered order to it. When you're done, click OK.**

    The column order is saved and you're returned to the Site Content Type information page; your new site content type is ready to use.

In addition to adding columns to a content type, a content type can be used to store the additional configuration settings:

- ✔ **A document template that's used every time a new document is created with this content type:** Say you have a standard template that you use for contracts. You can create a content type for contracts, add the columns that are relevant to contracts, and then upload your document template.

- ✔ **Associate workflows with the content type:** If your workflows are related to approving contracts, you can associate them with your Contracts content type.

- ✔ **Specify a custom form to display in Office documents:** You can create a custom form using InfoPath that displays in the information panel in Office clients, such as Word and Excel. This form may specify properties for the user to fill out and provide instructions on using your document template. InfoPath forms are very powerful.

- ✔ **Specify information policy settings:** These settings pertain to how long a document must be retained, what events are audited, and whether properties from your content type are inserted automatically as labels in a document.

    Information policy settings can also be configured at the top-level site to affect every document in your site.

Associating a content type with a list or library

Content types are an extremely powerful way to associate metadata and actions with your documents and list items.

The role of the content type is to separate the metadata, workflows, document template, and other settings from individual lists and libraries. However, content types by themselves aren't useful without lists and libraries. So you have to associate them with the lists and libraries where you want to use them to describe content.

To associate a content type with a list or library:

1. **Browse to the List Settings or Library Settings page for the list or library where you want to use the content type by selecting the List tab or Library tab and the List Settings or Library Settings button.**

2. **Click the Advanced Settings link.**

3. **In the Allow Management of Content Types section, select the Yes radio button and then click OK.**

   The Content Types section appears in the Settings page. All lists and libraries have at least one default content type associated with them, so this content type appears.

4. **To add another content type to the list or library, click the Add from Existing Site Content Types link.**

5. **On the Select Content Types page, in the Available Site Content Types section, select the content types you want to add to the list or library and click the Add button to move them to the Content Types to Add list.**

6. **Click OK.**

   The new content type appears in the Settings page.

When you add a content type to a list or library, it appears in the New Document drop-down list, as shown in Figure 22-9. When a user selects this content type, the columns associated with the content type determine metadata the user can enter to describe the content.

Remove any content types from your list that you aren't using. To do so:

1. **In the List Settings or Library Settings page, click the content type you want to remove.**

   See the preceding steps for how to access the Settings page.

2. **Click the Delete This Content Type link and then click OK at the confirmation prompt.**

   The content type is removed from the list or library. *Note:* You're removing only this content type from the list or library; it still exists as a site content type.

Publishing site content types

You aren't limited to using your content type in just your site collection. You can also publish your content type so that other site collections can use it. Conversely, you can consume content types published by other sites.

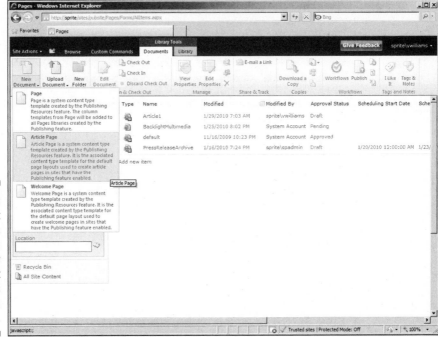

To publish your content types, your site must be designated as a content type publishing hub in SharePoint 2010. This is a task that your SharePoint administrator must perform.

To publish your content type:

1. **Create your content type and then choose Site Actions⇨Site Settings.**

   The Site Settings page appears.

2. **Click the Publish Content Type link.**

3. **Select the Publish radio button and then click OK.**

   Your content type is now available for other sites to consume.

You can consume a content type from another site by clicking the Content Type Publishing Hubs link in your site's Site Settings page.

Using Columns

SharePoint 2010 has a *site column* entity that allows you to reuse columns across multiple lists. When you create a new column in your list, you create a *list column* — meaning the column can be used only in that list. Site columns are created at the top-level of your team site and can be reused in any list or library within your entire team site, including subsites.

All columns you see in a list are technically list columns. When you add a site column to a list column, SharePoint copies your site column to the list to create the list column. A link is maintained between the list column and the site column. If you update the site column, you can opt to push your changes down to the list column.

Creating a new site column

To create a new site column that you can use in a list or library:

1. **Choose Site Actions⇨Site Settings from your top-level site.**

   The Site Settings Page appears.

2. **In the Galleries section, click the Site Columns link.**

   A list of site columns appears.

3. **Click the Create link to create a new column.**

   The New Site Column page appears.

4. **In the Column Name field, enter the name for your site column in the Name text box.**

   When naming your column, don't put any spaces in the name. The spaces make it hard to use your column later for queries. Instead, type the name using proper name casing, such as entering **ArtifactType**. You can rename the column later to Artifact Type, but the internal name remains as ArtifactType.

5. **Select the column type you want to use for your column by clicking a radio button next to an option in the Type of Information in This Column Is list.**

   You have many column type options, as I discuss in Chapter 4. You also have the Managed Metadata column type, which I discuss earlier in this chapter.

6. **In the Put This Site Column Into section, indicate into which group to place your column by selecting either the Existing Group or New Group radio button.**

   If you select the Existing Group radio button, choose a group from the drop-down list. If you choose New Group, enter a name for the group in the New Group text box.

A site column can be a member of one group. I like to use groups to help me quickly identify my custom site columns from those provided by the system.

7. **Enter any additional column settings that may be required by your column type by selecting radio buttons in the Additional Column Settings section.**

8. **(Optional) In the Column Validation section, enter a formula to use to validate the values that are entered into this column in the Formula text box.**

9. **Click OK.**

Your site column appears in the list of site columns.

Reusing site columns

You've probably already been using site columns. All the standard SharePoint lists — Calendar, Contacts, Announcements, and so on — use site columns. That's why each time you create a new Announcements list, you always get the same columns every single time.

Instead of creating your own site columns, you can reuse the site columns provided by SharePoint. Site columns are stored in the Site Column gallery. The Site Column gallery is accessible from the Site Settings page in your site collection. You can browse around this gallery and see what site columns already exist.

Sometimes the site columns that Microsoft provides are intended for use that's different than the name implies. For example, the Active Site column pertains to document routing. The actual internal name of the column is RoutingEnabled. Sometimes creating your own column is better than reusing Microsoft's columns.

I like to use site columns in content types as a way to group several columns in a meaningful (and reusable) way. You can also associate site columns directly with lists and libraries using the List Settings or Library Settings page of your list or library. (See the steps in the section "Associating a content type with a list or library," earlier in this chapter for details about accessing the Settings page.)

Figure 22-10 shows the columns section of a document library. Click the Add from Existing Site Columns link to add your custom site columns or the site columns provided by SharePoint to the list of columns that are available to your list or library.

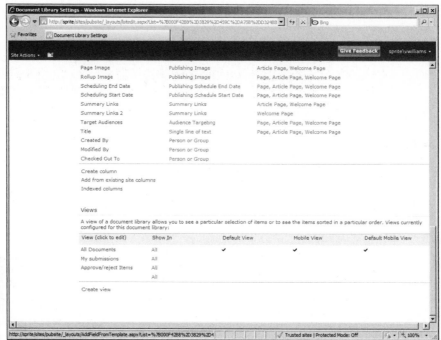

Figure 22-10:
Add existing
site columns
to a library.

Chapter 23

Exploring Enterprise Search

. . . .

In This Chapter

▶ Customizing SharePoint search capabilities

▶ Using search results

▶ Tweaking search

. . . .

*M*ost Web sites let you search the site. End users probably won't be surprised to see the familiar search box in the upper-right corner of all SharePoint sites. Users can use this search box to search the site or list they're viewing.

Chances are you may want a customized search experience for your site. In this chapter, I walk you through search configuration options.

Tweaking Search

Figure 23-1 shows the default search box found in most SharePoint sites. As shown in the figure, this search box is just a text box with the prompt Search This Site inside it. Type what you want to search for and then click the magnifying glass to execute a search.

Figure 23-1:
Share-
Point's
search box.

By default, the search box executes a contextual search. That is, the search box searches the particular site or list where your browser is sitting.

Here are the three things you can do immediately to configure your user's search experience:

- ✔ Create a custom search results page
- ✔ Define the set of scopes that appear in the drop-down list next to the search box
- ✔ Determine whether the search drop-down list appears on the page

You may be asking: Why would I ever want to do these things? Well, for a lot of reasons. You could change the way the search results page is laid out or how much information is displayed on the page. You could create new scopes that define a group of project sites, a group of departmental content, and so on.

Enabling search

You set all these options for search in one place, but you have some prep work to do first. By default, the search box is configured to use your site's search configuration settings. To configure your site's search settings:

1. **Choose Site Actions➪Site Settings to browse to the Site Settings page for your site collection.**

   The Site Settings page appears.

2. **In the Site Collection Administration section, click the Search Settings link.**

   The Search Settings page appears, as shown in Figure 23-2.

3. **(Optional) On the Search Settings page, select the Enable Custom Scopes radio button if you want to use a search center.**

   See the section "Using the search center" for details on creating a custom search center. Otherwise, all your site's searches will use SharePoint's default search page. By choosing to use custom search drop-down lists, you can target your search results to a search center, which is essentially a custom search results page.

4. **In the Site Search Dropdown Mode section, select the option that describes how you want all the search boxes in the site to behave.**

   For example, if you want all the search boxes to show Scope drop-down lists, choose Show Scope Dropdowns from the list.

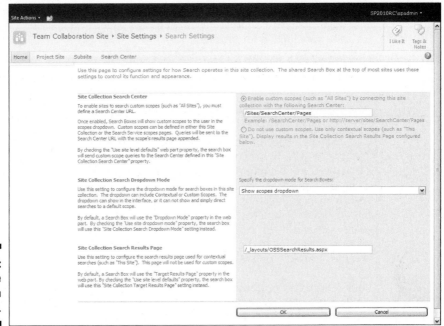

Figure 23-2:
Configure
search
settings.

Choose the option that you want to be the default for all search boxes in your site. You can configure individual search boxes to behave differently in the pages or page layouts where you use them. See the section "Customizing the Search Box Web Part" later in this chapter for more details.

5. **Set the default search box target results page by entering the path to a custom search results page in the text box.**

By default, all search results for *contextual searches,* meaning searches that use SharePoint's default search drop-down options, target SharePoint's default search results page. With this option, you can choose to target another page, such as the page you entered in Step 3.

Using the search center

SharePoint 2010 provides a site template that's built for delivering search results. You can use this template to create a branded search experience or to customize how results appear. You can choose among three search center site templates:

✔ **Basic Search Center** delivers a stripped down search experience in one page. This site template uses Web Part pages and is essentially a team site specialized for search.

✔ **Enterprise Search Center** provides multiple pages for displaying search results. This site template uses publishing pages, which make it easier to brand and customize than Basic Search Center.

✔ **FAST Search Center** is used with the add-on search product FAST Search for SharePoint 2010 to provide enhanced search results. Very large enterprises use the FAST search product. Any search solutions you create with SharePoint 2010's default search options continue to work even if your company chooses to deploy FAST.

You can follow the steps in Chapter 13 to create a new site using one of the search center templates. To configure your site collection to use your search center site, enter the relative URL to your search center in the Search Settings page, as I describe in the preceding section in Step 3. Anytime someone executes a search on your site, she's directed to the search results site.

Your search center doesn't have to be in the same site collection. You can create a new site collection using one of the search center templates and then configure multiple site collections to use that same search center.

The settings I describe in the preceding section set the default experience for all search boxes in your site. Individual search boxes found on the master page, in page layouts, or placed directly on Web pages can be configured to use the default settings or have their own custom settings.

The meat and potatoes of the search experience aren't the search center; it's the Search Web Parts that are used to display search results. These Web Parts can be configured to meet almost any search requirement you can dream up. Figure 23-3 shows the results page from the search center in Edit mode. The page has seven Web Parts on the page, each one with its own set of configuration options. Don't want your results page to include People Matches (as shown in the upper-right corner of Figure 23-3)? Delete that Web Part from the page.

You aren't restricted to using the Search Web Parts in the search center. You can create your own search results page and add the Search Web Parts to the page. In my projects, I usually create a results.aspx publishing page in the top-level site and use it for all my search results.

Figure 23-3:
Editing the
search
results
page.

Scoping out

The drop-down boxes that appear next to a search box are used to select the search *scope*. SharePoint uses *search scopes* as a way to filter the content index. By limiting the user's query to filter subsets of the content index, SharePoint increases the probability of returning a relevant results set. You can create your own custom search scopes to help users of your site get better search results.

Office SharePoint Server Search has a single content index that stores text from all the crawled content sources. SharePoint has two kinds of search scopes. *Shared* scopes are managed by your company's search administrator and are shared across site collections. (SharePoint provides two default shared scopes: All Sites and People.) In addition, though, each site collection can have its *own* set of scopes that are available for only that site collection.

Search scopes are built by creating a set of rules that determines what content is included from the content index. Here are four kinds of search scope rules you can create:

- ✔ **Web address:** Allows you to build rules based on locations, such as a site, list, or folder in a document library.

- ✔ **Property query:** Allows you to build rules based on *managed properties,* such as `author`. Managed properties define the set of metadata terms that can be used to build search scopes and queries. In other words, not every metadata term used in list and site columns can be used to build a property query. Instead, your company's search administrator must add terms to the list of managed properties. Thankfully, a good number of metadata terms are already available as managed properties. Chances are if you think a metadata term would be good to use for building search scopes and queries, other people probably will also. Don't hesitate to ask your company's search administrator to evaluate your metadata suggestions for use as managed properties.

  Rules based on managed properties use the IsExactly operator, which means that results aren't returned unless the search term exactly matches the value in the content source.

  You may be inclined to think using properties is of limited value. However, you can create properties for content sources based on data from the Business Data Catalog. Therefore, you have the opportunity to create properties based on business data, such as `Sales Territory` or `Product Category`.

- ✔ **Content source:** Allows you to limit the scope to a specific content source for shared search scopes. This option is available only to your company's search administrator.

- ✔ **All content:** Includes all content in the content index in the scope.

You create one rule at a time based on these rule types. You can include, require, and exclude items matching the rules to create the search scope's filter criteria.

Users need to understand how to use scopes. If you have too many scopes, their use might not be obvious. For example, the All Sites shared scope includes everything in the content index except People. If a user conducts a People search using the All Sites search scope, he won't get the same results he would if he were to use the People scope, which is limited to content from user profiles.

You can add scope rules to existing scopes. If you need to reuse your scope across multiple site collections, you may want to ask your search administrator to create a reusable scope for you.

To create scopes on a site collection, follow these steps:

1. **Browse to the Site Settings page (see the "Enabling search" section, earlier in this chapter) of the top-level site of the site collection where you wish to create the scope.**

2. **Click the Search Scopes link.**

   The View Scopes page appears.

3. **Click the New Scope button.**

   The Create Scope page appears.

4. **Type a title and description for the scope in the Title and Description fields.**

   The title appears in the drop-down list next to the search box.

5. **In the Display Groups section, place a check mark next to each display group where you wish to display the search scope.**

   By default, SharePoint 2010 includes two display groups — Search Dropdown and Advanced Search. These display groups correspond to SharePoint's default search options — search and advanced search, respectively. The scopes included in the Search Dropdown display group appear in the Scope drop-down list in the search box that appears on SharePoint sites (refer to Figure 23-1). Choosing to add your scope to the Search Dropdown display group displays the scope in the Scope drop-down list.

6. **Indicate whether to use the default search results page by selecting the desired option in the Target Results Page section.**

   The results page for People searches is an example of using a different results page.

7. **Click OK.**

The scope appears in the display group you selected on the View Scopes page.

Because no rules are defined for the new scope, no search results are returned when it's used. To add new scope rules, follow these steps:

1. **Click the scope from the list of scopes on the View Scopes page.**

   A drop-down list appears.

2. **Click the Edit Properties and Rules option.**

   The Scope Properties and Rules page appears.

3. **In the Rules section, click the New Rule link.**

   The Add Scope Rule page appears.

4. **Select the rule type from the Scope Rule Type section.**

5. **Enter the path for Web Address rules or the property for Property Query rules in the Web Address or Property Query section.**

6. **In the Behavior section, indicate whether to include, require, or exclude the content by selecting the proper radio button.**

7. **Click OK.**

   The rule appears.

You can click the New Rule link to add as many rules as necessary to properly limit the scope.

Adding your own search results

Wish you could add a page or another item to the search results? You can with SharePoint's best bets. A *best bet* is a Web address that you match to a search keyword. When someone searches for that keyword, your best bet appears in the search results. That is, assuming your search results page has the Search Best Bets Web Part.

Adding best bets is a two-part process. First, you have to create the keyword that you expect someone to search on. Then, you associate the best bet with the keyword. For example, say you want to make sure the Web address of the Human Resources portal appears as a best bet every time someone searches on the phrase *human resources.* You have to create the keyword for human resources and then add the best bet for the portal.

To add the keyword:

1. **Click the Search Keywords link on the Site Settings page of your site collection.**

   The Manage Keywords page appears.

2. **Click the Add Keyword link.**

3. **In the Keyword Phrase text box, enter your search keyword.**

4. **In the Synonyms text box, enter any synonyms that apply to your keyword.**

   For example, you might enter **HR** for the human resources keyword.

5. **Click the Add Best Bet link.**

6. **In the Add Best Bet dialog box, enter the URL, title, and description for your best bet in the URL, Title, and Description text boxes, respectively, and click OK.**

7. **Repeat Steps 5 and 6 to add up to three best bets for a single keyword.**

8. **In the Keyword Definition section, enter a description for the keyword.**

9. **(Optional) Enter the name of a contact and publishing start, end, and review dates in the Keyword Definition section.**

   The *contact* is the person responsible for managing the keyword and making sure its best bets are accurate.

10. **Click OK.**

When a user executes a search query for the keyword, the keyword's definition and best bet appear in the Search Best Bets Web Part on the search results page, as shown in Figure 23-4.

Removing search results

Sometimes you don't want items in lists and libraries to appear in search results. By default, items and documents in lists and libraries appear in search results. To keep these items out of search results, use the Advanced Settings page in your list or library, which you can access from the List Settings or Library Settings page in your list or library. Under Allow Items from This Document Library to Appear in Search Results?, select the No radio button.

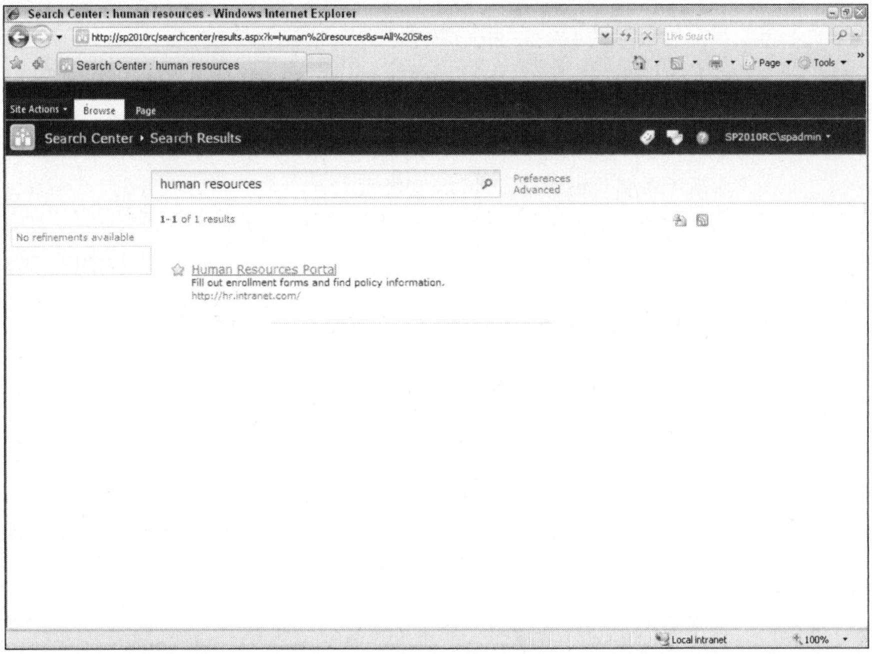

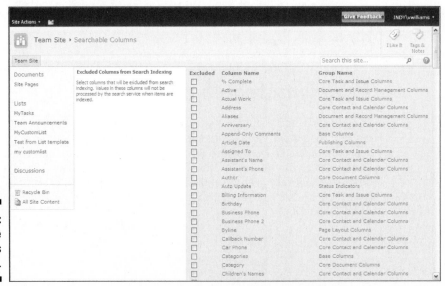

Figure 23-4:
Best bets
in search
results.

You can also exclude columns from being searched. Click the Searchable Columns button in the Site Settings page and then select which columns to exclude, as shown in Figure 23-5.

Figure 23-5:
Exclude
columns
from search.

Reviewing search analytics

SharePoint 2010 provides a number of reports you can use to review the searches people execute on your site. This is a great way to figure out what search terms people are using and whether they're getting the results you want them to get. Click the Site Collection Web Analytics Reports link in the Site Settings page to view reports related to search.

Customizing the Search Box Web Part

As I mention at the beginning of the chapter, the search box is where most of the searching action takes place. SharePoint's search box offers a large number of properties you can use to customize how searches are executed. One of my favorite uses of these properties is to create specialized search boxes. For example, you can specify one search box to use the People scope and another to search content. This allows you to place two separate search boxes on one page. Figure 23-6 shows the Search Box Web Part.

The search user experience is delivered using Web Parts, so everything you know about working with Web Parts applies to customizing the search experience. See Chapter 10 for details on Web Parts.

I recommend using this Web Part in a page layout or Web Part page so you can access additional properties with SharePoint Designer 2010.

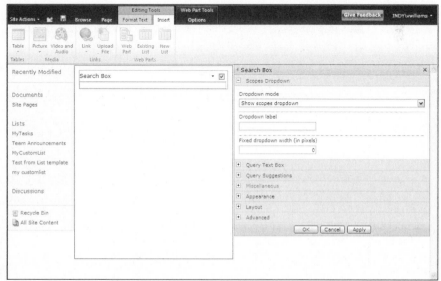

Figure 23-6: Configure the Search Box Web Part.

Chapter 24

Business Intelligence in SharePoint

In This Chapter

▶ Exploring business intelligence options in SharePoint 2010

▶ Using the Business Intelligence Center site template

▶ Introducing PerformancePoint Services

Decisions, decisions, decisions. Think about your life and how you make decisions, whether taking a trip, buying a house, or deciding where to eat dinner. Chances are you research and look at multiple pieces of information before making the decision. The price, the past experience, and the extras (for every vacation I take, boarding my dogs costs as much as airline tickets!) all need to be looked at before you can make the best decision. The good thing is that as an individual it's a bit easier to get your arms around the necessary parts and pieces. In a business, especially a large business, this can be much harder.

If you're an information worker, chances are you have more data than you know what to do with. Being able to make sense of it all is where the concepts of business intelligence (BI) and performance management come in. Much of the content you have in your SharePoint sites is technically business intelligence, but often this information may be stored and arranged to benefit a working team and may not be visible or integrate with other pieces of the data puzzle for your organization.

Business data can include enterprise databases, spreadsheets, lists, reports, charts, diagrams, presentations, and so forth. SharePoint supports all this content and includes new tools to work with specific types of content, such as Access Services and Visio Services. SharePoint also includes a new Business Intelligence Center site template, which includes the Microsoft PerformancePoint Dashboard Designer.

A specific site (or sites) that's focused on business intelligence and performance results using all the latest and greatest in dashboard visualization will be of particular interest for decision makers in your organization. Make sure you drop the new SharePoint BI support in your SharePoint 2010 conversations early and often to get extra brownie points!

In past versions, SharePoint introduced BI support with features like Excel Services, the Business Data Catalog, and lists to track key performance indicators (KPIs). Microsoft incorporated its *PerformancePoint* server product, a separate application dedicated to performance managements, into SharePoint 2010.

Calling All Data Wranglers

While working as an analyst, I used tools like Excel, Access, different report software, and enterprise (think large, company-wide) databases like SQL Server and Oracle. I wasn't much fun at cocktail parties unless you wanted to know our call center statistics or meter reading rates.

Getting the information to the user and management in a friendly, understandable format was always a struggle. Graphic representations, such as diagrams and charts, helped immensely, but I was always busy doing one-offs on reports and queries.

No matter how easy I thought building reports was (and of course I did, I did so every day), most of my managers didn't want to open an application they seldom used and then try to remember how to add a different sort or parameter. Now with SharePoint, these types of analytical tools and visualizations are at their fingertips, right where they do other work, allowing them to access and perhaps interact with the data in a user-friendly format.

Figure 24-1 shows a diagram of ways to think about BI and how SharePoint can bring it all together.

Like many topics in SharePoint, I could probably write another whole book on just this subject. Unfortunately, I can't do all the step-by-step instructions justice in this short chapter, so this chapter introduces you to these BI tools in your SharePoint toolkit, explains where they are located, gives you some of the basics, and shows you where you can find out more about them.

Figure 24-1:
Diagram
showing an
analyst and
products
of BI.

Business Intelligence Tools in the SharePoint Toolkit

Chances are you've already used many of these tools and applications in or out of SharePoint. Here are some of the major players in your SharePoint BI toolkit:

- ✔ **Analysis and ad-hoc reporting:** Creating one-off reports with reporting tools like SQL Reporting Services or Crystal Reports.

- ✔ **Excel spreadsheets:** Ahh, the old standby. I used to say if I were ship-wrecked and could take only one software application with me, I'd take Excel. If SharePoint is the Swiss Army knife of applications, Excel is the Swiss Army knife of analytical software.

- ✔ **Excel support in SharePoint:** If Excel is your application/file of choice, you can always upload Excel spreadsheets to a SharePoint library, espe-cially if multiple people need to be able to access and edit the file.

  - *New Pivot Table add-in:* Extra power for large spreadsheets that allow users to pivot large amounts of data in SharePoint.

- *Excel Services:* Perhaps you want users to use a spreadsheet you built and/or a tool you made with Excel, such as a calculator, but not have them change the file itself. That's what Excel Services is for. Plus, your users don't have to have Excel installed on their computers.

✔ **Other analytical support in SharePoint:**

- *Access Services:* A new feature that allows you to create an Access database on your own computer and then publish or convert it to SharePoint components. Your tables turn into SharePoint lists, and your forms and reports run in the browser.

- *SharePoint lists:* Don't forget that SharePoint lists are great for tracking, have built-in input forms, and allow for filtering, sorting, grouping, and totaling, as well as have calculated columns.

- *Business Data Services:* Allows you to connect to backend data sources and integrate the data into SharePoint without code.

✔ **Standard reporting:** Although some of your reports may be in Excel, chances are that your organization uses enterprise-wide databases, such as SQL Server, with a reporting tool to produce necessary reports generated on a schedule.

SQL Server has a Reporting Services component, which has multiple tools that integrate with Office and SharePoint Services. You can access data from the database, but you can also use it to access data from SharePoint lists and store the reports in SharePoint libraries. These kinds of reports are generally run at specific timeframes with well-defined outputs, as opposed to ad-hoc reports.

✔ **Business intelligence and performance management visualization (graphic stuff):** Uh oh, another buzz word — *visualization.* People have so many names for the ways they display their performance and business data, *visualization* covers the whole gamut.

A picture is worth a thousand words, right? So is a chart, diagram dashboard, scorecard, status list, and so forth. I've met some accountants who feel you're trying to fool them with charts and want to see the data, but for the most part, the status of your organization's KPIs and performance is going to hit home faster and resonate more with graphical representations.

If you're unsure where to start, see the following section, "The New Business Intelligence Center Site Template." Many of the BI supporting libraries and lists are pre-created in the template, as well as in the PerformancePoint Dashboard Designer.

However, if you wish to add BI functionality to another type of site template in SharePoint, look for these libraries/lists when you create new lists and libraries:

✓ Data Connection library

✓ Report library

✓ Status list

✓ Visio Processing Repository

These Web Part categories also enable you to add BI functionality (see Figure 24-2):

✓ Business Data Web Parts

✓ Office Client Applications Web Parts (InfoPath, Visio, Excel)

✓ PerformancePoint Web Parts

✓ Miscellaneous (Chart Web Part)

Figure 24-2:
Some BI
lists and
Web Parts.

You can also access commands in the Office 2010 clients of InfoPath, Visio, Excel, and PowerPoint for publishing content to SharePoint 2010.

You must have the Enterprise Edition of SharePoint Services to enable the SharePoint Server Enterprise Site Collection features, which include InfoPath Forms Services, Visio Services, Access Services, and Excel Services.

The New Business Intelligence Center Site Template

The new Business Intelligence Center site template brings together everything for you in order to monitor, analyze, and represent performance data and results in your organization.

To create a site based on the Business Intelligence Center template, you must have the PerformancePoint Services Site Collection feature turned on, as shown in Figure 24-3. If you aren't the owner of the site collection, ask the site owner to activate the feature for you.

The PerformancePoint Services Site Collection feature enables the PerformancePoint Services site, including associated content types and site definitions.

You can also create a new site collection using the Business Intelligence Center site template.

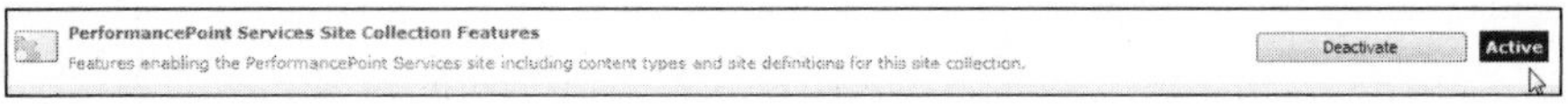

Figure 24-3:
Enable
Performance
Point
Services
Site
Collection.

PerformancePoint Services Site Collection Features	Deactivate	Active
Features enabling the PerformancePoint Services site including content types and site definitions for this site collection.		

Creating the site

The Business Intelligence Center site template choice is available from most SharePoint parent templates. To create a new site that uses the Business Intelligence Center site template, follow these steps:

1. **Choose Site Actions⇨New Site.**

   The Create dialog box appears. The Business Intelligence Center template is available from the All Categories or Enterprise Category below the Filter By: header on the left of the dialog box.

2. **Click the Business Intelligence Center icon.**

You see the types of sites (site templates) that you can choose from. Select the Business Intelligence Center template.

3. **Type a title and URL in the appropriate fields in the Create dialog box.**

   You can also click the More Options button to include a description and to decide on permission or navigation inheritance.

4. **Click the Create button.**

   Your new Business Intelligence Center appears with prepopulated help information and sample data, as shown in Figure 24-4.

From here, you can explore the pre-made lists and libraries. Use the links on the left navigation pane (or All Site Content) to investigate the pre-made libraries and lists. Use the links in the home page to find out more about what you can do with this site.

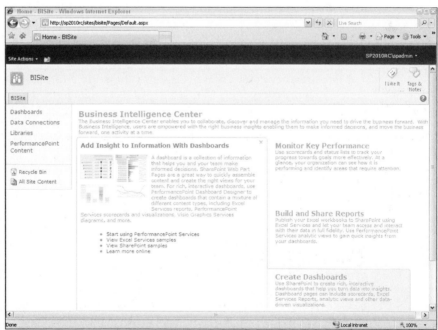

Figure 24-4:
The Business Intelligence Center site template.

Reviewing the site's pre-created content

As I mention in Step 4 in the preceding section, one of the great things about the Business Intelligence Center site template is that it already has some sample data to give you ideas and great help references to get you started.

This site includes these pre-made libraries and lists. Here are the libraries:

✔ **Dashboards:** A library for Web Part pages, Web Part pages with status lists, and deployed PerformancePoint dashboards.

✔ **Data Connections:** A library that includes the PerformancePoint Data Source, Office Data Connection File, and Universal Data Connection File content types.

   Store your data connection files here so you can reuse data connection information. Columns in the library supply metadata about the connection.

✔ **Documents:** A standard document library — includes an Excel Services Sample workbook.

✔ **Images:** A standard Images library.

✔ **Pages:** A standard Publishing Pages library. As part of the site creation, four pages are pre-created: `default.aspx` (home) page, `excelservices sample.aspx`, `mossbisample.aspx`, and `ppssample.aspx`. These pages are pre-created for help and tutorial assistance.

Here are the lists:

✔ **PerformancePoint Content:** Designed to hold PerformancePoint content including scorecards, KPIs, reports, filters, indicators, and dashboards.

✔ **Sample Indicators:** Three sample indicators are included in the list.

✔ **Workflow Tasks:** A standard list used for workflow tasks in a publishing.

The home page of the site contains three help sections listed on the right. As you hover your mouse over these sections, more details and helpful links appear on the left.

Monitoring key performance with status lists and scorecards

Status lists with their accompanying red/yellow/green stop light graphics are a great way to update decision makers on the current standing of a performance item. Think budget, safety incidents, manufacturing defects, and so forth. Great top-of-the rock visualization!

The indicators can be from a SharePoint list, a data connection, stored in Excel, or manually entered into the Web Part.

To explore the status list, follow these steps:

1. **Click the All Site Content link on the left navigation pane.**

   The All Site Content page appears. Note the Sample Indicators link under the List category.

2. **Click the Sample Indicators link.**

   Three sample items are included — Morale, Productivity, and Expenses. These are populated manually.

3. **Open any one of the three sample indicators by choosing Edit Properties from the Item drop-down list.**

   The Sample Indicators dialog box appears. Notice the indicator value and the status icon values used to determine what the values are for exceed, danger, or fail.

4. **Click the X button to close the Indicator Properties dialog box.**

5. **Click the New drop-down list to view your options for creating a new indicator.**

   Options include SharePoint Lists, Excel, SQL Server Analysis Services, and Fixed Value Based Status Indicator.

6. **Select the Fixed Value Based Status Indicator option.**

   The Sample Indicators dialog box appears.

7. **(Optional) Review the choices and add a new indicator.**

8. **Click OK to save your new indicator.**

You can use the Web Part for this list to show the status on a page with your other scorecards, charts, and dashboards.

The Create Scorecards with PerformancePoint Services section links to the PerformancePoint page, as do several other links in the help area, so see the section "Dashboards — PerformancePoint Services and Excel Services," later in this chapter, for details.

Dashboards — PerformancePoint Services and Excel Services

The home page of the Business Intelligence (BI) site provides two scenarios for using SharePoint for business intelligence. The two primary scenarios are Excel Services and PerformancePoint Services, as shown in Figure 24-4.

Excel Services makes it possible for you to display parts of your Excel spreadsheets on your SharePoint sites. You can see a sample of Excel Services in the BI Site by clicking the View Excel Services Samples link on the home page of the BI site.

Where to find out more about BI

I'm sure by the time this book comes out there will be books specifically about the BI offerings of Microsoft and SharePoint, so be sure to check your favorite online or local bookstore. The following Web sites are also good places to find out more about business intelligence in SharePoint:

✔ **Microsoft TechNet:** http://technet. microsoft.com/en-us/share point/ee692578.aspx

✔ **Microsoft Download Center:** www. microsoft.com/downloads/ details.aspx?FamilyID= fc97d587-ffa4-4b43-b77d- 958f3f8a87b9&displaylang=en

✔ **To the SharePoint:** This features the TechNet blog on BI — look for Business Intelligence. http://blogs. technet.com/tothesharepoint/ default.aspx

The home page of the BI site includes a link to the PerformancePoint Services specific tools in SharePoint. The PerformancePoint Dashboard Designer is an important new tool for creating scorecards, integrating dashboards, providing drill-down capability, and charting or graphing.

If the idea of scorecards or balanced scorecards is new to you, as well as any other dashboards that I describe in the Business Intelligence Center site templates, consider doing research on performance measurement and management processes as well as real-life implementations to find what types of metrics are right for your organization.

To access the PerformancePoint Designer:

1. **On the home page of the BI site, click the Start Using PerformancePoint Services link.**

   The PerformancePoint Services sample page appears.

2. **Click the Run Dashboard Designer button on the page, as shown in Figure 24-5.**

   The browser contacts the remote server where the PerformancePoint Designer application is hosted and launches the application on your machine.

3. **Use the Dashboard Designer to connect to data sources and create PerformancePoint content (see Figure 24-6).**

   The Designer provides templates for creating dashboards, scorecards, filters, indicators, and reports.

Figure 24-5: Performance Point Services page.

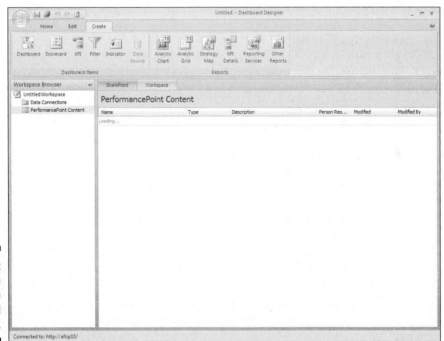

Figure 24-6: The Create tab of the Dashboard Designer.

Part VI
The Part of Tens

"I hate when you bring 'SharePoint' with you on camping trips."

In this part . . .

*H*ere I talk candidly about SharePoint, without any features or steps getting in the way. I cover big, bad *governance,* which is a word I hate. I provide ten governance considerations that give you tips on how to make sure you have business and technical ownership of SharePoint. This is important because governance helps you figure out who's responsible for funding projects, keeping content updated, and making sure the site is up and running as expected.

I also share with you my ten ways to SharePoint mastery. This is how I mastered SharePoint, and you can, too.

Chapter 25

Ten Governance Items

● ●

*G*overnance has gotten kind of a bad rap in part because of its association with the banking scandals of recent years. People hear the word and get all squirrely and anxious, especially when someone proposes governance that affects them. But a well-crafted Web site governance plan isn't about restricting people; in fact, it contains just enough detail to ensure a certain level of consistency and oversight. Web site governance is about the people, policies, and processes that craft your site. And your governance helps you figure out how to apply all the boffo new SharePoint features you can read about in this book.

In this chapter, I show you ten things that influence how you think about your SharePoint governance.

Failure Is Not an Option (Neither Is Looking Away and Whistling)

One of Microsoft's key SharePoint product drivers was the goal to put more control and configuration in the hands of the users; SharePoint was designed to be The Platform of the People.

And people, as you've probably noticed, tend to be unpredictable. So SharePoint + Human nature = Chaos. Sooner or later, an uncontrolled proliferation of sites and subsites, ways of doing things, ways of tagging and applying metadata, and ways of managing documents will produce a very unwieldy SharePoint installation indeed. Trying to identify and implement governance at that point can be an exercise in frustration.

This is a long way of saying that you'll have to address governance sooner or later. Take my advice: Make SharePoint governance a high priority and start now.

Get Executive Buy-In and Support

Successful governance plans usually have a high-visibility advocate to support and communicate them. So find an executive buy-in. You won't have too hard a time making the case to leadership; they've already invested in a powerful SharePoint platform, and it's probably supporting functions that are crucial to the success of your organization. Line up executive support and enlist that support to drive the formation of and participation in governance committee activities.

Build an Effective Governance Group

IT commonly dominates governance committees; they have to manage server space, deal with security groups, and implement new functionality. These are ample motivation to formalize much of what they do with SharePoint. But a governance committee comprised entirely or even largely of IT resources won't get you where you need to be.

I recommend that in addition to your executive sponsor, your governance group represent a diverse mix:

- ✔ **Include representatives from the business.** The information workers who use SharePoint all the time often are in the best position to produce realistic governance policies and to identify governance gaps, too.

- ✔ **Include representatives from any compliance areas.** They can advocate for governance that promotes adherence to regulations that affect your business.

- ✔ **Recruit folks from corporate communications and training.** These people are well placed not only to address governance in areas like branding but also can help craft a plan to publicize governance decisions and provide organizational change management to support those decisions.

Find the Right Level

Don't try to identify and address everything someone might do with SharePoint; provide guardrails to steer your users in the appropriate things to do or to avoid. Those things vary by organization; there's no magic list of what to address. (Larger organizations tend to need more governance than smaller organizations.)

Over time, your governance group will uncover areas that need governance, and this will be helped along if you already have a clear process in place to propose, evaluate, and implement governance when and where the need arises.

Yours, Mine, Ours: Decide Who Owns What

Kick-start a governance effort by thinking about the whos: Who can do what? Who owns what? So for example, you might start with identifying who can provision top-level sites and who can provision subsites. Or who should determine where certain types of documents belong. Or who decides what merits a new content type (and who owns the changes to it).

If you have global navigation, identify who decides what goes there. And so on. The whos will suggest the hows, so you can consider those next.

One of my favorite governance exercises is to project the home page on the screen for your governance group. Then ask who has the authority to update the page? Because the home page usually links to so many other pages, it naturally leads the discussion into other areas of the portal that need ownership.

(Re)visit Social Networking Policies

If you have a social media governance plan in place, it may have been developed to govern external social networking tools; if this is the case, you need to revisit it in the context of SharePoint.

When social media, such as instant messaging, started to become pervasive, a lot of companies responded by locking Internet access to those applications out of fear about what employees would say and how much time they'd waste using them. Likewise, Internet discussion boards and wikis were treated with suspicion, and all kinds of corporate rules and regulations rose around them, making a lot of corporate intranets more like prisons. Over time, some companies evolved governance around when and how employees used external social networking on company time or using the company name. The goal was to keep everyone focused on documents and data and to minimize interpersonal exchanges.

Eventually, forward-thinking organizations recognized that actively facilitating informal interactions between individuals could benefit the organization by making the exchange of information more efficient, uncovering hidden pools of expertise, and (oh, by the way) recognizing that people are social creatures who need a certain degree of human contact to feel happy at work.

SharePoint 2010 brings components of the social media we use in the real world into the workplace. And the ability for employees not only to connect with their peers but also use a corporate-sanctioned tool (SharePoint) to follow coworkers' activities (via live feeds and Twitter-like status updates), exchange opinions with peers (via social tagging and ratings), and pool information (wikis) represents a significant change from external social media. So if you have a specific governance policy around social media, revisit it in the context of internal communications. You'll probably find that you need a whole new strategy.

Design and Branding

Whether your SharePoint is an internal portal or a public-facing Web site, the interface should reflect your corporate image, present a certain level of design integrity, and provide users with a consistent navigation scheme that helps them find their way around.

Your governance plan should address look and feel and how things like global navigation persist across your site. (Master pages certainly can help define what's changeable and what's not — for more information see Chapter 20 — but the governance explains where those master pages should appear.)

The Content Managementy Bits

Metadata, content types, and taxonomies (oh my!) can help reduce the plague of duplicate-but-slightly-different information.

To leverage the content management of your SharePoint installation, encourage consistency around metadata and how things are tagged. Content types are a great way to ensure that a core set of tags are consistently applied to similar content, making the content easier to find, easier to reuse, and easier to filter. So identify key metadata that needs to be formalized via content types and applied across SharePoint sites, and then develop governance around them.

Reuse Web Parts

One great feature of SharePoint is the fact that someone can create a really useful Web Part and then export and import it for use somewhere else. Plenty of community Web Parts are available for download on the Web. Unfortunately, some Web Parts contain malicious code that can pose security problems or just simply don't work as advertised. Likewise, even some internally developed Web Parts can present problems if they allow users to configure them.

Web Parts need to be subjected to controls before they're added to your SharePoint sites. Develop governance around how they're tested and approved, what the change control process looks like, and how they're released and made available.

Keep Things Current: Web Operations Management

Web Operations Management is the care and feeding of your SharePoint sites. You may find it's easy to think about SharePoint sites as projects with defined beginnings, middles, and ends. But in reality, they're more organic than that. Web sites are living entities, which grow and change over time. And like decorative hedges, they require pruning and maintenance, or they get out of control pretty fast. The more traffic your site sees, the more important it is to stay on top of that maintenance. Web Operations Managers wield the pruning shears that shape SharePoint to reflect the strategic vision and technical goals of the company while ensuring that things like verifying that links still work or identifying and deleting irrelevant or outdated content get done. You need to designate someone with a green thumb to prune and water your SharePoint site.

Chapter 26

Ten Ways to Master SharePoint

. . . .

As a SharePoint consultant, you can add value to projects in two key ways. One way is continually reminding people that most problems aren't SharePoint problems. Or, as I like to say, if you don't know how to do it outside SharePoint, what makes you think you can do it inside SharePoint? Help clients figure out what skills they need and what problems to solve that don't require SharePoint product knowledge.

The second way to add value is with *encyclopedic knowledge* of SharePoint. By knowing where the bodies are buried in SharePoint, you can help clients get the most out of their SharePoint deployments.

In this chapter, I share with you some of the resources and approaches that I've used to master SharePoint. Even if your goal isn't mastery, these sugges- tions help you keep your bearings as you get up to speed in SharePoint.

Reading Developer Blogs

Now that SharePoint has been around for a while, you can easily find lots of good resources online. Plenty of Web sites are dedicated to SharePoint. And the blogosphere is chock-full of people blogging about SharePoint. Generally speaking, most of what you find about SharePoint 2007 still applies to SharePoint 2010. However, I recommend avoiding content related to SharePoint 2003.

Microsoft encourages its product teams and employees to blog about the products they're working on. These blogs give you an insider's track on announcements and tutorials that you can't get anywhere else:

- ✔ **SharePoint Team Blog:** This is the official blog of Microsoft's SharePoint Product Group. You can find SharePoint-related announcements at `http://blogs.msdn.com/sharepoint`.

- ✔ **Records Management Team Blog:** Read everything you ever wanted to know about records management in SharePoint at `http://blogs.msdn.com/recman`.

✔ **Enterprise Content Management Team Blog:** This blog covers the Enterprise Content Management features of SharePoint. You'll find a little bit about document management, Web content management, and records management at `http://blogs.msdn.com/ecm`.

Finding Local User Groups

Most major cities have a user group (or two) dedicated to SharePoint. If your city or town doesn't, look for a .NET or Windows group and ask about SharePoint. User groups are a great place to connect with other SharePoint junkies (or newbies). Groups in larger towns often have SharePoint celebrities visit from time to time.

Many user groups also have an online presence. If you can't find a group in your immediate area, go online and find the one closest to you. These groups often use SharePoint and post articles and content from their meetings. Maybe they'd be willing to use Live Meeting so you can connect online.

I also recommend keeping an eye on the Microsoft Events and Webcasts page (`www.microsoft.com/events`). You might find an event in your area or one worth traveling to. I often travel to Chicago to attend training and launch events.

Building a Virtual Lab

Sometimes, you just need a place to play. That's the role of a virtual lab. (And not the role of your personal My Site, I might add.) Running a virtual lab is easier than you think.

In the old days, you had to use dedicated hardware to run a lab. Now, you can use software in a virtual machine — a kind of machine inside a machine. I use a dedicated server to host lots of virtual machines, but I also run virtual machines on my laptop all the time.

You don't even have to build your own virtual machine. Here are two ways you can access off-the-shelf virtual labs:

✔ **Microsoft Virtual Labs:** Microsoft hosts labs online of all its popular products. Use your browser to access these labs. You can find a list of available labs at `www.microsoft.com/events/vlabs`.

✔ **Microsoft Virtual Hard Disks:** Microsoft provides preconfigured virtual hard drives that you can download and use in your own virtual environment. You can find a list of available virtual hard drives at `http://technet.microsoft.com/en-us/bb738372.aspx`.

If you're going to use virtual machines on your own hardware, you need to be aware of the two kinds of virtualization available. Older virtual hard drives use Virtual PC 2007 or Virtual Server 2005 and work with Vista and older operating systems. Windows 7 and Windows Server 2008 use a new Hyper-V technology. Newer virtual hard drives, such as the one for SharePoint 2010, are usually made available in both formats. Read carefully to make sure you get the format that will work for your setup.

Because SharePoint 2010 requires a 64-bit operating system, many people find they need to upgrade. Most new laptops are 64-bit systems, but they're running a 32-bit operating system. You have to wipe your hard drive clean and reinstall a 64-bit operating system.

Another option is to install SharePoint 2010 on your local hard drive. That's how I do it. I run a Hypersonic-PC Avenger Laptop with 4GB of memory and Windows Vista 64-bit. I paid less than $1,000 for this laptop, and I use it as my private SharePoint 2010 server for testing purposes.

Because I also need to run SharePoint 2007, I upgraded to a much fancier Lenovo T410S with 8GB of memory, running 64-bit Windows 7. I intend to run SharePoint 2010 from my hard drive and SharePoint 2007 as a virtual machine.

Getting Information from the Horse's Mouth

If you're an IT professional, chances are you've used Microsoft's TechNet site, which is dedicated to the technical aspects of its products. On TechNet, you find technical libraries and administrator guides for IT administrators for SharePoint and every other Microsoft product. The library includes loads of information on planning and deploying your SharePoint implementation. You also find dozens of worksheets you can use to assist in your planning.

You can use the TechNet SharePoint Products TechCenter to access the technical libraries, articles, and other IT Professional resources at this URL:

```
http://technet.microsoft.com/en-us/sharepoint
```

Microsoft's site dedicated to developers — the Microsoft Developer Network (MSDN) — features portals showcasing development-related articles and resources. You can find a Developer Center for SharePoint, along with all of Microsoft's other products. The home page for MSDN is `http://msdn.microsoft.com`. You can find the SharePoint Developer Center at `http://msdn.microsoft.com/en-us/sharepoint`.

Be sure to check out the latest edition of *MSDN Magazine,* the Microsoft Journal for Developers, while you're on MSDN. You'll find lots of detailed articles explaining how stuff works. Access *MSDN Magazine* at `http://msdn.microsoft.com/en-us/magazine`.

Software development kits (SDKs) are excellent resources for finding out how to develop custom SharePoint applications. Even if you never plan on writing one line of code, SDKs provide extensive documentation on product architecture. If you want to get your mind around what makes SharePoint work, poke your head into the SDK.

You can access the SharePoint SDKs online via the Developer Centers on MSDN. You can also find links that download the SDKs on the MSDN Developer Centers. When you download an SDK, it usually includes sample applications to demonstrate developer opportunities.

One of the best resources for accessing end user documentation is Office Online. You'll find walkthroughs of all sorts of tasks and resources for use with SharePoint clients and servers. Access Office Online at `http://office.microsoft.com/en-us/sharepointserver`. Click the Products tab to see a list of all the products you can peruse on the site.

You can also find Discussion Groups for all the products in the Office 2010 suite, including SharePoint, at `www.microsoft.com/office/community/en-us/default.mspx`.

The Microsoft Download Center is an excellent resource for finding all sorts of downloads. By conducting an advanced search, you can choose WSS or SharePoint Server from a list of products to see all relevant downloads. Sort by release date to see the most recent downloads first. Visit the Download Center at `www.microsoft.com/downloads`.

Anytime you download a file from Microsoft's Web site, be sure to scroll to the bottom of the page to see a list of related downloads.

Starting with a Good Foundation

If you really want to master SharePoint, you need a good foundation. SharePoint is built on the .NET Framework, which is a good starting place, but it also helps to know these skills:

- ✔ Web developer skills, such as XHTML, CSS, and JavaScript for creating visually interesting user experiences
- ✔ XML, XSLT, and XPath for manipulating content into the format you need to drive great user experiences

✔ ASP.NET for understanding how to get the most out of the SharePoint 2010 toolkit

✔ Silverlight for creating next generation visual presentation of content and building desktop SharePoint applications

Depending on what you're trying to master in SharePoint, you may need other domain-specific foundations. For example, knowledge of the Dublin Core and DITA are useful when trying to use SharePoint for building Enterprise Content Management solutions.

Borrowing from Others

The code-sharing site CodePlex is a great place to find utilities and add-ons that help you get the most out of SharePoint. Not only can you find useful tools, but you can also download the source code. Even if you aren't a coder, sometimes just reading through the help text and the code can give you insights as to how things work in SharePoint.

You can find CodePlex online at `www.codeplex.com`.

Getting Certified

Microsoft offers two kinds of certification in SharePoint — an administrative track and a developer track. Pursuing certification is a great way to really dig into any technology; it forces you to get familiar with all the dark corners of the software that you might otherwise ignore.

Taking a Peek under the Covers

One way to really get acquainted with SharePoint is to review the source of the Web pages rendered by SharePoint. I like to use Firefox or Internet Explorer 8 because they both color-code the text. You can look at different kinds of pages — publishing pages and Web Part pages — to see the differences. Or you can create a new Web Part page using SharePoint Designer 2010, and then methodically add and remove things from the page. Watching the source change in the browser, you start to see the naming conventions and figure out how things work.

I also like to use a tool like Firebug with Firefox to view the hierarchical structure of the page.

Digging Deeper under the Covers

When I'm trying to figure out how to do something in SharePoint, I always ask: How did Microsoft do it? All the site templates, pages, and Web Parts that come with SharePoint can be reviewed to see how they're implemented.

All these elements are stored the *14 Hive,* which is located at C:\ Program Files\Common Files\microsoft shared\Web Server Extensions\14. Most of what you want to review is in the Templates folder. This is where you'll find everything from the Publishing Portal template to the templates used to display menus on the Web page.

This is a look-but-don't-touch exercise. Don't change these files because they're used by the system.

Deconstructing a SharePoint Site

Visual Studio 2010 also provides some great new tools for deconstructing SharePoint sites. With Visual Studio 2010, you can explore a site and copy items, such as columns and content types, for reuse. One of my favorite features is the ability to import a site template into Visual Studio 2010. That means you can create a site with the browser, save it as a site template, and then import the template into Visual Studio 2010. Then you can see the underlying XML that SharePoint uses to define the site.

Index

• A •

access
  Edit menu, 32–33
  My Profile feature, 158
  My Site feature, 158
  team site, 13–14
  Web Part tool pane, 151
Access Services feature, 352
Access view, 70
activation, solution, 315
Ad Hoc view, 81
ad-hoc report, 351
administrative access, 180–184
administrative certification, 373
administrator, 180
advanced library settings, 124–127
advanced search, 161
alert
  approval workflow, 224
  Content Approval, 220
  Create Alerts permission, 92
  creating to list or library, 93
  deleting, 95
  delivery method, 93
  e-mail notification, 95
  managing from single page, 94
  subscribing to, 93
All Items view, 69
All Site Content link (Quick Launch
    bar), 162
analysis report, 351
announcements list, 42
appearance
  Look and Feel site setting, 280–281
  as Web Part property, 150
application
  business, 2
  CAML (Collaborative Application Markup
    Language), 85, 255
  MMSA (managed metadata service
    application), 321
  Web, 188–189

approval workflow. *See also* Content
    Approval
  accepting or changing options, 226
  adding stage to, 222
  alert, 224
  approval task, 222
  Approve button, 227
  Approvers assignment, 221
  Cancel button, 227
  cancellation status, 222
  cc notification, 222
  checking status of, 228–229
  configuration, 221–223
  Content Approval versus, 215–216
  description of, 221
  duration unit, 222
  e-mail notification, 226–227
  history, 224
  initiating, 225–227
  name, 224
  notification message, 222
  outcome, 228
  overdue task, 222
  permission, 223
  Reassign Task button, 228
  Reject button, 227
  rejection status, 222
  request author to make changes in, 228
  Request Change button, 228
  responding to approval request, 228
  serial task duration, 222
  setting up, 223–225
  starting manually, 224–227
  status, 228–229
  task details for Approver, 227
  task due date, 222
  uses for, 230
  viewing all tasks in, 229
  when to use, 215–216
Approve button, 227
Approve permission, 183
Approvers group, 172–173
Article page layout, 205
AspMenu control, 266

ASP.NET control, 249, 373
ASP.NET perspective, 3
audience targeting, 129
Authenticated Users domain group,
    173–174
authorization model, 180

• *B* •

back up, 39
background color, 286
Basic Search Center template, 340
best bet keyword, 344–345
BI (business intelligence)
  Access Services feature, 352
  ad-hoc report, 351
  analysis report, 351
  analyst and product diagram, 351
  basic description of, 2
  business data associated with, 349
  business data services, 352
  Business Intelligence Center template,
    354–356
  Dashboard library, 356
  Data Connection library, 353, 356
  Document library, 356
  Excel services in, 357–358
  Excel spreadsheet, 351
  graphic representation, 350–351
  home page, 357–358
  Images library, 356
  performance management visualization,
    352
  performance monitoring, 356–357
  PerformancePoint Content list, 356
  PerformancePoint services, 357–358
  pre-created content, 355–356
  Publishing Pages library, 356
  Report library, 353
  resource, 358
  sample indicator, 356
  scorecard, 356–357
  standard reporting, 352
  status list, 353, 356–357
  template, 349
  tool, 351–352
  Visio Processing Repository, 353

  visualization, 352
  Web Part category, 353
  workflow task, 356
Blank & Custom site template, 186
Blank Site template, 203
blog
  comment, 106
  content management, 370
  creating, 105–106
  Enterprise Content Management, 370
  example of, 105
  home page, 106
  post, 106
  records management team, 369
  SharePoint Team, 369
  social networking, 104–106
boxed style view, 78
branding
  collaboration option, 292–293
  CSS (Cascading Style Sheet), 294
  custom, 304–305
  description, 291–292
  governance, 366
  image, 294
  master page, 294
  page layout, 295
  parts and pieces, 293–296
  publishing option, 292–293
  resource file example, 308
  usability versus, 296
breadcrumb
  description of, 156
  heading, 159
  hierarchical folder, 160
  higher-level site connection, 160–161
  site, 160
  tracking back with, 159–161
breaking inheritance, 175–177
Browse button, 15
browser
  accessing team site through, 13–14
  Firebug, 299
  Firefox, 14, 299
  Internet Explorer, 14, 299
bulk operation, 72
business application, 2
Business Data Web Part, 148, 353

business intelligence. *See* BI
business representative, 364
button
  Approve, 227
  Browse, 15
  Cancel, 227
  Check In, 21, 37
  Check Out, 20, 35
  Check Permissions, 179
  Choose Folder, 31
  Configure Styles and Layout, 259
  Create, 44
  Create View, 71
  Datasheet View, 27
  Edit, 20
  Edit HTML Source, 206
  Grant Permissions, 175
  I Like It, 18, 98
  Image, 22
  Import, 64–65
  Library Settings, 87
  Link, 22
  List Settings, 46
  Modify This View, 83
  New Event, 16
  New Folder, 31
  New Group, 259
  New Item, 47
  New Link, 259
  New Scope, 343
  Preview Theme, 284
  Reassign Task, 228
  Reject, 227
  Reorder, 259
  Reply, 112
  Request Change, 228
  RSS Feed, 88
  Searchable Columns, 346
  Stop Editing, 21–22
  Stop Inheriting Permission, 175
  Sync, 51
  Table, 22
  Tag & Notes, 99–100
  Upload Document, 15, 25
  View Item, 49
  Web Part, 22

• C •

.cab file extension, 197
calculated column, 59, 65–66
calendar
  adding new event to, 16
  End Time field, 16
  Start Time field, 16
  Title field, 16
Calendar list, 42
Calendar view
  creating, 81–82
  day, week, and month selection, 82
  description of, 70
  filtering choices, 82
  time interval, 81
CAML (Collaborative Application Markup
    Language), 85, 255
Cancel button, 227
cancellation status, approval workflow, 222
Cascading Style Sheet (CSS)
  alternate style sheet, 302–304
  custom class style, 297
  description of, 280, 294
  HTML element, 297
  resource, 298–299
  rule, 294, 297–298
  selector, 297
  style, 298–299
  Style library, 299–300
Central Administration feature, 191–192
certification, 373
Chart Web Part, 353
check box, 72
Check In button, 21, 37
Check Out button, 20, 35
Check Permissions button, 179
checked out column, 74
checking document in/out, 34–37
choice column, 59
Choose Folder button, 31
class style, 297
closing Web Part, 151
CMP (content migration package), 197
code solution feature, 312
Code view, page layout, 232
CodePlex Web site, 373

collaboration
  basic description of, 2
  how this book is organized, 5–6
collaboration branding option, 292–293
Collaboration site template, 186
Collaborative Application Markup
    Language (CAML), 85, 255
color
  background, 286
  color palette, 284
  hexadecimal number of, 284
  selection consideration, 287
  text, 287
  theme, 284–285, 288
  Web safe, 284
color scheme. See theme
column
  adding to custom list, 56–62
  built-in column type, 59
  calculated, 59, 65–66
  checked out, 74
  choice, 59
  content type, 74, 330–331
  currency, 59
  date, 59
  excluding from search result, 346
  external data, 59
  hyperlink, 59
  ID, 74
  list, 333–334
  list column data type, 57–60
  lookup, 59, 66–67
  managed metadata, 59
  metadata, adding to list or library, 324–326
  multiple line of text, 59
  name, 56
  number, 59
  person or group, 59
  picture, 59
  reusing, 58, 335
  single line of text, 59
  site, 58
  time, 59
  Title, 62–63
  type, 57–59
  validation, 335
  version, 74

  view, 72–74
  yes/no, 59
command
  contextual, 20, 123
  list, 46
  Ribbon, 157
comment, blog post, 106
Communications list, 41
comparison operator, 75
compliance, 364
configuration
  approval workflow, 221–223
  Content Approval, 217–218
Configure Styles and Layout button, 259
Contact list
  in Datasheet view, 79–80
  uses for, 42
content
  content file example, 308
  default locations for storing, 310
  deploying in folder or library, 311
  document library storage, 309
  resource versus, 308
  what to put where, 307–308
Content & Data site template, 186
Content Approval. See also approval
    workflow
  alert, 220
  approval workflow versus, 215–216
  approved item status, 219–220
  basic description of, 216
  configuration, 217–218
  document property with approval
    note, 218
  Draft Item Security settings, 217
  enabling, 217–218
  pending approval status, 219–220
  rejected item status, 219–220
  security groups, 218
  specifying approvers for, 218–219
  turning on, 217
  uses for, 230
  version history settings, 217
  when to use, 215–216
content management
  basic description of, 2
  blog, 370

description of, 201
governance, 366
content migration package (CMP), 197
content placeholder, 235
Content Query Web Part
  CAML query, 255
  content type, 254
  description of, 191, 253
  displaying all tasks not started, 254–255
  fields to display setting, 257
  grouped results in, 256
  list type, 254
  location source, 254
  presentation options, 255–256
  target audience setting, 254
Content Rollup Web Part, 147–148
content source, search scope, 342
content type
  associate workflow with, 331
  associating with list or library, 331–332
  column, 330–331
  defined, 328
  deleting, 332
  description, 329
  Document, 329
  information policy setting, 331
  Item, 329
  name, 329
  new site, 329–331
  from other site, 333
  parent, 329
  publishing site, 332–333
  role of, 331
  site column in, 333–335
Content Web Part, 148
contextual command, 20, 123
contextual navigation, 266
contextual search, 337, 339
Contribute permission, 176, 183
conversion, document, 208
copying
  link, 37
  template, 196–197
Create Alerts permission, 92
Create button, 44
Create View button, 71
Crystal report, 351

CSS (Cascading Style Sheet)
  alternate style sheet, 302–304
  custom class style, 297
  description of, 280, 294
  HTML element, 297
  resource, 298–299
  rule, 294, 297–298
  selector, 297
  style, 298–299
  Style library, 299–300
currency column, 59
current navigation, 268–269
custom branding, 304–305
custom list
  adding column to, 56–62
  calculated column, 65–66
  category, 54
  column data type, 57–60
  column validation, 60–62
  creating basic, 55–56
  description of, 53
  header, 63
  lookup column, 66–67
  name, 64
  planning the, 54
  spreadsheet as, 63–65
  Title column, 62–63
  uses for, 43
Custom view, 71
customization
  list form, 49–50
  Ribbon, 157
  team site, 19–22
  theme, 288–290
  Top Link bar, 157

• *D* •

Dashboards library, 356
Data Connection library, 353, 356
Data Form Web Part
  data source selection, 262–263
  inserting, 261–262
  layout, 263–264
  new item form, 263
  single/multiple item form, 263
  single/multiple item view, 263

database and referential integrity, 67
database driven perspective, 3
Datasheet view
  Contact list in, 79–80
  description of, 70
  uses for, 79
Datasheet View button, 27
date column, 59
deleted document, 38–39
deleting
  alert, 95
  content type, 332
  Top Link bar tab, 158
  Web Part, 151
Design permission, 176, 183
Designers group, 172–173
developer
  certification, 373
  who can benefit from this book, 4
directive, 234
discussion board
  creating, 110–111
  creating new subject in, 111–112
  Flat view, 112
  name, 111
  replying to subject in, 112
  Subject view, 112
  Threaded view, 112
  viewing discussion in, 112
Discussion Board list, 42
DIV tag, 248
document
  checking in/out, 34–37
  conversion, 208
  editing properties of, 33–34
  name, 33
  properties, 18
  recovering deleted, 38–39
  restoring, 38–39
  sending link to, 37–38
  tag, 17–18
  template, 124, 126
  title, 33
  uploading to folder, 30–32
  uploading to team site, 15–16
Document content type, 329
document library. *See also* library; list
  advantages of, 24
  description of, 15

folder, 30–33
  moving document between, 29
  storing content in, 309
  uploading documents with Windows
    Explorer to, 28
  uploading multiple documents to, 25–27
  uploading single document to, 25
document workflow, 23
domain group, 173–174
domain-specific foundation, 372–373
Draft Item Security settings (Content
    Approval), 217
duration unit, approval workflow, 222
dynamic navigation, 265–266

• *E* •

Edit button, 20
Edit HTML Source button, 206
Edit menu access, 32–33
Edit mode, 20
Edit mode panel, 250–251
editing
  home page, 20–22
  inline, 76–77
  publishing site page, 204
  theme, 283–286
  view, 83
  wiki page, 108–109
e-mail notification, 226–227
End Time field, calendar, 16
Enterprise Content Management blog, 370
enterprise keyword, 327–328
Enterprise Search Center template, 340
enterprise service, 6
Enterprise Wiki, 140, 202
Enterprise Wiki page layout, 205
Enterprise Wiki template, 106
equality operator, 75
equation
  comparison operator, 75
  equality operator, 75
  filtering list with views, 74–76
  substring operator, 75
Excel
  business intelligence services, 357–358
  spreadsheet, 351
executive buy-in and support, 364

Extensible Stylesheet Language (XSLT), 85, 91, 372
external data column, 59
External list, 43
extranet, 12
extrinsic metadata, 319–320

• F •

FAST Search Center template, 340
feature, solution, 311–312
file share. *See* document library; social networking
Filter Web Part, 148, 153–154
filtering equation, 75
filtering option, view, 74–76
Firebug browser, 299
Firefox browser, 14, 299
Flat view, 112
folder
  deploying content in, 311
  document library, 30–33
  library, 125
  Local Drafts, 35
  permission, 32
  restricting access to, 32
  uploading document into, 30–32
  uploading files into, 31
folksonomy, 326–328
font
  sans-serif, 286
  selection consideration, 286–288
  serif, 286
  style, 286
form setting, 131
formula, 65–66
forward-thinking, 366
foundation, 372–373
Full Control permission, 12, 183

• G •

Gantt view
  creating, 82
  description of, 70
  split view, 82

global navigation
  child site, 267
  common settings in, 268
  configuration, 266–267
  parent site, 267
  press release option, 267
  subsite, 267
governance
  committee, 364
  compliance, 364
  content management, 366
  design and branding, 366
  executive buy-in and support, 364
  forward-thinking, 366
  as high-priority, 363
  keeping things current, 367
  large versus small organization, 364–365
  social networking, 365–366
  Web Operations Management, 367
  Web Part reuse, 367
  who owns what exercise, 365
Grant Permissions button, 175
graphic representation, 350–351
graphical status indicator, 43
Groove product, 50
group membership
  adding users to Members group, 170–171
  description, 169
  domain group, 173–174
  list of, 170
grouping results, 76

• H •

header
  custom list, 63
  team site home page, 14
heading, 270–271
Help icon, 162
hexadecimal number of color, 284
hiding column, 62–63
hierarchical folder breadcrumb, 160
Hierarchy Managers group, 172–173
hierarchy, site, 188–191
home page
  adding image to, 21–22
  adding link to, 21–22

home page *(continued)*
  adding table to, 21–22
  adding Web Part to, 21–22
  BI (business intelligence), 357–358
  blog, 106
  changing text in, 21
  checked out, 20
  editing, 20–22
  left navigation pane, 14
  locking, 20
  page content, 14
  placing in Edit mode, 20
  team site, 13–14
HTML (HyperText Markup Language), 297
hyperlink, 42
hyperlink column, 59

• I •

I Like It button, 18, 98
icon
  about this book, 7
  site, 281–282
ID column, 74
image
  adding to home page, 21–22
  branding, 294
Image button, 22
Images library, 356
IMG tag, 248
Import button, 64–65
Import Spreadsheet list, 43
importing
  spreadsheet as list, 63–65
  term set file, 322–323
information policy setting, 331
information portal
  basic description of, 2
  how this book is organized, 6
inheritance, breaking, 175–177
inline editing, 76–77
Internet Explorer, 14, 299
intrinsic metadata, 319–320
issue tracking list, 43
IT professional, 4
Item content type, 329

• J •

JavaScript, 372

• K •

key filter, 130
keyword
  best bet, 344–345
  enterprise, 327–328
  tag, 98–99
KPI (Key Performance Indicator)
  list, 43, 350

• L •

landing page, 254
laptop, 371
layout. *See* page layout
left navigation pane, 14
library. *See also* document library; list
  adding managed metadata column to,
      324–326
  advanced setting, 124–127
  associating content type with, 331–332
  audience targeting setting, 129
  configuration, 117
  content approval, 123
  content type, 124
  creating alert to, 93
  deploying content in, 311
  description, 121
  document destination, 126
  document template, 124, 126
  enabling RSS feed for, 87–88
  folder, 125
  form setting, 131
  general setting, 120–121
  metadata navigation setting, 129–130
  navigation, 121
  offline client availability, 125, 127
  Pages, 310
  per-location views setting, 130
  permission and management options,
      131–136
  rating setting, 129

removing from Quick Launch bar, 163
search result, 125
search visibility, 127
Style, 299–300
title, 121
validation setting, 128
versioning setting, 122–124
Web Part as, 149
workflow setting, 133–136
Library Settings button, 87
Limited Access permission, 183
link
    adding to home page, 21–22
    copying, 37
    hyperlink, 42
    sending to document, 37–38
Link button, 22
Links list, 42
list. *See also* custom list; library
    accessing list settings, 118–119
    adding managed metadata column to,
        324–326
    announcements, 42
    associating content type with, 331–332
    Calendar, 42
    column, 333–334
    commands, 46
    Communications, 41
    Contact, 42, 79–80
    creating alert to, 93
    creating new, 44–46
    Discussion Board, 42
    draft version, 123
    enabling RSS feed for, 87–88
    entering data in, 47–48
    External, 43
    filtering option, 74–76
    header, 63
    Import Spreadsheet, 43
    Issue Tracking, 43
    KPI (Key Performance Indicator), 43
    Links, 42
    list form customization, 49–50
    Manage Lists permission, 44
    name, 46, 119
    offline access, 50–51
    permission, 181

Project Tasks, 43
    prototyping, 42
    removing from Quick Launch bar, 163
    Survey, 43
    Tasks, 43
    Tracking, 41
    Transaction, 66
    types of, 41–43
    with view, 74–76
    Web Part as, 149
List Settings button, 46
List tool, 69
List View Web Part, 84–85, 145
Live Meeting, 370
Local Drafts folder, 35
locking home page, 20
logo, 294
Look and Feel site setting, 280–281
lookup column, 59, 66–67

• *M* •

malicious code, 367
Manage Hierarchy permission, 183
Manage Lists permission, 44
Manage Permissions permission, 177
managed metadata, 320
managed metadata column, 59
managed metadata service application
    (MMSA), 321
managed property, 342
manager, 4
master page
    branding guidance, 214, 294
    Night and Day, 213
    page layout relationship, 237–238
    predefined, 300–301
    publishing site, 213–214
    v4, 213
    viewing contents of, 301–302
Master Page gallery, 246–247
media data, 241
Media Web Part, 148
Members group
    adding users to, 170–171
    permission, 173

member, team site, 12
memory, 371
metadata
  column, adding to list or library, 324–326
  defined, 319
  enterprise keyword, 327–328
  extrinsic, 319–320
  folksonomy, 326–328
  intrinsic, 319–320
  managed, 320
  navigation, 328
  set of terms, 321–322
metadata navigation setting, 129–130
Microsoft Developer Network (MSDN),
      371–372
Microsoft Download Center Web site, 358
Microsoft Journal of Developers, 372
Microsoft Outlook, 89–90
Microsoft TechNet Web site, 358
Microsoft Virtual Hard Disk, 370
Microsoft Virtual Lab, 370
Miscellaneous Web Part, 353
MMSA (managed metadata service
      application), 321
Mobile view, 84
moderation. *See* Content Approval
Modify This View button, 83
moving
  document between document library, 29
  Web Part, 147
MSDN (Microsoft Developer Network),
      371–372
MSDN Magazine, 372
multiple line of text column, 59
My Content feature, 101
My Newsfeed feature, 101
My Profile feature
  access, 158
  described, 103
  My Site feature versus, 102
  tab, 102
My Settings feature, 159
My Site feature
  access, 158
  described, 103
  My Profile feature versus, 102
  sections of, 101

My Site Host feature, 102

• N •

name
  approval workflow, 224
  content type, 329
  custom list, 64
  discussion board, 111
  document, 33
  list, 46, 119
  list column, 56
  naming convention, 309
  site template, 195
  team site, 12
  Title column, 62
  view, 72
  workflow, 134
navigation
  contextual, 266
  current, 268–269
  dynamic, 265–266
  generating menu for, 272–275
  global, 266–268
  metadata, 328
  primary, 266
  static, 269–271
  Tree View, 164, 280
network file share. *See* document library;
      social networking
New Event button, 16
New Folder button, 31
New Group button, 259
New Item button, 47
New Link button, 259
New Scope button, 343
newsfeed, 101
newsletter style view, 78
Night and Day master page, 213
note
  private, 99
  viewing, 18, 103
notification message, approval workflow,
      222
no/yes column, 59
number column, 59

• O •

Office Client Applications Web Part, 353
Office Online Web site, 372
Office Web Part, 149
offline client availability, 125
opening page layout, 232
organization, about this book, 5–7
outcome, approval workflow, 228
Outlook (Microsoft), 89–90
owner permission, 12
Owners group, 170, 172–173

• P •

package, 311–315
page field, page layout, 249
page layout
  adding containers and control to, 248–250
  adding site column to, 243–244
  additional content fields, 239–242
  Article page, 205
  ASP.NET controls, 249
  branding, 295
  Code view, 232, 236–237
  content controls, 249
  content placeholder, 235–237
  creating new, 245–248
  custom content type, 241–242, 245
  default, 210–212
  defining, 210
  description, 231
  directive, 234
  Edit mode panel in, 250–251
  Enterprise Wiki page, 205
  HTML controls, 248
  master page relationship, 237–238
  media data, 241
  opening, 232
  orange highlighted text in, 234
  page field, 249
  prototype, 239
  publishing image controls, 241
  publishing page, 207–209
  Redirect page, 205

site column creation, 240–241
splitting view of, 236
standard registrations, 234
style, 237
summary file, 232
summary link, 241
versioning status, 232
Web Part, 150, 248
Welcome page, 205
wiki page, 109
WYSIWYG display, 235
Page Layouts and Site Templates link, 187
Page Layouts Gallery, 301–302
Pages library, 310
paragraph tag, 248
pending approval status, 219–220
People Web Part, 149
performance monitoring, 356–357
PerformancePoint server, 350
PerformancePoint Web Part, 353
permission
  to access, 12
  administrative access, 180–184
  approval workflow, 223
  Approve, 183
  Approvers group, 173
  breaking inheritance, 175–177
  checking, 179
  Contribute, 176, 183
  Create Alerts, 92
  creating unique, 177
  default, 176
  Design, 176, 183
  Designers group, 173
  folder, 32
  Full Control, 12, 176, 183
  grant, 175–176
  Hierarchy Managers group, 173
  level, 181–183
  library, 132–133
  Limited Access, 183
  list, 181
  Manage Hierarchy, 183
  Manage Lists, 44
  Manage Permissions, 177
  Members group, 173

permission *(continued)*
  owner, 12
  Owners group, 172–173
  personal, 181
  Read, 173, 176, 183
  Read Only, 12
  re-inherit, 176
  Restricted Read, 183
  Restricted Readers group, 173
  restricting access to folder, 32
  SharePoint Designer 2010, 183–184
  site, 181
  View Only, 183
  viewing, 178, 180–182
  Visitors group, 173
permissions inheritance, 170, 172, 174
person or group column, 59
personal permission, 181
Personal view, 70
picture column, 59
platform, as SharePoint model, 3
portal, 201
Portal Site Connection feature, 160–161
post, blog, 106
press release option (global navigation), 267
preview
  pane style view, 78
  theme, 284
Preview Theme button, 284
primary navigation, 266
private note, 99
private view, 72
private, marking tag as, 18, 99
product, as SharePoint model, 3
Project Tasks list, 43
property
  document, 18, 33–34
  managed, 342
  Web Part, 150–152
property query, 342
prototyping, 42
public Web site
  basic description of, 2
  how this book is organized, 6
publishing branding option, 292–293
publishing page
  adding content to, 205–207
  description of, 140

page layouts, 205, 207–209
  text box, 206
Publishing Pages library, 356
Publishing Portal template, 202–203
publishing site
  adding to existing site, 202
  content type, 332–333
  creating new page in, 204
  creating site template from, 196–197
  editing pages in, 204
  master page, 213–214

• *Q* •

query, 191, 342
query string, 148
Quick Launch bar
  adding/removing list or library from, 163
  All Site Content link, 162
  disabling, 162–163
  Recycle Bin link, 162

• *R* •

rating setting, library, 129
Read Only permission, 12
Read permission, 173, 176, 183
readability, 286–287
Reassign Task button, 228
records management team blog, 369
Recycle Bin
  restoring document from, 38–39
  time period of file stored in, 39
Recycle Bin link (Quick Launch bar), 162
Redirect page layout, 205
Reject button, 227
rejected item status, 219–220
rejection status, approval workflow, 222
Reorder button, 259
Reply button, 112
report
  ad-hoc, 351
  analysis, 351
  Crystal, 351
  search, 347
  SQL Reporting Service, 351
  standard, 352

statistical, 315–316
Web Analytic, 315
Report library, 353
Request Change button, 228
request, team site, 11–12
resource
  BI (business intelligence), 358
  branding resource file example, 308
  content versus, 308
restoring document, 38–39
Restricted Read permission, 183
Restricted Readers group, 173
results
  search, 338
  totals, 76
return on investment (ROI), 296
reuse
  column, 335
  Web Part, 367
Ribbon
  command, 157
  customization, 157
  description of, 156
  features of, 19–20
  Share & Track group, 98
ROI (return on investment), 296
root site, 188
RSS feed
  displaying from other site, 90–91
  enabling for list or library, 87–88
  reading with Outlook, 89–90
  RSS Viewer Web Part, 90–91
  viewing, 88–89
RSS Feed button, 88
RSS view, 84

• *S* •

sample indicator, 356
sans-serif font, 286
scope, search, 342–344
scorecard, 356–357
SDK (Software Development Kit),
    95, 312, 372
search
  advanced, 161
  Basic Search Center template, 340

best bet keyword, 344–345
contextual, 337, 339
custom results page, 338
custom search center, 338
drop-down list, 338
enabling, 338–339
Enterprise Search Center template, 340
excluding columns from, 346
FAST Search Center template, 340
index of properties, 18
reports, 347
result, removing, 345–346
scope, 342–344
search box configuration, 339
template, 339–340
widening/narrowing search scope, 161
Search Box Web Part, 347
Search site template, 186
Search Web Part, 148, 340
Searchable Columns button, 346
security. *See* permission
security group, 218
selector, CSS rule, 297
Self-Service Site Creation feature, 191–194
serial task duration, 222
serif font, 286
server
  administrator, 180
  PerformancePoint, 350
shaded style view, 78
Share & Track group, 98
shared document/file. *See* document
    library; social networking
SharePoint Designer 2010, 183–184
SharePoint Foundation 2010 platform, 3
SharePoint Foundation 2010 SDK, 95
SharePoint Server 2010, 3
SharePoint Team blog, 369
SharePoint Workspace 2010, 50–51
Silverlight content, 241, 373
single line of text column, 59
Site Actions menu, 165–166
site administrator, 180
site breadcrumb, 160
site collection administrator, 180
Site Collection Web Analytics Reports link,
    315–316

site column, 58. *See also* column
Site Column gallery, 335
site hierarchy, 188–191
site icon, 281–282
site permission, 181. *See also* permission
Site Settings page, 165–167
site template. *See also* template
  Blank & Custom, 186
  Collaboration, 186
  Content & Data, 186
  creating from existing site, 192, 194–195
  creating from publishing site, 196–197
  creating from template, 194–197
  description of, 185
  Page Layouts and Site Templates link, 187
  Search, 186
  Tracking, 186
  Web Databases, 186
Site Web Analytics Reports, 315–316
sitemap path, 189
social bookmarking. *See also* tag
  My Site feature, 101
  tag, 98–100
social networking
  basic description of, 2
  blog, 104–106
  discussion board, 110–112
  governance, 365–366
  My Profile feature, 102–103
  My Site feature, 101–103
  services, 97
  tagging a document, 16–18
  wiki, 106–109
social tag, 327
Software Development Kit (SDK), 95, 312, 372
solution
  activation, 315
  code solution feature, 312
  creation, 312–314
  feature, 311
  uploading, 314
Solution Explorer, 312–313
Solution gallery, 312
sorting view item, 72

splash page, 205
split view, 82
spreadsheet
  Excel, 351
  as list, 63–65
SQL Reporting Service, 351
standard reporting, 352
Standard view, 70
standards-based Web site, 1
Start Time field, calendar, 16
static navigation
  displaying text as ToolTip, 271
  global and current navigation settings, 269–270
  heading, 270–271
  hiding items in hierarchy, 271
  target audience setting, 271
  title, 270
statistical report, 315–316
status list, 353, 356–357
status, approval workflow, 228–229
Stop Editing button, 21–22
Stop Inheriting Permissions button, 175
.stp file extension, 195
streamlined format table, 78
style
  CSS (Cascading Style Sheet), 298–299
  font, 286
  page layout, 237
  view, 78
Style library, 299–300
style sheet. *See* CSS
Subject view, 112
substring operator, 75
summary link, 241
Summary Link Web Part
  adding as field control, 259
  creating custom displays with, 258–260
  description of, 253
  example of, 261
  toolbar, 259–260
Survey list, 43
Sync button, 51
system master page, 213

• T •

table
  adding to home page, 21–22
  display style, 78
  streamlined format, 78
Table button, 22
Table of Contents Web Part
  content section, 258
  description of, 253
  displaying site hierarchy, 257–258
  organization section, 258
  presentation section, 258
table style view, 78
Tabular view, 76–77
tag
  adding wiki page, 142
  arranging, 104
  DIV, 248
  document, 17–18
  HTML controls, 248
  IMG, 248
  keyword, 98–99
  marked as private, 18, 99
  paragraph, 248
  predefined, 99
  social, 327
  social networking, 98–100
  viewing, 18, 103
Tag & Notes button, 99–100
tag cloud, 142
task due date, 222
Tasks list, 43
task, workflow, 356
team blog, 369
team site
  access, 13–14
  adding calendar items to, 16
  basic description of, 11
  contributing to, 14–18
  corporate communications use of, 11
  customization, 19–22
  department member use of, 11
  home page, 13–14
  home page editing, 20–22
  how this book is organized, 5
  member, 12
  name, 12
  navigation, 155–159
  owner, 12
  permission to access, 12
  project member use of, 11
  requesting, 11–12
  template, 12
  Top Link bar, 157–158
  uploading document to, 15–16
  user type, 12
  visitor, 12
  Web address or URL, 12
  Welcome menu, 158–159
  written justification for, 11
TechNet Web site, 371
template. *See also* site template
  Basic Search Center, 340
  BI (business intelligence), 349
  Blank Site, 203
  Business Intelligence Center, 354–356
  document, 124, 126
  Enterprise Search Center, 340
  FAST Search Center, 340
  Publishing Portal, 202–203
  search, 339–340
  team site, 12
  workflow, 134
term store
  adding new items to, 322
  creating, 321–322
  importing term set file, 322–323
  term group, 323
Term Store Management tool, 321–322
text
  color, 287
  editing in home page, 21
text box, 206
theme
  advantages of, 287
  color, 284–285, 288
  customization, 288–290
  customize, 284
  description of, 279
  editing, 283–286

theme *(continued)*
  Office Theme file creation, 288–290
  previewing, 284
  readability, 286–287
  selection, 283
Threaded view, 112
three-state workflow, 133
time column, 59
title
  document, 33
  library, 121
  static navigation, 270
  view column, 73
Title column
  hiding, 62–63
  name, 62
Title field, calendar, 16
tool
  BI (business intelligence), 351–352
  List, 69
toolbar
  Summary Link Web Part, 259–260
  as Web Part property, 150
toolkit, as SharePoint model, 3
ToolTip, 271
Top Link bar
  customization, 157
  description of, 156
  tab, 157–158
top-level site, 188
totals, 76
Tracking list, 41
Tracking site template, 186
training and launch event, 370
Transaction list, 66
Tree View
  adding new terms to an item in, 322
  navigation, 164, 280
  Term Store Management tool, 322
trouble ticket, 43

• *U* •

Upload Document button, 15, 25
uploading
  document to folder, 30–32
  document to team site, 15–16
  document with Windows Explorer, 28

file in document library folder, 31
multiple documents to document library, 25–27
single document to document library, 25
solution, 314
URL, 12
usability, 296
user group, 370
User Solution gallery, 195

• *V* •

validation
  column, 335
  custom list column, 60–62
  library, 128
version column, 74
version history
  Content Approval configuration, 217
  description of, 23
versioning setting
  draft version, 123
  library, 122–124
versioning status, page layout, 232
v4 master page, 213
view
  Access, 70
  Ad Hoc, 81
  adding items to, 72
  All Items, 69
  allowing editing options in, 76–77
  boxed style, 78
  Calendar, 70, 81–82
  changing current, 70–71
  check box, 72
  column, 73–74
  column order, 72
  creating standard, 71–73
  Custom, 71
  Datasheet, 70, 79–80
  displaying via Web Parts, 84–85
  editing, 83
  filtering lists with, 74–76
  Flat, 112
  Gantt, 70, 82
  grouping data in, 76
  Mobile, 84
  name, 72

newsletter type, 78
per-location views setting, 130
Personal, 70
predefined format, 70–71
preview pane style, 78
private, 72
RSS, 84
setting default, 83
shaded style, 78
sorting items in, 72
split, 82
Standard, 70–73
style, 78
Subject, 112
table style, 78
Tabular, 76–77
Threaded, 112
View Definition page, 71
View Item button, 49
View Only permission, 183
viewing
note, 18, 103
permission, 178, 180–182
RSS feed, 88–89
tag, 18, 103
virtual lab, 370
Virtual Lab (Microsoft), 370
Visio Processing Repository, 353
visitor, 12
Visitors group
description, 170
permission, 173
Visual Aids toolbar, 236
Visual Studio 2010, 374
visualization, 352

• W •

Web address
create, 189
search scope rule, 342
team site, 12
Web Analytic report, 315
Web application
description of, 188
root site, 188
site collections, 188
top-level site, 188
when to use, 189

Web application perspective, 3
Web Databases site template, 186
Web Operations Management, 367
Web page. *See* page layout; Web Part; wiki
Web Part
adding to home page, 21–22
advanced property, 150
appearance property, 150
asynchronous behavior, 151
Business Data, 148, 353
Chart, 353
closing, 151
connecting two, 152–154
Content, 148
Content Query, 191, 253
Content Rollup, 147–148
Data Form, 261–264
deleting, 151
description of, 137–139
displaying views via, 84–85
Filter, 148, 153–154
inserting, 146–147
layout, 150
list and library as, 149
List View, 84–85, 145
malicious code, 367
Media, 148
Miscellaneous, 353
moving, 147
Office Client, 149
Office Client Applications, 353
page creation, 143
page layout, 248
People, 149
PerformancePoint, 353
property, 150–152
reuse, 367
RSS Viewer, 90–91
Search, 148, 340
Search Box, 347
Summary Link, 253, 258–260
Table of Contents, 253, 257–258
tool pane access, 151
toolbar type property, 150
What's New, 316
wiki content page versus, 139
zone, 146
Web Part button, 22
Web safe color, 284

Web site. *See also* team site
  CodePlex, 373
  Microsoft Download Center, 358
  Microsoft TechNet, 358
  Office Online, 372
  popularity of, 1
  standards-based, 1
  TechNet, 371
Welcome menu, 158–159
Welcome page layout, 205
What's New Web Part, 316
wiki
  adding pages to, 107–108
  adding tag to, 142
  content page, 138
  content page creation, 140–141
  creating, 106
  defined, 105
  description of, 137
  editing, 108–109
  Enterprise Wiki, 140, 202
  Enterprise Wiki template, 106
  finding and linking other page, 141–142
  page layout, 109
  recently modified page, 141
  Web Part page versus, 139
Wikipedia, 105, 138
workflow. *See also* approval workflow
  associate with content type, 331
  configuration, 133–136

history list, 135
name, 134
task, 356
template, 134
three-state, 133
.wsp file extension, 195
W3C (World Wide Web Consortium), 298
WYSIWYG (what you see is what you get)
    display, 235

XHTML, 372
XML document, 264, 372
XPath language, 264, 372
XSL language, 264
XSLT (Extensible Stylesheet Language),
    85, 91, 372

yes/no column, 59

• Z •

zone, Web Part, 146